DATE			

FOUNDATIONS OF LIBERALISM

FOUNDATIONS OF LIBERALISM

Margaret Moore

CLARENDON PRESS · OXFORD

1993

Oxford University Press, Walton Street, Oxford OX2 6DP
Oxford New York Toronto
Delhi Bombay Calcutta Madras Karachi
Kuala Lumpur Singapore Hong Kong Tokyo
Nairobi Dar es Salaam Cape Town
Melbourne Auckland Madrid
and associated companies in
Berlin Ibadan

Oxford is a trade mark of Oxford University Press

Published in the United States
by Oxford University Press Inc., New York

British Library Cataloguing in Publication Data
Data available

Library of Congress Cataloging in Publication Data
Moore, Margaret.
Foundations of liberalism/Margaret Moore.
Includes bibliographical references and index.
1. Liberalism. 2. Individualism. I. Title.
JC571.M775 1993 320.5' 13—dc20 92-22186
ISBN 0-19-827385-1

Typeset by BP Integraphics Ltd., Bath, Avon
Printed in Great Britain
on acid-free paper by
Biddles Ltd, Guildford and King's Lynn

To

My Mother and Father

Acknowledgements

I HAVE incurred a number of debts in the course of writing this book which I am happy to acknowledge. I am grateful to the Social Science and Humanities Research Council of Canada and the London School of Economics for four years of financial support while doing my Ph.D. It was during this time that I began to formulate the ideas in this book. I learned an enormous amount about political philosophy from my Ph.D. supervisor, John Charvet. His thoughtful and challenging comments on numerous drafts of this work have made it much better than it would otherwise have been. Brian Barry, Ronnie Beiner, David Braybrooke, Les Green, Will Kymlicka, Steve Newman, and especially Raymond Plant read all or some of this manuscript and their support and criticisms have been extremely helpful. I am indebted to the anonymous referee at Oxford University Press whose incisive comments and criticisms prevented me from falling into worse error than I have. And I am grateful to my husband John McGarry for support throughout and helpful criticism. Both he and our son Sean helped to remind me that there are some attachments that cannot be explained in terms of either self-interest or impartial justice.

Naturally, I accept full responsibility for any errors or mistakes which this book may contain.

M.M.

March 1992

Contents

1. Introduction   1

PART I. INDIVIDUALIST LIBERAL THEORIES

2. Gewirth and the Project of Entailment   9
3. Rawls and the Abstract Contract   34
4. Gauthier and the Full-Knowledge Contract   79

PART II. REVISIONIST LIBERAL THEORIES

5. Contextual Arguments for Liberalism   115
6. Perfectionist Arguments for Liberalism   144

PART III. AN ALTERNATIVE FOUNDATION

7. An Alternative Foundation for Political and Ethical Principles   165

Bibliography   206

Index   217

1

Introduction

THIS book is principally concerned with theories of justice, theories of the defensibility of social or institutional arrangements for the distribution of the basic goods of society—money, power, status, leisure, and so on. Liberal theories are theories of justice *par excellence*, and Parts I and II of this book are devoted to examining different justificatory arguments for *liberal* social arrangements.

At the heart of my argument is the familiar problem of relating the personal point of view of the individual to the impersonal or impartial perspective of morality. This problem is common to all ethical theories and frequently surfaces in terms of the relation between the two when they conflict. Different moral theories have different strategies for dealing with conflict: act-utilitarianism, for example, prescribes that one should always act to increase the greatest happiness, thereby according primacy to the impartial standpoint of morality when it conflicts with the things desired from the personal perspective. Plato and Aristotle, by contrast, were concerned to show that each person has reasons (from the personal perspective) for endorsing the demands of morality, thus making morality a subset of individual well-being (properly understood). Liberal rights theorists often claim that their theories achieve a delicate balance between the two perspectives: utilitarianism is criticized for being too demanding and sacrificing the interests of the individual in its quest to attain the best overall state of affairs from the impartial perspective;[1] Greek ethical theories are considered primitive, in not understanding the distinctive perspective of morality and the notion of moral obligation.[2] My concern in this book is not directly with the relationship prescribed by ethical theories in cases where the requirements of morality conflict with those of self-interest, but with the more fundamental problem of conceptualizing the relationship between the personal and impersonal standpoints at the level of the individual.

The problem of the relationship between the personal and impartial perspectives is frequently discussed in moral philosophy and the philosophy of action, but it also arises in political theory. This issue is probably most familiar to political theorists in the form of questions of political obligation: members of a political community are typically conceived as adopting some form of the impartial perspective when they voluntarily subordinate themselves to the authority of government; and explaining how this is possible or describing the circumstances under which government is legitimate is one of the enduring themes of political philosophy. The problem of integrating the personal and impartial standpoints is exacerbated in contemporary liberal political theory because liberal principles purport to adjudicate not just between actions based on different self-interested reasons but actions based on different moral theories which also claim to apply impartially to all.[3] At the same time, contemporary political liberalism eschews appeals to specific conceptions of religious truth, for example, or particular conceptions of the good for human beings as justificatory support for political principles or structures. Thus, while liberalism requires a strong justificatory argument to defend its claim to decide which actions, and implicitly which moral theories, are permissible and which are not, it seems to have denied itself the justificatory avenues typically used to support other political philosophies.

The arguments discussed in Part I all attempt to justify liberalism as an interpretation of impartiality itself. Three kinds of arguments for liberal principles are identified: (1) the Kantian argument, put forward by Alan Gewirth in *Reason and Morality*, that morality, which is identified with liberal principles of justice, is entailed in the standpoint of self-interest, and can be discerned through the exercise of theoretical reason; (2) Rawls's argument in *A Theory of Justice*, which attempts to derive liberal rights and rules of justice from an original position or contract among people denied full knowledge of their identities; and (3) Gauthier's contractarian argument in *Morals by Agreement*, in which people with full knowledge of their identity agree to certain (liberal) principles of justice. The reason for selecting only these arguments from the many theories that have been characterized as 'liberal' is that each represents a distinct type of argument in support of liberal political principles and institutions. Each one is concerned to justify political principles which can be described as liberal in that they function to protect a sphere of action attaching, as it were, to each individual. They must therefore provide liberal principles with the justificatory leverage to adjudicate between actions based not only on self-interest but also on different ethical conceptions. The three arguments examined in Part I claim that liberal principles are impartial in the (higher-order) sense that they are derived from a starting-point which is itself neutral between different conceptions of the good, for this is what justifies them in adjudicating between conceptions of the good.

Each of the arguments in Part I can be seen as an improvement over the previous argument. Gauthier's formulation of a full-knowledge contract self-consciously attempts to avoid the difficulties which Rawls faced concerning the adoption of a contract between selves conceived abstractly. Similarly, Rawls's argument in *A Theory of Justice* is an improvement over Gewirth's, in that it attempts to link more effectively than Gewirth's theory the standpoint of self-interest with the standpoint of morality through the idea that there are (self-interested) reasons to adopt the impartial perspective described by the original position.

This examination of the justificatory arguments for liberalism focuses on its claim to be based on a higher-order impartiality. The central theme is that it is not possible to attain to this kind of impartiality, and the attempt by contemporary liberals to achieve this vantage-point has left their theories unable to explain how the personal and impartial perspectives are related (the integrity problem), and, following from this, unable to provide the person with reasons to act in accordance with the requirements of impartiality (the motivation problem). Because no proponent of any of the three arguments for liberal principles is able to deduce the principles of justice from the standpoint of self-interest, the theories are left with two distinct perspectives from which the person might act: the moral standpoint, which is identified with action in accordance with the principles of justice; and the self-interested standpoint, which describes action motivated by the person's particular ends, aims, and goals. The inability of liberal theories to derive a substantive ethical or political theory from their starting-point in self-interest leaves them with an incoherent account of human agency and no way to relate the requirements of liberal impartial justice to people in the real, empirical world.

Part II turns its attention to two quite different kinds of justificatory argument for liberal principles, both of which are designed to overcome the difficulties encountered by the individualist liberal theories of Part I. Rawls, in essays published since *A Theory of Justice*, and Charles Larmore, in his 1987 book *Patterns of Moral Complexity*, both reject the derivation of liberal principles from a neutral starting-point and claim that their liberal principles are justified because they are the most appropriate response to the circumstances that obtain in modern society. This emphasis on the contextual character of liberalism is, in part, a response to the argument, put forward by prominent communitarian critics of liberalism, that liberalism presupposes an implausible or indefensible conception of the person as identified with her capacity for pure rational autonomy.

Chapter 6 examines another, quite different revisionist argument for liberalism: this argument attempts to ground political liberalism in terms of a specific ideal of the person and of the good life. This perfectionist argument is put forward by Joseph Raz in *The Morality of Freedom*: he claims that liberal political principles do not need to be derived from an argument neutral among all ethical conceptions, as the individualist theories of Part I supposed, but can be justified as an essential, constituent element of a particular ideal of human flourishing. In Chapters 5 and 6, I argue that these contextualist and perfectionist arguments for liberalism are more defensible than the arguments of Part I, because not subject to the problems associated with the neutral starting-point of these individualist theories, but that they are inappropriate for liberal political principles.

I argue in this book that theories of liberal impartiality have left us with a series of unbridgeable dualisms: between self-interest and morality, the particular perspective and the impartial perspective, desire and reason. Some of these arguments have been anticipated by communitarian critics of liberalism who have suggested that Kantianism is a problem for liberalism.[4] This, I think, is a kind of shorthand which communitarians use to identify a whole set of related problems with liberal theory, and liberals have been right to complain about the lack of precision in many communitarian arguments. Will Kymlicka, in his book *Liberalism, Community, and Culture*, dismisses some communitarian criticisms because they have not been developed through a careful exploration of various liberal theories. Rorty and Walzer 'make claims in advance of the arguments', Kymlicka complains, and MacIntyre's 'examination' in *After Virtue* is altogether 'too hasty'.[5] One of the aims of this book is to address this criticism, to show through a detailed examination of various liberal arguments the problems that communitarians such as Rorty, Walzer, MacIntyre, and Taylor have identified in liberal political theory.

The argument of this book is not wholly negative: the critical first two sections are a necessary precursor to the elaboration of an alternative approach to political and ethical theorizing. In Part III I examine the implications of the failure of liberal neutrality, for both our political theory and our philosophical approach to political theorizing. One possible implication of the failure of liberal neutrality is the view that, because there are numerous conversations, but none are privileged in the sense of being neutral amongst various conversations, there can be no way to justify a particular tradition or conception or theory. On this view, such disputes are in principle *not* rationally arbitrable. Another, related reaction to the failure of liberal neutrality is to conceive of our social life and practices, and indeed every arena of human endeavour, as essentially aesthetic; and to glorify this individual self-creation. This Romantic conception also eschews any objective foundation for social life, viewing it instead as the product of individual self-formation. In the final chapter I conclude by rejecting both this more far-reaching relativism and the Romantic emphasis on individual self-creation to urge a return to a more modest justificatory approach to political and ethical life.

The justificatory approach adopted in the final chapter incorporates the insights of revisionist liberals such as Rawls, who, in his recent essays, presents his theory as within a particular historical or cultural context, and Raz's attempt to ground political principles in a perfectionist ideal of human flourishing. It takes as its starting-point a conception of the person as within communities, within traditions, and thereby ensures that the account of morality will be intelligible to the people subject to it. It overcomes the motivation and integrity problems which plagued the individualist versions of liberalism examined in Part I by conceiving of moral and social relations as constitutive of the person's identity. This chapter argues that conceiving of ethical reasoning as internal to a particular tradition is not merely designed to overcome the problems associated with individualist liberalism but is justified on the grounds that this is the only place from which reasoning can proceed.

At the same time, I argue that the starting-point internal to a particular tradition does not involve a denial of the person's autonomy. Community beliefs, practices, and institutions are judged in relation to a conception of human well-being or flourishing, according to which community and the human powers of reason and autonomy are objective goods. In the final sections of this chapter, the superiority of this justificatory approach over the liberal conception is explicitly argued for: I claim that this approach to justifying political and ethical principles avoids the difficulties associated with individualist liberal theories by presenting a coherent account of the relation between the personal and impartial standpoints.

NOTES

1. See John Rawls, *A Theory of Justice* (Oxford: Oxford University Press, 1972), 28–9.
2. See Bernard Williams, *Ethics and the Limits of Philosophy* (London: Fontana, 1985), 32.
3. For an excellent discussion of this issue, see Thomas Nagel, 'Moral Conflict and Political Legitimacy', *Philosophy and Public Affairs*, 16/3 (Summer 1987).
4. Communitarians such as Rorty, MacIntyre, Taylor, and Walzer have pointed out the affinity between contemporary liberalism and Kant's ethical theory. See Will Kymlicka, *Liberalism, Community, and Culture* (Oxford: Clarendon Press, 1989), 69.
5. Ibid.

PART I

Individualist Liberal Theories

2

Gewirth and the Project of Entailment

THERE are, broadly, two types of liberal approaches to the issue of justice: justice as mutual advantage and justice as impartiality.

According to the theory of justice as mutual advantage, the principles of justice are regulative principles governing the pursuit of self-interest, adherence to which is self-interestedly rational. The moral subject is viewed for the purposes of this theory as a rationally self-interested non-tuist, who considers the principles of justice from the perspective of her own particular interests, aims, and situation in the world. This conception of justice was first put forward by Glaucon in the *Republic* but is now most closely associated with Hobbes's theory in *Leviathan* and with contemporary Hobbesians such as David Gauthier.

The principles endorsed by the theory of justice as mutual advantage may be described as intrinsically fair in the sense that they are mutually beneficial to those subject to them; and they require mutual restraint on (narrowly) self-interested behaviour. The animating idea behind this conception—that the principles of justice have to be acceptable to each person subject to them—can be expressed through the metaphor of a contract, specifically by the contractual requirement that each person must consent to the principles of justice. Of course, a contractual device is not essential to this type of theory: it is sufficient to show that it would be self-interestedly rational to adhere to the principles of justice.

On the theory of justice as impartiality, the principles of justice are acceptable to each person when that person is viewed impartially, as just one person among others. This conception of justice can also be modelled in contractual terms, as long as the contract or agreement is between people defined abstractly, so that their choice represents, not what is self-interestedly rational for them, but what is best from the impartial point of view.

The theory of justice as impartiality has historical roots in Kant's ethical theory and is given contemporary expression in Rawls's conception of the original position, Ackerman's device of a rational conversation, Hare's impartial sympathizer, and, especially, Gewirth's argument in *Reason and Morality*. Gewirth moves from the self-interested ('prudential') claim of rights (to freedom and well-being) to the impartial recognition of everyone's rights to freedom and well-being by applying the Criterion of Relevant Similarities, which embodies the impartial perspective, in which each person is viewed abstractly, as equal to all others.

It is essential to both types of liberal theories of justice that the theory be neutral or impartial at its very core: its principles are justified, not in terms of some narrow sectarian doctrine, such as Christianity, or some particular controversial ethical conception, but in terms that are neutral among all ethical conceptions. This claim to represent a higher-order impartiality distinguishes liberal theories of justice from other ethical conceptions which are impartial in the sense that the principles apply impartially, but which do not claim to be impartial because derived or justified in terms which are neutral (impartial) among all substantive ethical conceptions.

What is interesting about Gewirth's argument for impartial justice from the point of view of this book is its clear treatment of both the motivation and integrity problems. Gewirth begins his argument from the self-interested standpoint, from the point of view of the agent about to act, who requires to be shown that reasons other than self-interested ones have binding force for her. This is a paradigmatically liberal starting-point, which defines the terms of Gewirth's project: what he must do is integrate the two standpoints—that of self-interest and that of morality—into a coherent conception of agency; and he must show why the person, who is initially defined in self-interested terms, would act in accordance with morality. Obviously, this second task—of demonstrating the motivational force of morality—would be accomplished if the first task were successful, and a coherent conception of agency, encompassing both the self-interested and the moral standpoints, were developed.

1. Outline of Gewirth's Argument

In its goals and main outlines, Gewirth's theory is a modern version of Kantianism. Kant's central aim was to justify the supreme moral principle, the Categorical Imperative, and so make morality binding on all agents.[1] Kant argued that traditional ethical theory supposes that moral action is possible because of the presence or absence of certain feelings, such as sympathy. Presupposing a feeling such as sympathy does serve to explain why people behave morally, but it also has the (in Kant's view) undesirable effect of making the entire structure of ethics rest on something which is contingent and subjective, namely the presence or absence of a certain feeling or desire in the person. In contrast to these theories, Kant sought to develop an ethical theory which relates the moral will to the good in such a way that it preserves the autonomy of the will while affirming an objective and unconditioned good. Such an ethical theory could not be grounded on presupposed desires in the person nor on the attainment of some end, for these relationships of the moral will to the good make the good subjective (in the sense that the good is good only because the person desires it) and contingent (on whether the faculty of desire is moved to feel pleasure rather than, say, aversion when considering the object in question).[2] Gewirth's version of liberal theory follows Kant's in conceiving of morality not as grounded in presupposed desires in the person nor on the attainment of some end but as rationally justified, unconditioned, objective, and universally valid. Gewirth seeks to ground his supreme moral principle in reason, and so justify it in arbitrating between different and competing conceptions, aims, and interests, and in serving as a standard by which principles can be tested and (lesser) moral principles derived. Gewirth argues that the supreme moral principle must be justified in rational terms if it is to have the justificatory force to claim this role of arbiter over conceptions of the good:[3] it must be prior to any particular conception of the good that a person may hold, because derived in a way that does not presuppose any contingent desires or contingent states of affairs.

This is achieved in Gewirth's theory by employing his dialectically necessary method, a mode of argument which proceeds by positing a rational agent in abstraction from all contingent circumstances, such as her position in society or her culturally acquired conceptions, aims, and beliefs.[4] Gewirth eschews all rational-choice justificatory models which rest on contingent circumstance, insisting instead that the supreme principle must be derived from a foundation independent of all contingency, from the neutral starting-point of action and appealing only to the logical implications of the concept of an action. The independence which this formulation confers on the supreme moral principle means that the virtue of Gewirth's Principle of Generic Consistency, like Kant's supreme principle, the Categorical Imperative, does not consist in the ends it promotes but in being prior to all other ends and regulative with respect to them. Rational foundations are, then, uniquely appropriate to Gewirth's project, not only because they are necessary to support the claim that these principles hold without exception, regardless of the particular desires, interests, and beliefs of the people subject to them, but also to support the relationship of primacy which holds between the supreme moral principle and all other principles.

Although both Kant and Gewirth emphasize that morality is grounded in terms of reason, this, in itself, gives us little insight into the way in which reason and morality are connected, or the kinds of actions Kant and Gewirth have in mind. The function of linking the general concept of rationality with the specifics of morality is performed in Kant's theory by the Categorical Imperative and in Gewirth's theory by the Principle of Generic Consistency. The Categorical Imperative states: 'Act only on that maxim through which you can at the same time will that it should become a universal law';[5] while Gewirth's Principle of Generic Consistency is: 'Act in accord with the generic rights of your recipients as well as yourself.'[6] Both principles serve as a test of principles or maxims, a method by which the person can imaginatively universalize either the maxims on which she acts, as in Kant's theory, or the rights she claims for herself, as in Gewirth's theory, in order to determine whether, when universalized, the maxim or the denial of the right to others is self-contradictory. Both universalization principles are forms of impartiality principles, for they involve considering every person, including oneself, as just one person among others. In both theories, the rational test of the supreme principle is that its denial (to others, to everyone) involves one in self-contradiction;[7] and in order to show contradiction, the principle must have some material content which can be contradicted. In other words, if the test of non-contradiction is to work, the principle must have some substantive elements which the person is both affirming and denying. In Kant's theory, the goods which are incorporated into the material content of the supreme principle are goods which the person desires, which take the form of maxims of self-interested action. But if, as in Kant's theory, the principle takes as its substantive content goods which are good because desired, then it seems that his supreme principle has a certain element of contingency at its very core. And here Gewirth's theory can claim superiority over Kant's, for the material content of his supreme principle, the Principle of Generic Consistency, is goods which are *necessarily* desired, i.e. desired by all regardless of their conceptions of the good.

This claim to superiority over Kant's theory is only part of Gewirth's case for having rescued the Kantian project from the dualisms and incoherences which bedevilled it. What Gewirth is attempting to do is to make morality autonomous but not too autonomous: on the one hand, he does not want to make morality a mere servant of desire and so wholly absorbed by self-interest, but on the other hand he does not want to characterize moral considerations in a way that makes them so transcendent from the self that the person has no reason or motive for acting morally. He seeks, in other words, to make the supreme moral principle binding on all human agents and yet not related to the person by being desired by her, and this involves explaining not only the categorical nature of the moral principle but also how morality can be a motive for action. And this may seem an impossible task: for, if morality is to be a motive for the person, it must be related in some way to the person, to the desires and interests and beliefs which are unproblematic motives for action; but if it *requires* a link to the contingent contents of the self-interested standpoint to move the person to action, the principle is not categorical or unconditioned. Gewirth must, in other words, overcome the divisions that he sets up between the desirous self-interested self and the rational moral self and explain how the former self can be brought to recognize the rationally grounded supreme moral principle. Even if we accept the (questionable) assumption that pure reason can itself somehow move the person to action, we still require a coherent conception of moral agency, of how this recognition is possible and how it can be a motive for action.

Kant's theory, notoriously, was unable to explain the grounds on which a person, conceived of as divided between two strikingly different selves, the egoistic, pleasure-seeking, sensuous self and the rational moral self, can make a decision to act morally.[8] If the person decides on moral grounds, this presupposes the answer to the question at issue; if the person is simply moved by stronger inclinations in one direction rather than another, then her action is not rational, not autonomous, and not moral. Kant's explanation of how the person is able to act morally depends on the sensuous self's recognition of its own humility and its respect for the moral law. In his *Critique of Practical Reason*, Kant writes that this feeling of 'humiliation occurs proportionately to the purity of the law; for that reason the lowering of the pretensions of moral self-esteem (humiliation) on the sensuous side is an elevation of the moral, i.e., practical, esteem for the law on the intellectual side'.[9] Yet this solution only reformulates the question: why should the sensuous self respect the moral law? For, in order to feel respect for the moral law, it must already have accepted the standards of morality. Thus, Kant's solution fails because it *presupposes* the acceptance of morality rather than explains it. The failure of Kant's theory to provide a coherent account of moral agency is directly due to his conception of the person as radically divided between two different aspects, each with its own source of action. Because there is no point at which the two selves meet, no unifying ground, his theory cannot give a coherent account of how the person 'decides' to act morally or non-morally, autonomously or heteronomously.

Gewirth's solution to this, the principal problem in Kantian ethical theory, is to relate the prudential and the moral standpoints in terms of entailment. The entire first half of Gewirth's book is taken up with demonstrating the thesis that the self-interested standpoint on which all people act necessarily involves or entails the moral standpoint. He adopts as the starting-point of *Reason and Morality* the standpoint of the self-interested agent and considers what is involved in that standpoint. Through this analysis of the concept of action, Gewirth argues that there are certain things which the agent necessarily must regard as good and then shows that regarding these as (prudentially) good entails moral considerations.

The first step of Gewirth's argument consists of the claim that, if an agent's action is to regarded as her action at all, it must be supposed to be free; and if the action is free or unforced, it must be that the agent has some end or purpose or intention which is her reason for acting. Purposiveness, then, is necessarily or conceptually involved in all human action, and freedom and well-being are necessary conditions for the pursuit of the agent's purposes.

In the second step of his argument, Gewirth analyses the conceptual connection between rights and necessary goods. The goods of freedom and well-being are prudential goods in the sense that the agent regards her freedom and well-being as good for her; indeed, it is because they are necessary to action that, at least from her standpoint as a prudential agent, the person must claim that she is entitled to freedom and well-being, that she has a prudential right to them. Gewirth's argument for the transition from these goods being prudentially good for her to her having a prudential right to them is that there is a logical contradiction involved in the denial of such rights. Gewirth believes that the denial of a prudential right to freedom and well-being is equivalent to a denial of these goods as good. That is, if the person denies that she has a prudential right to freedom and well-being, then she is giving a licence to all other people to interfere with her freedom and disregard her well-being. If she does that, she cannot regard her freedom and well-being as good; but then she is involved in a contradiction, for, as the first stage of the argument has shown, she *must* regard her freedom and well-being as good because they are necessary conditions to the achievement of purposes that she regards as good.

The third step of Gewirth's argument involves the transition from the self-interested prudential claim of rights to the impersonal standpoint of morality. Gewirth applies the criterion of relevant similarities to the agent's prudential right-claim: if the agent from within her own prudential standpoint claims freedom and well-being as rights that others ought not to interfere with, consistency requires that she acknowledge her obligation to respect the similar rights of others.[10] Only at this stage of the argument, where prudence is universalized and where self-interest is superseded by appeal to rational consistency, does Gewirth's argument become a moral one. Only when the rights are conferred on all and regulate interaction among people are they given the status of moral principles. From this standpoint of the impartial recognition of everyone's right to freedom and well-being, Gewirth derives the supreme moral principle, the Principle of Generic Consistency (the PGC): 'Act in accord with the generic rights of your recipients as well as yourself.'[11]

By making the transition from self-interest to morality in terms of entailment, Gewirth is able to argue that all self-interested agents—which, in his conception, are all persons who act to fulfil any purpose or desire—are necessarily led into morality. Thus, it seems that Gewirth is able to realize the Kantian project, for this procedure ensures that morality is binding on all agents because entailed by inescapable characteristics of action. If Gewirth's argument from entailment is successful, he will have resuscitated the Kantian project; he will have grounded ethics on the firm and necessary foundation of reason, thereby justifying a universal moral principle and showing that each person has reason to act morally.

2. PROBLEMS WITH THE ARGUMENT

But has he? Is it really the case that the standpoint of self-interest *entails* other-regarding considerations? Can action in fulfilment of one's desires really, logically, require acceptance of a principle which involves accepting the goods desired by other people—i.e. their reasons—as reasons for one's self to act?

At the first stage of his argument, Gewirth remains entirely within the agent's standpoint in establishing that freedom and well-being are prudential goods, i.e. good in the service of the agent's aims and desires. From within this standpoint, the use of the term 'good' may be misleading, for it seems to imply a common recognized evaluative standard, whereas Gewirth's argument has demonstrated only that freedom and well-being are instrumental to the fulfilment of the agent's desires, and therefore that the agent must desire freedom and well-being also.

At the basis of Gewirth's theory, then, is a theory of the good: indeed, a theory of the good such as this is necessary to the success of any deontological programme. It is not possible to derive a full-fledged theory of rights and obligations without some theory of the good, for a theory of the good is needed to distinguish which interests ought to be protected by rights and so also to derive correlative obligations. Within the structure of Gewirth's particular brand of liberalism, a theory of the good is necessary in order for the principle of non-contradiction to work, which in turn is necessary to derive particular rights and duties from the supreme moral principle. In specifying his theory of the good, it is essential to the success of Gewirth's project that he avoid biasing the neutrality of his derivation and confine his theory of the good to those goods which do not presuppose a particular substantive moral conception. Gewirth does this by abstracting from the aims, projects, and desires of particular agents and viewing what is good in terms of the necessary conditions for fulfilling the agent's purposes, regardless of what they are. Gewirth calls this abstraction from the agent's particular purposes and desires to the necessary conditions for the fulfilment of purposes and desires in general the 'generic-dispositional' view of the good.[12] By confining his theory of the good to all-purpose goods such as well-being and freedom, Gewirth successfully avoids jeopardizing the neutrality of his argument; but he does so at the cost of setting up a potential opposition between what is good from the standpoint of the agent and what is good from the point of view of the theory. The reasons that Gewirth gives for confining his theory of the good to the all-purpose goods of freedom and well-being—that this avoids the problem of relativity, that these goods are 'necessarily' i.e. universally, good[13]—all stem from the perspective of Gewirth's particular Kantian conception of morality; but he gives no reason from the point of view of the agent for adopting this theory of the good. Indeed, because what makes prudential goods good is the fact that they are subjectively desired, it seems arbitrary to limit the goods to just these and not consider things the agent might desire other than or in addition to freedom and well-being. Since freedom and well-being are only instrumental to the achievement of other goods, and prudential goods are defined in terms of what is desired, it seems that Gewirth should include also the objects of the agent's actions, the things desired, in his list of prudential goods.

This issue can also be raised at the next stage of Gewirth's argument, where he applies the Criterion of Relevant Similarities to derive the supreme principle of morality. Gewirth's argument at this stage is that it is irrational to claim entitlements or rights to goods for oneself and to deny the similar claims to entitlements or rights of other people. But one could object that it is not self-evident nor necessary to apply Gewirth's universalization principle, the Criterion of Relevant Similarities, only to the goods which are necessary for action to be possible at all. It seems at least as reasonable to focus on the ends and aims and goals that are the motives for action, rather than on the requirements for purposive action in general, for these are only instrumental to achieving the purposes that the agent regards as the primary good. The openness of the Criterion of Relevant Similarities to varying contents has implications both for the success of Gewirth's argument and for the usefulness of this principle. Some of these difficulties have been pointed out with respect to Kant's very similar universalization principle, the Categorical Imperative.[14]

One very serious difficulty with using the Categorical Imperative as a test of the maxims on which to act involves the precise wording of the maxim, for some actions can be accurately described at different levels of abstraction. At one quite high level of abstraction, a maxim might contradict itself when it is universalized, thus signalling that acting on this maxim would be wrong. However, at another, lower level of abstraction, at a level which specifies more qualifications, the same maxim might be willed as a universal law without contradiction. For example, Kant might argue that 'I will tell lies' cannot be willed as a universal law since there would be some contradiction if everyone told lies. But qualifications could be built into the wording of the maxim which name expressly when one can tell lies, in which case the maxim would not yield contradictory results.

Gewirth's universalization principle, the Criterion of Relevant Similarities, is subject to similar difficulties. For, like the Categorical Imperative, it is a formal principle which requires substantive content to yield its results. And changes in the material content of the criterion would result in a different list of the prudential goods that would then be universalized and form the basis of his ethical theory. Now, of course, it is necessary to the success of his argument that Gewirth confine his goods to all-purpose goods; but there is nothing in his argument which necessitates such a blinkered conception of what counts as a prudential good. It is at least as reasonable for the person to view as prudentially good or valuable to her the fulfilment of her desires, say, to be a lawyer or desires for a luxurious, aesthetically pleasing environment, surrounded by beautiful works of art. (Here the universalization principle requires that the prospective lawyer and art-lover grant the right-claims of other people with similar subjective conceptions of the good, i.e. people who wish to be lawyers or surrounded by beauty.) But protecting these prudential goods with rights would be counter-intuitive, for it would involve imposing duties on others either to protect or positively aid the fulfilment of one's subjective desires. Why, after all, should others be required to help A realize her expensive prudential goods of a beautiful and luxurious environment or even B's prudential good of fulfilling her ambition to be a lawyer, when she has no talent in that direction and there are too many lawyers anyway? The prudential goods of malicious, envious, and sadistic people pose even more serious problems for subjectivist theories of the good, because fulfilling their primary desires (what is good for them) would be injurious to others. Although Gewirth avoids these difficulties by arbitrarily limiting his theory of the good to goods which are necessary for action, these are the natural implications of any theory (such as his) which determines what is good, i.e. what should be protected by rights, by universalizing what is considered to be good from the subjective, self-interested standpoint.

Thus far, it seems that Gewirth's thin theory of the good is just an arbitrary list of two goods which are chosen only because they are neutral enough not to jeopardize the success of Gewirth's theory. But the idea of neutrality in this case is that they are necessary to all conceptions of the good, and this implies a deeper theory of the good, one which rests on a particular view of the human person. Freedom and well-being are necessary to human agency, and human agency is central to Gewirth's right-based theory, because underlying his theory or implicit in it is a conception of the person as autonomous chooser. Only if one adopts this view of the person as primarily an autonomous agent who is related to her ends by having chosen them does Gewirth's theory make sense.[15] Only such a deeper theory can make sense of Gewirth's starting-point in human action and the limitation of his theory of the good to those things which are necessary for the exercise of choice or human agency. But if this is the case, then Gewirth's theory is not neutral between different conceptions of the good, as it purports to be, but incorporates, in a more radical way than hitherto suggested, a particular conception of the moral subject. On this interpretation of Gewirth's theory, the rules of justice—i.e. the PGC and the rights and duties derived from it—are justified because they represent a way of organizing society compatible with Gewirth's conception of the person. There is nothing wrong with this procedure in itself, when it is fully explicit and justified, but it is certainly a radically different conception of moral philosophy from the one Gewirth officially endorses. For it means that what is really happening in Gewirth's theory, the real moving force behind his argument, has relatively little to do with the dialectically necessary method and the logical entailment of morality by self-interest, and almost everything to do with a conception of the person which is never made explicit and never argued for but absolutely central to Gewirth's thin theory of the good and derivation of rights from that.

From the very beginning of his argument, in his derivation of a thin theory of the good, Gewirth's theory threatens to collapse. He needs a theory of the good to give substantive content to his moral theory, but any criterion that he employs to choose some goods over others, to distinguish something as good because valuable (in terms of a theory of human nature, for example), will threaten the theory's neutrality and scuttle Gewirth's programme of making morality logically necessary, undeniable even for the moral sceptic because entailed by action itself. On the other hand, if Gewirth does not employ a criterion to distinguish goods on the basis of their value but instead describes things as good merely because they are desired, his theory must include all objects of the agent's actions, all objects of desire merely because desired, in his list of prudential goods. And it would be impossible to base a theory of human rights or of justice on goods which are good because desired, not only because people may desire many different and conflicting things but because the resulting principles would not be universal. Instead, Gewirth employs a tactic of equivocation: he purports to employ the second method and base his theory of the good on those things which are good because desired, but in fact he limits the objects of desire, the goods, by introducing, through the back door as it were, a criterion of value other than desire—a criterion based on a particular theory of the human person—to limit his list of human goods to freedom and well-being.

In the concluding pages of *Reason and Morality*, Gewirth antici-pates precisely this criticism, namely that the premises from which he begins are not morally neutral but imply a particular substantive moral theory. Gewirth outlines this objection in terms of the validity of his deductive enterprise: since the argu-ment for the supreme moral principle has been primarily deduct-ive, its conclusion must have been implicit in its premises. And if that is so, his argument must be circular and his premises, neither morally general nor neutral.[16] Gewirth responds to this potential criticism by reaffirming the integrity of his derivation: his argument is morally neutral because it begins from the start-ing-point of action, which is a universal concept, in the sense of being central to all moralities; and the moral rights and duties that he has discovered in his analysis of the concept of action do not represent a particular evaluative commitment or prescrip-tion that he has put into the premises. 'The commitment is there in the nature of the case,' Gewirth writes, 'and all he [the deriver] is doing is recognizing it.'[17] But, on the interpretation of Gewirth's theory presented here, the (non-neutral) conception of the person on which his argument relies is not a natural, inevitable conception that everyone must accept. What Gewirth has done in the first step of his theory is to present two distinct and incompatible conceptions of the self. By taking action from the person's particular purposes and aims, desires and commit-ments, as his starting-point, Gewirth suggests that there is a special and very close relation between the person and the per-son's interests, desires, and concerns: he suggests that the per-son's motivational basis and values, and indeed her very identity, are closely bound up with her central aims, desires, and interests. But the transition from the concrete objects of the person's purposes and desires to the conditions for achieving any purpose whatsoever suggests another, radically different conception of the self. This conception requires that the person abstract from herself all contingent features, including of course the special relation that she feels from the subjective point of view to her central beliefs and interests and projects, viewing herself instead merely in terms of her capacity as an agent. And the problem with relying on this conception of the person, even apart from the fact that it represents a departure from Gewirth's dialectically necessary method and his project of showing that moral considerations are entailed by self-interest, is that the conception of the person as rational agent is too abstract a conception to do the work required by Gewirth's theory.

The problem with this conception is that Gewirth has given the person no reason to adopt this highly abstract view of herself and conceive of herself as stripped of all identifying features. There is nothing at the level of action, nothing in the standpoint of self-interested desire-fulfilment from which Gewirth begins, which necessitates the adoption of this standpoint. Like Kant, it seems, Gewirth has presented us with two distinct and unrelated conceptions of the person: there is the prudential self, with her own commitments and projects and ends, moved to act by desire; and the moral self, which conceives of itself in abstraction from its particular features, as essentially identical to all others, and which acts in obedience to reason. And because these two aspects of the person are completely distinct, because there is no reason to conceive of one's self in the abstract way required by Gewirth's moral standpoint (and crucial to his derivation of morality from self-interest), his theory has the consequence of being irrational at its core, for it can offer no reason for people to adopt the moral standpoint, and hence no reason to act morally rather than self-interestedly.

3. The Transition from Self-Interest to Morality

But let us for the moment accept that the person would regard her freedom and well-being as good, and put aside the serious difficulty of limiting the prudential goods to just these two without employing a non-neutral criterion of value. Let us suppose that the person would regard her freedom and well-being as good for her, i.e. as subjectively good, because they are necessary conditions for the successful pursuit of purposes that the agent regards as good. From this claim that freedom and well-being are subjective goods, Gewirth seeks to show that the agent must claim that she is prudentially entitled to them and then, by applying the criterion of relevant similarities, enter into the moral standpoint of impartiality, recognizing the similar rights of similar agents. But here the question of the nature of the goods of freedom and well-being raises its head and threatens once again Gewirth's derivation of rights. It is easy to accept Gewirth's claim that freedom and well-being are goods for the agent in the sense that she subjectively values or desires them, but Gewirth has not shown that they are good independently of these subjective desires. It is, of course, the case that freedom and well-being are subjective goods for A, because instrumental to purposes that she regards as good; and also subjective goods for B, because instrumental to her purposes; and so on. Gewirth is correct to say that, from the standpoint of the agent, these goods are valued or are prudential goods; and he is even right to say that they are necessarily prudentially valuable in the sense that they are necessary to self-interested action. But none of this suffices to establish a ground of entitlement to these goods, a justification for the judgement that others ought not to interfere.

Sometimes Gewirth writes as if the fact that these goods are necessary goods, or necessary for action, somehow serves as a ground for entitlement. That would be the case if his argument proceeded from a conception of human nature and argued, say, that certain goods are necessary to the realization of this nature. But Gewirth's theory takes as its starting-point the standpoint of the self-interested agent and argues that these goods are necessary to self-interested action. It does not follow from the fact that something is necessary to fulfil the desires of A that A is entitled to that thing or that others ought not to interfere with the fulfilment of her desires. It does not follow because the fact that something is subjectively desired does not show that it is valuable in an objective sense, and any claim to entitlement, any ought-judgement that has practical import for someone other than the self-interested agent, requires an objective standard, a standpoint which can be entered into by any agent.[18] And the standpoint of self-interest, of desire-fulfilment, or even what is necessary for desire-fulfilment, does not provide a ground of entitlement or a justification which has force for any person other than the person who has the desires in the first place. This is implicit in Gewirth's own theory of action.

The reason why Gewirth begins from the standpoint of the self-interested agent is that desire-fulfilment is an unproblematic motive or reason for action. The fulfilment of my subjective desires gives me a reason to act, and the fulfilment of your desires gives you a reason to act; but the fact that you desire something does not make any claims on me. There is no duty on me to provide you with what you regard as prudentially good (for example, freedom and well-being), for these goods are good only for you and only from the standpoint of fulfilling your desires. It does not follow from the fact that something is good from a subjective standpoint, i.e. good from the standpoint of subjective desire-fulfilment, that it is good from an objective (or inter-subjective) standpoint; for example, that it has the characteristics or qualities which make it objectively valuable or worthwhile. And it is the latter kind of claim which Gewirth needs in order to claim that there are duties incumbent on each person to enable or ensure that others secure the goods of freedom and well-being.

4. THE DERIVATION OF PRINCIPLES

Thus far, we have seen that the starting-point of Gewirth's argument, in terms of an individual abstracted from all relations to others, makes it difficult for him to integrate this standpoint with the impartial standpoint of morality. Not only does Gewirth import into his theory a non-neutral conception of the self, which undermines the neutrality of his derivation, but, more seriously, the conception of the self on which his argument relies is not one that the person need accept. And this renders his theory into an optional one: it is a matter of choice whether to adopt the moral standpoint, whether to view oneself in a highly abstract way as just one person among others. The failure of Gewirth's argument from entailment leaves his theory without any connection between the self-interested self, which is the starting-point of his argument, and the moral self, which acts in accordance with the requirements of morality. And this problem with his theory does not emerge only at a highly abstract level of analysis: it is not confined to the foundational level of his argument with no effect on the liberal moral and political theory which Gewirth develops. The incoherence at the base of Gewirth's theory affects the liberal principles that emerge at its conclusion: because the (moral) principles are based on Gewirth's conception of a rational moral self, which has no relation to the self-interested self, Gewirth has difficulties explaining why the self-interested self would act morally, and relating this conception of freedom and well-being to the person as she is constituted in society.

Although the main justification for the PGC is his argument from entailment, Gewirth considers the coherence and comprehensiveness of the PGC's application to situations to be an important a posteriori justification for his supreme principle. For what Gewirth is claiming for the PGC is that it alone is capable of resolving all moral issues at the level of both individual actions and social and political rules and institutions: in short, he is claiming that this single, rather slim principle provides a rational basis for decision in all cases of moral conflict.[19] To support this ambitious claim, Gewirth, in the second half of his book, seeks to demonstrate the adequacy of this principle in dealing with a host of diverse moral issues.

Many critics of the kind of liberal theory put forward by Gewirth, in which morality is derived from a single principle or particular circumscribed (impartial) perspective, have questioned the logic of the derivation. They have argued that these principles are either not directly *derived* from the argument or that many other principles are equally compatible with the derivation. Both kinds of arguments have been made with respect to John Rawls's derivation of the two principles of justice from the original position, and are also applicable to Gewirth's derivation of ethical and political principles from the impartial standpoint embodied in the PGC.

Gewirth's fundamental principle of morality states: 'Act in accord with the generic rights of your recipients [to freedom and well-being] as well as yourself.'[20] The right to well-being involves both the duty not to hinder others in pursuit of their well-being and the duty to assist others if they are unable to provide themselves with the basic pre-conditions for successful action. Gewirth argues that this involves rights to basic education, medical care, housing, equality of opportunity, and income protection. Gewirth interprets the right-to-freedom component of the PGC primarily as a sphere of non-interference in action which attaches, as it were, to each individual. He arrives at this conception of freedom by employing a distinction between occurrent and dispositional freedom, and opts for the dispositional interpretation: freedom, Gewirth writes, 'consists not only in exercising control over one's behavior by one's unforced choice in particular situations, but also in having the long-range effective ability to exercise such control'.[21] At the level of individual action, this means that freedom is limited 'only where they [agents] coerce or harm other persons, that is, where the agents violate the rights of their recipients to freedom and well-being'.[22] At the social level, Gewirth derives from the right to freedom the conclusion that 'prospective agents have rights to a vast area of protected actions of their own, including physical movement, speech and other forms of expression, assembly, religion and sexual conduct'.[23]

The problem with Gewirth's conception of a right to freedom and its application to individual interaction and social life is that there is a gap between freedom understood as a necessary precondition of action and freedom defined in terms of a sphere of unforced choice which attaches to each agent. It is, as Gewirth recognizes,[24] a conceptual truth about the notion of action, as distinct from mere behaviour, that it is free. The freedom ascribed to action is posited: we assume an action is free if the person performs it intentionally. We assume that actions are performed with free will even in cases where the action is *not* the outcome of complete deliberation and full knowledge of the facts, a wide range of desirable options and no external pressure. There is nothing puzzling or unnatural in saying, 'X acted under duress'. We recognize that X is acting, not merely behaving or being acted upon, even in cases where duress is present. But it does seem paradoxical to claim that 'X acted autonomously under duress'. And this indicates that what Gewirth's rights to freedom from coercion are designed to protect is personal autonomy, not freedom understood as a necessary pre-condition of action.[25] And it does not follow directly from the goodness of the former kind of freedom that the development of individual personal autonomy is a good.

Even if we set aside doubts concerning whether Gewirth can argue directly from the notion of freedom as a necessary precondition of action to a full range of social and political freedoms, there remains the difficulty of whether Gewirth's argument naturally gives rise to the choice conception of freedom that he seeks to derive from it, that is, whether the foundations on which his theory is built support the identification of freedom with choice as such. The tension in Gewirth's theory between his commitment to a negative or procedural conception of freedom and his substantive moral conclusion emerges in his discussion of the Christian Scientist who will not consent to a blood transfusion. This is presented in Gewirth's theory as a case where freedom and well-being are in conflict, but it is even more illuminating as an example of the tension between negative or procedural freedom and positive freedom or freedom defined in terms of rational or moral choice. Gewirth imagines a Christian Scientist who 'on deeply felt religious grounds' refuses to consent to a blood transfusion that is needed to save her life.[26] This seems to be a case of a dilemma between freedom defined procedurally, i.e. in terms of the person's choices over her life, and the well-being requirement, which prescribes a medical operation. But, Gewirth argues, this dilemma is only apparent: the freedom component of the PGC does not apply in this case because the Christian Scientist's religious commitment prevents her from assimilating the 'relevant knowledge'; hence she cannot give her informed consent.[27]

The first point to be noted is that Gewirth's conception of well-being in terms of the capabilities of action is extremely impoverished. It is a conception of well-being defined apart from or in abstraction from the subject's own sense of well-being; it is blind to the projects and aims and desires that define a person's life and whether it goes well from the subjective point of view. Gewirth unhesitatingly states that the Christian Scientist's well-being requires that the transfusion operation be performed, thus completely ignoring the person's own beliefs or point of view as a component of her well-being. But if the person's life is saved by means of an operation which she feels is dirty, evil, and degrading, if flowing in her veins is something she regards as the product of the Devil, then it is doubtful whether she could be described as living a life of well-being. Gewirth's notion of well-being suggests a conception of the person abstracted from all particular aims and interests and desires—in other words, a person essentially identified with her capacity for rational choice, and so potentially at odds with the well-being of real, empirical human beings, with their particular desires and beliefs and commitments. This parallels the division at the foundational level of Gewirth's theory between the rational moral self and the empirical sensuous, desiring self. Gewirth's criterion of well-being is based on the rational self, who is concerned solely with maintaining her capabilities of action, and so, when it is applied to real human beings like the Christian Scientist, with deeply felt beliefs and projects and commitments, what is done in the name of well-being for the person seems to be the very opposite of promoting well-being to her.

The same division between the rational and empirical aspects of the person emerges in terms of the conception of freedom underlying the example of the Christian Scientist. Gewirth claims to be committed to a procedural conception of freedom such that an action is free if it is the product of the person's uncoerced choice.[28] On this conception of freedom, it is always possible that the person's choice will be wrong from the moral point of view, as in the case of the Christian Scientist who chooses a course of action not endorsed by the PGC. The rational choice in this example is the moral choice: there is no conflict between a perfectly rational choice and the PGC. But because people are not perfectly rational, moral agents—because they have beliefs and commitments which reflect their faith or cultural tradition or upbringing, which are not derived from pure reason—there is always the possibility of a gap between the outcome of pure procedural freedom and the requirements of the PGC. In this case, it seems that the Christian Scientist has considered the relevant facts and decided that the most important thing for her is her religious faith. But what indicates to Gewirth whether or not the person is making a choice rationally and with full knowledge is whether the choice is the right one. He has a substantive moral conception, which is derived from reason, by which to test the rationality and knowledge with which the choice was made. There is nothing in this example *except* the divergence between the Christian Scientist's choice and the rational moral choice to indicate that the knowledge requirement has not been met. On this interpretation, the procedural term 'knowledge requirement' is extremely misleading. The freedom that is not being violated by requiring the Christian Scientist to have the operation without her consent is the person's rational freedom—the freedom of the person's rational moral self. Her empirical self, with its particular beliefs and conceptions and projects, on which her actual choice is based, is of course being coerced and the person feels from the subjective point of view that her freedom is being violated. There is here a deep division between the objective or moral point of view, which conceives of people in terms of their capacity as rational moral agents, and people in the real, empirical world. And the problem with this division, like the division in Kant's theory between the noumenal and phenomenal selves, is that there seems no way of bridging the two standpoints, nothing to convince the Christian Scientist that her freedom and well-being are being respected, or to make the impartial moral point of view sensitive to the commitments and projects and beliefs which give meaning to the person's life.

At one level, the tension between negative and positive freedom or negative freedom and well-being (which is defined in terms of the conditions for choice) is an instance of tension between procedural and substantive goods, and will arise whenever agents use their freedom in ways opposed to their well-being or opposed to the rationally justified ethical life. In Gewirth's theory, the negative freedom component of his principle is at odds not only with the well-being component, but, more fundamentally, with his project of deriving morality from rationality: if the person's negative freedom or choice is respected, the rational (moral) result may not obtain; and if Gewirth directly applies the PGC to obtain the morally justified result, the actual choices of individuals may not be respected. What makes Gewirth's formulation unusual is that in his theory reason is identified with morality and so, if the person arrives at conclusions not endorsed by the PGC, it follows that that person's choice is irrational or non-rational. But since the exercise of reason and full knowledge of the relevant facts are necessary procedural conditions for free choice even on Gewirth's negative freedom conception, any choice that is the wrong choice must have been flawed at the deliberative phase. Because any gap

between a (procedurally) free choice and the ethical life represents a failure of rationality or full knowledge—represents, that
is, a lack of one of the necessary conditions for free (procedural)
choice—there is a tendency for Gewirth's theory to condemn
morally wrong choices on the procedural grounds that the full
knowledge and rationality conditions were not met, and in this
way identify freedom with the ethical life.

This division between the two conceptions of freedom is a
reflection of a deeper division in Gewirth's theory, namely his
conception of the person as divided between two aspects, the
rational moral self and the real, empirical desiring self with its
particular aims and beliefs and commitments. The relationship
between the two conceptions of the person and the two conceptions of freedom is clearly revealed in Gewirth's discussion of
the application of the PGC to the political and institutional
arrangements of social life. Gewirth argues that the PGC justifies
a constitutional state with redistributive functions (to meet the
well-being component of the PGC) and retributive function (to
maintain equality of generic rights), and a democratic form of
government (which is justified by the freedom component of
the PGC).[29] But this raises the question: why is the empirical
consent of people needed to justify a state that is already justified
in terms of a rationally justified supreme moral principle? And
what would happen in the case of conflict, as when the people,
in exercising their democratic choice, decide against the equaliz-
ing, redistributive laws of Gewirth's welfare state?

Gewirth recognizes the possibility of conflict between the
requirements of the PGC and the democratic choice of the elector-
ate and argues that the constitutional framework and overall
structure of the society are too important to be subject to the
vagaries of shifting allegiances: in being justified by the PGC,
he argues, they have the people's 'rational consent, because as
intrinsic parts, or logical consequences of the PGC, they share
its inherently rational justification'.[30] Only laws other than the
criminal law and the officials who administer the Gewirthian
state can be subject to the empirical consent provided for by
a democratic vote. This does not, of course, address the underlying problem: it merely relegates people's choices to the less
important spheres and so ensures that choices based on the concrete desires and interests and conceptions of people, which may

not be rationally justified and endorsed by the PGC, cannot do much damage to the rational moral structure Gewirth has derived. This serves to bring into sharper focus the radical opposition in Gewirth's theory between the requirements of the ethical life, based on an abstract conception of the self as purely rational and moral, and the desires and interests and commitments of real, empirical people. This division at the level of the person deeply affects the coherence of the principles which Gewirth derives from his theory. By deriving morality from the undeniable foundation of reason, Gewirth sought to answer conclusively the question, 'Why be moral?' But because his theory is committed to a conception of the person that real empirical people need not accept, he fails in his aim of solving the motivation problem: his theory cannot explain why people would be moral. And because the freedom and well-being which Gewirth's theory purports to protect are goods only for abstract, rational selves, there is a parallel difficulty at the social and political level in explaining why real, empirical people would be committed to Gewirth's principles and social institutions and political state.

5. CONCLUSION

The failure of Gewirth's attempt to derive the supreme moral principle from an analysis of the concept of action is not a failure in ingenuity of argument nor a failure to think clearly about a certain stage of the derivation but a failure rooted in the conception of morality with which Gewirth begins. Because Gewirth conceives of morality in terms of impartiality, and self-interest as an unproblematic motive for action, he is led to the Kantian oppositions between self-interest and morality, desire and reason. And it is extremely difficult, if not impossible, to overcome the gap between self-interest and morality when they are defined as so radically different, as characterized by such different and even opposed motives as desire and reason respectively. Gewirth's attempted transition from prudential goods to prudential rights or being prudentially entitled to these goods fails: in the weak sense of being prudentially entitled, the concept does not do the work Gewirth's theory requires it to do; and in the strong sense of prudential rights or entitlements, where having a right involves correlative duties, it simply does not follow from Gewirth's conception of prudential goods.

The failure of Gewirth's argument that morality is logically entailed by self-interest leaves his theory with two distinct and unrelated conceptions of the person: there is the prudential self, with her own commitments and projects and ends, moved to act by desire; and the moral self, which acts in obedience to reason. Because these two aspects of the person are completely distinct and unintegrated, it is difficult to conceive how the person could be moved to act morally at all, for on this view moral action is completely removed from the person's own desires, emotions, and interests—removed, indeed, from the person's own particular individuality. Gewirth's theory can only posit the existence of a rational moral self, an aspect of the person which acts morally on the basis of reason untainted by desire, but he cannot explain how formal, abstract reason can perform this function, nor how the person decides whether to act morally or self-interestedly. And this juxtaposition of two unintegrated aspects of the person, each with its own motivational basis and centre of concern, does not advance his theory beyond Kant's. Gewirth has not after all discovered a way to unite the two aspects, to rationally ground ethics by showing that morality is entailed by self-interest, but has presented instead a theory riddled by impossible, unbridgeable dualisms.

NOTES

1. Immanuel Kant, *Groundwork of the Metaphysic of Morals*, trans. H. J. Paton (New York: Harper & Row, 1964), 59–60.
2. Immanuel Kant, *Critique of Practical Reason*, trans. Lewis White Beck (Indianapolis: The Bobbs-Merrill Company, 1956), 87–8.
3. Alan Gewirth, *Reason and Morality* (Chicago: University of Chicago Press, 1978), 199.
4. Ibid. 25.
5. Kant, *Groundwork*, 88.
6. Gewirth, *Reason and Morality*, 135.
7. Ibid. 48; Kant, *Groundwork*, 101–2.
8. Terence Irwin, 'Morality and Personality: Kant and Green', in *Self*

and Nature in Kant's Philosophy, ed. Allen W. Wood (Ithaca, NY: Cornell University Press, 1984), 46. Irwin drew my attention to this objection and the passage in the second *Critique*.

9. Ibid. 46.
10. Gewirth, *Reason and Morality*, 104–5.
11. Ibid. 135.
12. Ibid. 58.
13. Ibid. 59.
14. J. Kemp, 'Kant's Examples of the Categorical Imperative', in *Kant: A Collection of Critical Essays*, ed. R. P. Wolff (London: Macmillan, 1968), 257.
15. The conception of the person on which Gewirth's theory relies is also noted by Richard B. Friedman, 'The Basis of Human Rights: A Criticism of Gewirth's Theory', *Nomos XXIII, Human Rights* (1981), 156.
16. Gewirth, *Reason and Morality*, 355.
17. Ibid. 357.
18. This point is also made by Henry B. Veatch, 'Book Review of Alan Gewirth's *Reason and Morality*', *Ethics*, 89/4 (July 1979).
19. Gewirth, *Reason and Morality*, 199–200.
20. Ibid. 135.
21. Ibid. 249.
22. Ibid. 270–1.
23. Ibid. 256.
24. Ibid. 31.
25. From D. D. Raphael, 'Rights and Conflicts', in *Gewirth's Ethical Rationalism*, ed. Edward Regis Jr. (Chicago: University of Chicago Press), 86.
26. Gewirth, *Reason and Morality*, 262.
27. Ibid.
28. Ibid. 249–50.
29. Ibid. 249, 308–9.
30. Ibid. 320.

3
Rawls and the Abstract Contract

THE central thesis of Brian Barry's *Theories of Justice* is that many arguments for liberal justice have attempted to combine elements from theories of both justice as mutual advantage and justice as impartiality. Barry argues that mutual advantage theorists such as Hume and Gauthier have attempted to incorporate impartial elements into their theories, perhaps in an attempt to avoid the counter-intuitive implications of justice as mutual advantage. And theories which are predominantly theories of justice as impartiality, such as Bruce Ackerman's theory in *Social Justice in the Liberal State* and Rawls's *A Theory of Justice*, include elements which are commonly associated with justice as mutual advantage.

Rawls is perhaps the best-known contemporary exponent of justice as impartiality, but his description of society as a 'cooperative venture for mutual advantage'[1] and of justice as relevant only when certain empirical circumstances obtain suggest that it must be self-interestedly rational for the parties to the contract to make the agreement. Rawls, following Hume, argues that

there are objective circumstances which make human cooperation both possible and necessary. Thus, many individuals coexist together at the same time on a definite geographical territory. These individuals are roughly similar in physical and mental powers; or at any rate, their capacities are comparable in that no one among them can dominate the rest. They are vulnerable to attack, and all are subject to having their plans blocked by the united force of others. Finally, there is the condition of moderate scarcity understood to cover a wide range of situations. Natural and other resources are not so abundant that schemes of cooperation become superfluous, nor are conditions so harsh that fruitful ventures must inevitably break down.[2]

In addition to these external or objective circumstances, which Rawls believes are virtually certain to obtain, he describes the subjective circumstances of justice: these involve the fact that people have different plans of life and different conceptions of the good. Principles are therefore necessary to adjudicate among the inevitable conflicts that arise among people.

On this description of the circumstances of justice, different people converge on the same principles from very different perspectives (from 'different plans of life' and 'different conceptions of the good'). The principles of justice represent constraints that each would accept as the price of gaining the co-operation of others. Because such restraints are seen by each to be beneficial, there is no difficulty explaining why each person would be motivated to act in accordance with justice.

Although Rawls's discussion of the circumstances of justice suggests that he endorses a conception of justice as mutual advantage, Rawls does not follow this idea to its logical conclusion by presenting the principles of justice as the outcome of a bargain among people with full knowledge of their situation and identity. On the contrary, the basic organizing idea of *A Theory of Justice* is the original position, which is not a full-knowledge bargain but a bargaining situation with abstract selves, ignorant of their distinguishing features and position in society. In such a situation, self-interested reason cannot be used by any person to gain advantages for herself: because the parties in the original position are denied crucial features of their identity (i.e. they do not know which self they are), they agree to principles in the interests of every, and therefore *any*, self. The original position is conceived as modelling moral choice on the grounds that it embodies impartiality: each constraint on choice in the original position is carefully argued for as a neutral or impartial constraint; and the information on which the choice is based is limited to purely empirical 'facts' about the world. The principles of justice are impartial, not only in the sense that they apply impartially, but also in the sense that they are chosen from the standpoint of the original position, which is an interpretation of impartiality itself.

The obvious question which presents itself in any interpretation of Rawls's theory is: how are these various elements related together? What is the function of the circumstances of justice within a theory which otherwise appears to be a conception of justice as impartiality?

While the two types of liberal theories of justice share the fundamental premiss that the principles which govern interaction in society must be acceptable to the individuals subject to those principles, the interpretations which each gives to that premiss differ sharply. On the theory of justice as mutual advantage, justice extends only to those capable of entering into relations of mutual advantage. This is because the motive for reaching agreement is self-interest, and self-interested people would agree to constrain their behaviour only if it is advantageous for them to do so, that is, only when there is something to be gained from obtaining the co-operation of another. A person who is so weak or so powerless that her co-operation would not benefit anyone else is therefore beyond the scope of justice as mutual advantage.[3] In contrast to the limited scope of mutual advantage theories, theories of impartial justice apply to all people (impartially) merely in virtue of their personhood. The weak and powerless are not conceived of as beyond the scope of justice but as precisely the kind of people to whom justice must extend.

This point of contention between the two types of theories is an expression of a more fundamental difference, namely the conception of the person on which the theory is based. Theories of justice as mutual advantage conceive of the individual concretely, as a person concerned to advance her own aims, interests and conceptions from her particular situation in the world. Hobbes's theory of justice as mutual advantage focuses on the person's position in the state of nature to show that agreement by all on the institution of a sovereign power would be beneficial to each person. And Rawls's discussion of the circumstances of justice also describes a situation in which justice would be beneficial for each person, given her vulnerability to attack and the (moderate) scarcity of resources. In contrast, the theory of justice as impartiality depends on viewing each person in an abstract way: someone who adopts the impartial standpoint must abstract from the differences between people, such as unequal strength or talents or bargaining leverage, and view each person as equal to all others. This is dramatically represented in Rawls's theory by the 'veil of ignorance', which excludes from consideration all 'morally arbitrary' or morally irrelevant aspects of the person, leaving us with a perspective which emphasizes the moral equality of persons.

In *Theories of Justice*, Brian Barry argues that Rawls's combination of elements from both types of theories of justice creates a tension in his work, which is most evident in his discussions of international and intergenerational justice and justice toward the handicapped. The difference between the two theories is not apparent when Rawls is considering the 'standard case' of justice, i.e. justice between competent adults who are contemporaries in the same society. However, when we examine justice between the able-bodied and the infirm or justice between generations, the theories pull in different directions, because in these cases there are arbitrary inequalities between people who are not co-operating for mutual advantage.

Barry argues that Rawls's difficulties arise because he retains some commitment to the idea of justice as involving mutual benefit and that it would have been better if he had left out all references to the circumstances of justice and straightforwardly present his theory as one which embodies impartiality. In Barry's view, the impartiality requirement is best represented, not by a self-interested choice in ignorance of one's identity, but by a debate on terms that no one could reasonably reject. And by 'reasonably reject', Barry seems to mean that the terms must be acceptable to everyone, providing that each abstracts from the inequalities of power that characterize real-life relations between people and views each person, including oneself, impartially, as just one person among others.

It is true, as Barry argues, that what does the work in Rawls's theory is his conception of justice as impartiality, and that his references to the circumstances of justice make his theory more confused and confusing. But Barry presents Rawls's commitment to certain elements associated with justice as mutual advantage as quite inexplicable, and that does not reflect the depth of Rawls's theorizing. Rawls is concerned in *A Theory of Justice* to ensure the priority of liberal principles over other conceptions of the good, and for that he needs a theory which embodies higher-order impartiality. Yet the two theories which claim to embody higher-order impartiality are both subject to serious flaws. Rawls does not, on the one hand, wish to base his theory on the slim and deniable foundation of a rational moral self and so introduce into his theory the Kantian dichotomies between desire and reason, self-interest and morality, which plagued both Kant's and Gewirth's theories of impartiality. But the principles which he seeks to justify have an important redistributive element and this seems to presuppose the fundamental moral equality of persons and the impartial standpoint of Gewirth's and Kant's theories. Rawls's solution is to construct the original position in a way which models the requirements of impartiality—that is, the most important element of Kant's moral theory—in a procedure which enables him to make the choice in the original position relevant to people in the real, empirical world. This is done by arguing, first, that justice is necessary, given the circumstances that each finds herself in. He then claims that the Kantian conception of morality that is embodied in the original position is one that we do in fact accept, thereby avoiding the charge that his theory is abstract and irrelevant to ordinary, empirical human beings.

The central theme of this chapter is that Rawls's project of arriving at Kantian principles without Kantian metaphysics does not work. The first section of this chapter argues that Rawls's theory requires an independent or neutral starting-point to justify the priority he gives to the rules of justice over the good. I hope to explain the attraction of the Kantian conception of justice as impartiality for liberal theory, and, at the same time, to cast doubt on the quest to arrive at a starting-point that is neutral among all conceptions of the good. The main movement in this section is backwards, from the original position and the principles of justice to an examination of the basic presuppositions of Rawls's theory, which are justified in terms of the method of reflective equilibrium. The organizing idea of this first section is that liberal principles are *not* neutral or impartial in the sense that liberalism requires. In the second section of this chapter, the argument reverses direction and examines the derivation of the principles of justice from these assumptions and from the original position. Two central problems are identified: the motivation problem, which can be described as Rawls's inability to explain why people would act in accordance with the principles of justice, when their knowledge is not constrained by the veil of ignorance; and the integrity problem, which refers to Rawls's related difficulty in integrating or relating the standpoint of the original position with the standpoint of the person in full knowledge of crucial features of her identity. I argue that, in an effort to avoid these problems, Rawls combines a theory of justice as impartiality with a theory of justice as mutual advantage. I conclude with a brief discussion of the problems inherent in Rawls's dominant conception of justice as impartiality.

1. Presuppositions of the Theory

Impartiality and the Independent (Neutral) Starting-Point

According to Rawls's description of the circumstances of justice, people will disagree with each other not only because they have different personal interests at stake but also because they disagree on the values that they and the institutions of government should promote. Principles of justice are necessary to adjudicate such disputes; and the principles must be impartial not only in the sense that they are derived in a way which is neutral with respect to each person's particular interests but impartial also in the higher-order sense that they can be appealed to in case of disputes between people acting on other moral values.

Rawls justifies most of the constraints on choice in the original position on the grounds that they are necessary to guarantee impartiality. He argues that, to secure impartiality in the original position, certain features of the rational contractors, such as their race or class, must be kept behind the veil of ignorance and excluded from the deliberative process in the initial situation. This is designed to prevent the parties to the original position from constructing principles that will be biased in favour of their own particular class or race.

The conception of impartiality that underlies the original position is extremely rigorous: Rawls requires his rational contractors to be impartial not just between persons but between moral ideals, and he expresses this requirement by denying the parties to the original position knowledge of their conceptions of the good. The exclusion of moral ideals from the original position is difficult to justify, for here Rawls cannot claim, as he does with respect to race and gender and class, that they are arbitrary from a moral point of view. It seems intuitively obvious that one's deeply held beliefs, commitments, and values are not only relevant to determining the kinds of principles which should govern one's society but are also central to personal identity: they serve, or they should serve in a well-integrated person, to anchor one's choices, as the basis on which one decides what things to do, and what kind of person one wants to be. In *A Theory of Justice*, Rawls's only argument is that this move is necessary to secure unanimous agreement;[4] but this explanation is inadequate, for it precisely begs the question. Of course it is the case that Rawls's theory will not work unless he excludes conceptions of the good, but we want to know whether there is a justification within the context of his theory for disallowing moral conceptions. We want to know whether we should accept Rawls's theory in the first place, and that involves asking whether each move in it is justified.

One obvious explanation (though *not* justification) for Rawls's concern to exclude moral ideals is that this is necessary to support the liberal public–private dichotomy. Rawls begins *A Theory of Justice* by drawing a distinction between the right and the good, a distinction which he seems to understand as unproblematic.[5] The core idea behind this division of morality into two parts is that the right or rules of justice should serve to regulate the institutions of society, while the promotion of ideals of the good is not a legitimate aim of the state but should be confined to the private or personal sphere. Sometimes Rawls expresses this distinction in terms of deontological or teleological theories or principles. In Rawls's theory, deontological principles apply to the basic structure of society: they outline the basic duties and rights which attach to individuals and which govern individual interaction; while teleological principles refer to particular (good) states of affairs which individuals sometimes strive to promote. Conceptions of the good are therefore viewed as properly personal or private, while the principles outlining the basic duties and structure of society (public principles) are conceived as expressing a higher-order impartiality in the sense that they are not justified by appealing to a particular conception of the good or particular moral ideal.[6]

In supporting the public–private distinction and the relegation of moral conceptions to the private sphere, Rawls in effect is claiming that the fact that a conception of the good is a coherent, intuitively attractive moral ideal is not sufficient to justify its political promotion. On what possible grounds, then, can Rawls claim that the rules of justice should be given political embodiment? Are there grounds on which Rawls can exclude perfectionism, say, without also excluding the principles of justice? Rawls's answer is that the principles of justice, principles of right, are qualitatively different from conceptions of the good because they are derived independently from all conceptions of the good, independently of all contingent features and attributes. This is Rawls's idea of an Archimedean point, an independent vantage-point from which he can assess moralities and derive principles and rights. On this claim hinges Rawls's anti-perfectionist argument, his functional distinction between the right and the good, his Kantian claim to have arrived at universally valid principles and rights. In short, it is crucial to the success of Rawls's theory that the right is prior to the good, that justice is morally prior to all other moral conceptions.

One may, of course, object that it does not follow in any direct way from the independence of a derivation that the principles which are the outcome of the argument have priority over other principles. But what Rawls is appealing to here is a powerfully attractive Kantian conception of morality as identified with impartiality. The regulative role of the rules of justice over other moral principles is justified on the grounds that they are derived independently of all socially acquired and so contingent moral ideals and conceptions, and so are impartial between them. This does not, of course, constitute a refutation of alternative ethical theories such as perfectionism,[7] but it does present an alluring alternative image of a morality derived from a foundation which is secure because beyond contingency, a foundation which gives the resulting principles a strong claim to assess socially acquired and so contingent moral ideals, and conceptions. On this view, the principles of justice are prior to other moral conceptions because more fully embodying impartiality, and this gives them the leverage to assess and adjudicate among socially acquired conceptions, ideals, and attributes.

The Method of Reflective Equilibrium

The relation of the original position to the principles which are its outcome is expressed by Rawls's claim that we accept the outcome of the original position because we accept that the conditions of the original position (i.e. the constraints designed to ensure impartiality) accurately model moral conditions, and we accept that the choice made there is a rational one under those conditions. But what justifies this conception of morality? Here Rawls employs the method of justification which he calls reflective equilibrium. In his own account of this justificatory method, Rawls emphasizes that moral principles should have independent appeal to our sense of right and wrong and be consistent with our standards and convictions. A moral principle may be initially attractive, but if it can be shown to lead to unacceptable consequences or if a standard we accept can be shown to suggest an unacceptable principle, we must bring into question our principles and convictions, altering both sides of the theory until they are in a state of reflective equilibrium, and we are reasonably satisfied with the resulting moral theory.

While Rawls's method of reflective equilibrium seems to describe in a rough way the process of thought of ordinary women and men when reflecting on particular judgements and principles, it does not take the resulting moral theory—the principles or standards or moral conception arrived at—beyond the morality of a particular society and confer universal validity on it. The method of reflective equilibrium involves testing the adequacy of the guiding principles of morality, of what is just or unjust, right or wrong, by reference to whether they match our ordinary considered moral intuitions. This characterization of the relation of the original position to real people in the empirical world is designed to ensure that his theory does not face the problems of Gewirth's and Kant's impartial theories, namely the problem of a deep division between the principles arrived at by the rational moral selves (the parties to the original position) and the principles accepted in the real, empirical world.

However, the problem of the relation between these two perspectives re-emerges in terms of our understanding of the original position as embodying a higher-order impartiality and our conception of the principles of justice as justified in adjudicating among disputes based on alternative moral conceptions. The theory of the original position, of what constitutes the moral point of view, is constructed, Rawls writes, out of 'our moral sentiments, as manifested by our considered judgments in reflective equilibrium'.[8] The term 'our' here cannot plausibly be intended to refer to the intuitions of all human beings, for Rawls has done nothing to show that the original position is a model of morality on which all people would agree. Rather, the considered convictions that serve as the basis for constructing the theory of the original position are shared by a much more limited group, namely by Rawls's readership, which is comprised largely of educated Western, and specifically Anglo-American, liberal democratic individualists. There is nothing wrong with this in itself, if the theory being sought is a theory for such people, a theory that articulates a specific shared moral understanding and is to apply to people who understand themselves and the world in that way. The problem is that Rawls seems unwilling in *A Theory of Justice* to accept the limitations of his communitarian foundations. He uses the considered convictions of a particular group, a particular community, to construct a theory that he then seems to treat as normative for all humankind. The tension between the particularistic grounding of the conception of the original position and the universalist aspirations of the principles that emerge from the hypothetical contract is a problem for Rawls's theory because, presumably, the point of the theory is to consider whether the views held by some, i.e. the convictions shared by the community, are correct. Only this would justify the extension of these views to all, including those who do not share them. But the attempt to *ground* moral theory in the views of some would not seem to justify any claim to truth for that theory, and so would not justify its universal application.

The tension between the universalist and particularist elements in Rawls's theory is also evident in his exclusion of conceptions of the good from the original position. We have seen that the method of reflective equilibrium works by articulating the moral conception that underlies a particular society, thereby rendering the deep theory on which people in that society act and the categories in which they think into a coherent and accessible theory. But if the justification for, and indeed basis of, the conception of the original position is a (deep) theory of the good, as is implied by the method of reflective equilibrium, on what grounds can Rawls exclude from the original position all other conceptions of the good? It cannot be because moral ideals are irrelevant to morality because he himself constructs his conception of the original position from a particular (communal) conception of the good. Thus, the method of reflective equilibrium contradicts Rawls's claim that the original position embodies impartiality, because that method works by appealing to a particular, i.e., sectarian, conception of the good. The problem for Rawls's theory is that, if he understands justice itself as an essentially contested concept,[9] and each theory of justice as expressing a particular moral understanding or particular theory of the good, he will have no ground, no Archimedean point, from which to assess and adjudicate among rival moral conceptions.

Behind the Original Position

Thus far, we have seen that Rawls conceives of his principles of justice as justified on the grounds that they embody a higher-order impartiality, that they are the product of a situation which is an interpretation of impartiality itself. The issue that I wish to raise in this section is whether the impartiality requirement is itself an impartial requirement, that is, whether it is possible to arrive at an understanding of impartiality which is independent of all substantive ethical conceptions. If it is not possible, then there can be no appeal to a higher-order impartiality: rather, all adjudicating principles are based on a particular (deeper) conception of the good and there is no language, no principles, which are neutral between them.

This issue can be approached by considering Rawls's conception of impartiality. One criticism which has been made of Rawls's theory is that his veil of ignorance is thicker than is necessary, that conceptions of the good should not be excluded from the initial situation. In *A Theory of Justice*, Rawls did not adequately deal with this problem, but he responded to this criticism four years after the publication of his book. Rawls writes:

It is not for reasons of impartiality and simplicity alone that these [conceptions of the good] are not known. Our final ends ... depend on our abilities and opportunities, on the numerous contingencies that have shaped our attachments and affections. That we have one conception of the good rather than another is not relevant from a moral standpoint. In acquiring it we are influenced by the same sort of contingencies that lead us to rule out a knowledge of our sex and class.[10]

In this passage, Rawls equates one's conception of the good with one's class and gender, lumping them all together as morally arbitrary. By 'morally arbitrary', Rawls cannot mean that these things are irrelevant to all moralities and so should be excluded from the original position. That could justify the exclusion of class and sex but is not applicable to conceptions of the good. There is a long tradition, stemming from Aristotle, of moral theories which have been based on conceptions of what is good, valuable, or important in life. What Rawls must mean by 'morally irrelevant' or 'morally arbitrary' is far more stringent than that: he wants to exclude conceptions of the good because they are influenced by the society in which one is born and that is as much a matter of chance or arbitrary fate as being born working-class, a woman, and black. Behind this requirement is a quest for principles which are impartial in the sense of being based on something absolute and non-contingent, which holds necessarily, for all people. What this quest assumes, without any argument or basis, is that the way in which a belief is acquired determines its relevance to moral theory, that moral principles must for some reason be based exclusively on what is necessarily the case.

The same Kantian quest for absolute non-contingent principles, which is itself motivated by his identification of liberalism with higher-order impartiality, also explains Rawls's rejection of desert as a basis for distribution. Rawls argues that favourable genetic endowment—being born intelligent or beautiful or talented—is a matter of good fortune or arbitrary luck, and the propensity to exercise one's capacities and develop one's abilities is affected in great measure by one's family and class background. This leads Rawls to argue that distribution should not be based on factors which are 'arbitrary from a moral point of view'.[11] And again he means by this that the talent or skill or intellect which is the basis of the desert claim is acquired in a contingent way and so cannot serve as a criterion of distributive justice. The products which flow from the exercise of a person's talents and abilities are not deserved because the assets and abilities which are the conditions of their exercise are not deserved.

To this argument, Robert Nozick, Michael Zuckert, and Michael J. Sandel have all persuasively argued that Rawls's requirement that things be deserved *all the way down* reveals a basic misunderstanding of desert-based claims.[12] Nozick and the others argue that the fact that talents and abilities are not deserved does not undermine the argument that the products of their exercise are deserved. Indeed, it is central to the concept of desert that there is a basis for desert not itself deserved, from which the deserving action proceeds, and which is ultimately prior to it.[13] There is an analogy here with the notion of possession, which requires a subject of possession not itself possessed.

Rawls's view that the person's moral ideals, her natural abilities and capacities and the propensity to exercise them, are not central to her identity but mere products of social and natural contingency, suggests a conception of the person underlying Rawls's theory.[14] In his justification of the difference principle and of the exclusion of moral ideals, Rawls implicitly draws a distinction between the person's autonomous core and contingent attributes and talents and ideas which is equivalent to a distinction between the self and what is external to the self.[15] Behind both these arguments is a conception of the self divorced from its attributes, a conception of a choosing core only contingently related to its abilities and ideas and talents. And so it seems that Rawls's search for a foundation beyond contingency, independent of all accidental features and ideas of the good, leaves him with a conception of the self identified only with the capacity for choice. It is this capacity for autonomy which serves as the basis for the rights and principles of justice in Rawls's theory.

The central problem with basing his theory of justice and rights on a certain conception of the person as an autonomous rational being is that it violates the neutrality of Rawls's starting-point.[16] If Rawls's rules of justice are to be justified in regulating people's interactions and conceptions of the good, his theory requires an independent starting-point, neutral among all conceptions of the good. He strives to achieve this in his quest to get behind all contingency and so arrive at a conception of the person as pure chooser or pure agency, stripped of all empirical features, of all ends and interests and particular content. At the bottom of Rawls's theory, behind his argument for the difference principle, is a particular conception of the person. And this conception is not a neutral one, for it defines the person in a radically individualistic way. It is individualistic in the sense that the identity of the person is given in advance, apart from the society in which she is a member, apart from the person's particular interests and ends. The person's identity is constituted by the antecedently given capacity for choice, rather than the ends the self believes in, which are, on other views, central to personal identity.

Though Rawls's theory purports to be neutral among divergent conceptions of the good, it is so only if the conceptions concern one's own plan of life.[17] But many conceptions of the good do not fit this individualistic mould; many can be realized only in certain types of social structures or if certain types of economic relations exist between people (for example, religious conceptions, or communism). Rawls's individualistic theory of each person choosing her own good cannot accommodate these goods; it is not neutral among them. This can be illustrated through a brief consideration of Aristotelian theory. On an Aristotelian conception, personal identity is defined in terms of the person's conception of the good, which is mediated through a theory of the virtues. The person identifies with the virtues because they exemplify individual excellence, and she strives to attain these virtues herself; but what counts as a virtue, what counts as an excellence, is relative to a conception of the good embodied in or underlying the practices and institutions and traditions of the community. It is because the virtues are defined as virtues by reference to an overall conception of the good, and they are virtues of the individual's dispositions—i.e. they are not straightforwardly chosen, but, rather, the result of cultivating and disciplining the person's affective responses over an extended time—that it is impossible to conceive of the capacity for choice as defining identity, as prior to the person's conception of the good. On an Aristotelian view, the person defines her identity through identifying with a particular conception of the good, and makes choices on the basis of this. Moreover, the virtues do not develop in the person spontaneously but are the product of moral education: it is necessary, therefore, to encourage in children the development of certain affective responses in certain circumstances and the discouragement of others, and in this way convey not merely a certain conception of the good at the cognitive level but an appreciation for and identification with that way of life by the person's whole being. This means that the achievement of this conception of morality is possible only if society is organized to promote it, that is, to develop in children the virtues which are necessary to live a good life. And so, by conceiving of conceptions of the good as solely a private matter, to be chosen by each person, Rawls denies the conditions which make the development of the Aristotelian virtues possible.

Although Rawls does not address the point that his theory is extremely antithetical to, say, an Aristotelian conception of morality, he does attempt to deny in general terms the charge of non-neutrality. His central argument here is that part of one's plan of life may include feelings or aspirations for other people.[18] He does not rule out the possibility of altruism or benevolence once the veil of ignorance is lifted, or that people will choose to organize their economic system collectively, but for the purposes of the original position, for arriving at the principles of justice, Rawls's theory treats each person as a distinct individual and attempts to secure to her rights to the unimpeded pursuit of her own good. But Rawls cannot have it both ways, for if people are essentially other-regarding, or if they are committed to a certain moral ideal which involves a certain type of social or economic structure, they will feel constrained by principles which frustrate their moral convictions and force them to view each person as the central shaper of her own identity. Rawls cannot say that within the original position we can treat people as identified with their capacity for choice while at the same time admitting that outside the original position they may consider their moral values, goals, commitments, and communal ties as essential constituents of their identity. He can accommodate the latter view only to the extent that he admits that the former view, i.e. the central assumption of the original position, is empirically false. It is not good enough for Rawls to claim that at the private level people can be altruistic or other-regarding, but at the public level, where the principles of justice apply, the central concern is with the protection of individual autonomy. It is not good enough because it is that division of morality which is precisely in question and which is supposed to be justified by the neutrality of Rawls's starting-point.

We began this section by raising the question of whether the impartiality requirement is an impartial requirement, and our examination of Rawls's conception of impartiality suggests that his conception is not impartial but presupposes acceptance of certain moral ideals, such as the value of individual autonomy and rationality. I wish to conclude this section by noting that Rawls's identification of morality with impartiality is also not impartial among ethical conceptions, but assumes a particular relation of self-interest to morality.

In requiring the person to abstract from specific features of her identity, and so assume a vantage-point where her particular desires and interests are not at stake, Rawls is following Gewirth and of course Kant in distinguishing self-interest and morality according to their internal relation to the individual's will. The underlying conception here is that actions on the basis of one's desires or interests or beliefs, while not, Rawls admits, necessarily selfish, are nevertheless self-interested;[19] while the impartial standpoint of morality abstracts from all such features, viewing each person, including the moral reasoner, as just one person among others.

One of the most striking aspects of this conception of morality is that it is extremely individualistic: it treats each person as a distinct individual, who is formally equal to all others from the moral point of view. It denies by fiat the relational conception of morality, according to which moral actions and the moral point of view involve identifying with one's whole being with a particular community, a particular conception of the good. Implicit in the identification of morality with impartiality is a conception of the person as divided between her self-interested, egoistic, desirous self and the impartial, rational, moral self. It is implicit in this conception because, in order to conceive of each person as equal to all others, as just one person among others, all particular differentiating features must be abstracted from the person. This, in effect, identifies moral actions with the standpoint that one can adopt through a cognitive process of abstraction, and identifies all actions based on particular interests, particular aims or desires or conceptions, as self-interested. The impartiality requirement is not, as it may seem to be, an innocuous constraint on the original position: not only is a radically individualistic conception of morality assumed, but a Kantian one, with Kantian

divisions at the level of the person, between reason and morality
on the one hand and desire and self-interest on the other.

2. THE DERIVATION OF PRINCIPLES FROM THE ORIGINAL POSITION

Let us for the moment set aside the difficulty that Rawls's individualistic conception of the person poses for the neutrality of
his theory, and consider the derivation of the principles of justice
from such an abstract conception. The parties to the original
position must choose the principles of justice in ignorance of
their bodily and social situations, their temperament, personality, beliefs, and values. So much needs to be abstracted from
the choosers to attain such absolute autonomy and equality and
thereby justify the principles agreed to that the parties to the
agreement do not have any distinguishing features, any particular mental content; they are just like Kant's noumenal selves:
pure, disembodied, rational agency. This raises the question to
which Kant could not provide a satisfactory answer: on what
can such abstract rational selves base their decision? How is it
possible to derive moral principles from pure, contentless
reason? Here Rawls's theory claims superiority over Kant's, for
Rawls claims to be able to derive moral principles by his method
of incorporating a Kantian moral conception into a traditional
contractarian argument. In the original position, Rawls's rational
contractors employ reason, not as a purely formal, and so empty,
power, as Kant conceived it, but reason as it is employed in
everyday life, in considering the advantages or disadvantages
of a particular course of action and weighing it against the alternatives.[20] This conception of reason, as an instrumental, utility-
maximizing capacity, serves the function of linking reason with
the real, empirical world. In considering the best course of action
from the self-interested maximizer's point of view, Rawls's rational contractors base their choices on empirical considerations
and so avoid the abstractness and the radical dualisms—between
desire and reason, the causal laws of nature and the autonomous
action of reason, self-interest, and morality—which plague Kant's
theory. Since the parties in the original position do not know
what their preferences are, what kind of life they would like

to lead, or their conceptions of the good, they must choose the principles of justice on the basis of those things which are means to a variety of different plans of life.

Rawls's theory, like Gewirth's liberal theory, requires a theory of the good to give content to his principles and rights, to determine such things as the objects of distributive policy, the interests which need to be protected by rights, the weight and scope of these rights, and the obligations correlative to the rights and rules of justice. But this theory of the good which underlies rights theories must be what Rawls calls a 'thin theory' of the good, that is, a theory which distinguishes certain things as good, without presupposing a deeper moral ideal, and so jeopardizing the neutrality of his theory.

Rawls formulates his thin theory of the good by appealing to the objectives of prudential calculators. Although his rational contractors do not know anything in particular about themselves or their society, they have access to general empirical knowledge, to the results of the most advanced work in the social and physical sciences to guide them. They isolate certain things as good by applying the criterion of what 'every man is presumed to want [because] ... they ... have a use whatever a person's rational plan of life'.[21] This criterion is similar to the criterion employed by Gewirth to distinguish freedom and well-being as good, namely that they are necessary for any plan of life, any action whatsoever. Rawls regards such things as health, intelligence, and imagination as goods in this sense (primary goods), but they play little part in his theory since they cannot be controlled by the basic structure of society.[22] Those things which do depend on the institutions of society, and which Rawls regards as in everyone's interest, are 'rights and liberties, powers and opportunities, income and wealth'[23] and self-respect.[24] Rawls argues that these are primary goods because they are means to a wide range of ends. Income, wealth, and power contribute to a higher standard of living, and will enable a person to pursue things which a poorer person might be debarred from doing; and greater opportunities in the institutions of society increase the likelihood that people will be able to realize their plan of life. Self-respect is a means to whatever ends an individual may have in the sense that, 'without it, nothing may seem worth doing, or if some things have value for us, we lack the will to strive for them'.[25] It is quite obvious why people in the original position desire liberty: since they cannot distinguish the relative value of different kinds of life (for the original position excludes this from consideration), they can provide only for the greatest possible latitude to fulfil whatever conception they will have, without interfering in the plans of life of others. The right to liberty can be viewed as a device to ensure that people's choices will be respected whatever they are (although, as we have seen, Rawls's individualistic conception of freedom is not in fact neutral among divergent conceptions of the good life).

It is on the basis of this list of primary goods that Rawls constructs his principles of justice, granting citizens basic liberties, such as freedom of speech and conscience, freedom from arbitrary arrest, and so on. And he combines his equal liberty principle with a principle of distribution which recognizes the importance of maximum income and wealth and powers, and so justifies inequalities if they benefit the least advantaged. We can see, then, that Rawls's thin theory of primary goods is crucial to his argument: he needs a thin theory of the good to rescue his theory from the problems of a purely formal and abstract theory like Kant's, but at the same time he must do so in a way which does not presuppose a full theory of the good and violate the neutrality of his argument. The list of primary goods provides him with an interpersonal standard to measure everyone's relative positions in the hierarchy for the purpose of applying the difference principle, without reducing all value scales to one, as Rawls accuses utilitarians of doing, and without introducing a teleological conception of the relative worth of different people's lives and conceptions of the good.

It is here, in his thin theory of the good, that the incoherence of Rawls's project of combining Kantianism with empirically based contractualism becomes evident. The only basis on which the rational contractors can call any state of affairs good is if it contributes to overall want-satisfaction, for wants are the only common factor left to the parties to the original position. Rawls's noumenal selves cannot deduce principles of morality from the standpoint of pure autonomous reason, abstracted from the world. In *The Liberal Theory of Justice*,[26] Brian Barry argues that Rawls's contractors cannot appeal to any standard of excellence or moral ideals in arriving at primary goods and so the only way they can distinguish certain things as good is by appealing to wants (content unknown). But Rawls's claim in *A Theory of Justice*, that primary goods are empirically derived goods necessary to all plans of life, is difficult to sustain. A moment's reflection will confirm that there are plans of life which would be frustrated by the possession of income, wealth, or power; indeed, there are plans of life whose central feature is the denial of these 'goods'. And there are, as J. S. Mill recognized,[27] certain types of societies, such as traditional tribal societies, in which people are not adjusted to political liberties, so that granting people in such societies the Rawlsian liberties could destroy the fabric of their society and contribute to these individuals' maladjustment and alienation. Indeed, it is hard to see how one could greatly expand the list of primary goods beyond good health, mental stability, security for one's physical safety and for the future. The criterion of good Rawls employs is a minimal one, for plans of life and types of societies are so diverse that very few things are necessary means to all plans of life in all societies. (A much more expansive conception of primary goods would use as a criterion of good those things which are necessary to human well-being, but this criterion would jeopardize the neutrality of Rawls's argument.)

If Rawls's primary goods are not all-purpose means to all plans of life, then what is the criterion that distinguishes these things as goods? Once again it seems that Rawls's theory is much more intimately bound up with his conception of the person as an autonomous agent than he wants to admit.[28] Rights to basic liberties can be explained as necessary to protect the interest in autonomy that Rawls believes all people have. Wealth, income, and power are means for the person to realize her individual plans and goals, to exercise her autonomy in the world. Similarly, increased opportunities are necessary to expand the choices open to the agent, thus providing greater scope for the exercise of autonomy. And self-respect is the necessary subjective condition for the individual to be able to carry out her choices and realize her capacity for autonomy. The problem with this interpretation of Rawls's primary goods is that it changes the nature of the primary goods from all-purpose means to want-satisfaction to essentially moral goods, justified by their contribution to realizing the autonomous essence of the person. But basing his theory of primary goods, and indirectly his principles of justice, on such a conception of the person involves a complete denial of Rawls's claim to neutrality, which is necessary to support the priority of the right over the good.

This tension between subjective and objective value, want-regarding and ideal-regarding considerations, surfaces again in a different way in Rawls's discussion of his first principle of justice, the liberty principle.[29] Rawls formulates the principle in the following way: 'Each person is to have an equal right to the most extensive total system of equal basic liberties compatible with a similar system of liberty for all.'[30] Rawls's appeal to 'the most extensive total system' of equal basic liberties suggests that he believes that the liberties of speech, of conscience, political liberty, and so on, can occur independently, and that it may be justified to limit one liberty for the sake of increasing another, as long as this yields the 'best total system of equal liberty'.[31] The goal here is maximum liberty and that may involve, as in Rawls's example,[32] limiting the occasions in which one may speak in accordance with certain rules of order to preserve the purpose of the right to free speech.

The problem with Rawls's formulation is that he is speaking in aggregative terms about freedom of speech to convey ideas that are not essentially aggregative at all, but involve differences in value. The formula of limiting liberty for the sake of liberty obfuscates the fact that the aim cannot be maximum liberty, what-ever that is, but maximally valuable liberty. Limiting the occasions in which one can speak, in accordance with rules of order, does not increase or decrease the amount of liberty, as if this could be computed along a single scale, with only greater or lesser amounts of the same thing. It does, however, enhance the value of the discussion. One must appeal to a standard to measure which system of liberty is most extensive, that which allows extensive political liberties such as self-government but does not protect freedom of religion or association in a trade union; or a dictatorship which denies the political liberty of self-government to its citizens but protects the other individual liber-ties. To decide which of these two 'systems of liberties' is more 'extensive' is not an aggregative question but a question of value. It can be answered only by considering which liberty is more important; and that means appealing to a standard of value, a deeper ethical theory.

Each time the question of value emerges in Rawls's theory, it poses a problem, for his theory purports to be neutral among different conceptions of the good, different ideas of value. He can attempt to deal with the issue of value by appealing to subjective value, i.e. value to the person, but this raises the problem of differential distributions based on subjective differences between people. Alternatively, he can rely on an objective standard of value and so implicitly on a particular conception of the good society, perhaps supported by an appeal to a conception of the person. Rawls wants to avoid both strategies by avoiding the issue of value altogether, but this proves extremely difficult. Rawls succeeds to the extent that he does only because his thin theory of the good enables him to give content to his principles and rights without making any claims about the (intrinsic) value of these primary goods. But within the list of primary goods, in decisions about trading one good for another, or one right against another, or in considering the importance to the individual of particular liberties and goods, the issue of value raises its head again.

To secure the primary good of liberty, Rawls's just society provides that citizens have equal basic formal rights, equal political liberties; but he also allows for the unequal exercise of these rights. 'Some have greater authority and wealth,' he writes, 'and therefore greater means to achieve their aims.'[33] In Rawls's view, this does not mean that they have less liberty, merely that the value of the formal liberties is not the same for everyone. 'The inability to take advantage of one's rights and opportunities as a result of poverty and ignorance, and a lack of means generally is sometimes counted among the constraints definitive of liberty. I shall not, however, say this, but rather I shall think of these things as affecting the worth of liberty.'[34] Significantly, Rawls does not provide any reasons for his distinction between liberty and the worth of liberty. This is puzzling, especially in light of the fact that Rawls accepts the view that the concept of liberty is best understood as a triadic relation between the agents who are free, the obstacles that they are free from, and what it is that they are free to do or not to do.[35] There does not seem to be any reason why poverty and ignorance (which, after all, can be overcome through social arrangements) do not count as obstacles in the relevant sense.

Rawls attempts to mitigate the inegalitarian thrust of his distinction between liberty and the worth of liberty by pointing to the second principle of justice, the so-called difference principle, which addresses the issue of social and economic inequalities. He concludes his discussion of the unequal worth of liberty by reminding his readers that the basic structure is to be arranged to maximize the worth to the least advantaged of the complete scheme of equal liberty shared by all.[36] This appeal to consequentialist reasoning does not, however, explain or justify Rawls's distinction between liberty and the worth of liberty. The issue here is not merely the fairness of the distinction or the inequalities that could be justified under it: it runs much deeper than that. It is not just that Rawls arbitrarily rules out such things as poverty and ignorance as obstacles to freedom: it is that Rawls does not want to consider at all the subjective value of these goods and rights to the individual. But if the primary goods and rights which are based on them do not have any intrinsic value, but only instrumental value in enabling the individual to fulfil the life-plan she chooses, then it follows that equal liberty can be realized only by ensuring that the goods are equally instrumental to fulfilling each person's life-plan. Of course, Rawls does not want to consider the primary goods from the point of view of their subjective value to the individual, because this greatly complicates his theory, making interpersonal comparisons between degrees of advantage almost impossible, and it has the counter-intuitive consequence of justifying differential distributions of primary goods on the basis of the expense of the person's particular life-plan. Thus he employs the distinction between liberty and the worth of liberty as a kind of Maginot line against the collapse of his objective list of primary goods into purely subjective goods, valuable for the individual because they enable her to realize her (subjectively valuable) life-plan. But within the context of his theory, Rawls's distinction between the equal formal liberties and the unequal value of these liberties to the individual is completely arbitrary. Here we must recall that Rawls founds his argument for justice on the equal value of human beings. It is this assumption which underlies the original position where persons are abstracted from their bodily and social situation, from any abilities or qualities which might suggest that some are worthier than others. If, as Rawls argues, all lives are equally valuable, then it follows that the rights which protect moral personhood should be equally valuable to the individuals who hold them.

A similar problem arises in Rawls's argument for the priority of the liberty principle over all other principles. In *A Theory of Justice*, Rawls's primary goods are presented as empirically de-rived interests that all people have. This description of the primary goods does not enable Rawls to distinguish in importance among the goods, for they are all supposed to be instrumentally necess-ary to all plans of life. But Rawls does not want to leave the adjudication of his principles to intuitionistic balancing in cases of conflict. Indeed, Rawls considers the assignment of weights or priority to his principles as one of the important achievements of his book.[37] How, then, does he distinguish in importance among principles which protect equally important interests?

Rawls introduces what he calls the Aristotelian Principle to justify the lexical priority that he ascribes to the political liberties over economic interests once a certain level of prosperity is attained. According to the Aristotelian Principle, 'human beings enjoy the exercise of their realized capacities (their innate or trained abilities) and this enjoyment increases the more the capa-city is realized, or the greater its complexity ... human beings take more pleasure in doing something as they become more proficient at it, and of the two activities they do equally well, they prefer the one calling on a larger repertoire of these intricate and subtle discriminations.'[38] This principle is not put forward by Rawls as an ideal of human nature: he is not saying that it is desirable for people to exercise their capacities, to engage in more complex, skilful, or intellectual activities, for that would be to base his principles of justice on a perfectionist ideal. Rather, Rawls is saying here that people do as a matter of empirical fact enjoy more demanding activities to less demanding ones.

One question which arises concerning Rawls's attribution of this motivational principle to all people concerns the coherence of this motivation with the self-interested utility-maximizing motive that Rawls ascribes to the parties to the original position. It seems doubtful that Rawls would have arrived at the principles that he does if his rational contractors had reasoned as people who preferred more complex and more demanding activities to less demanding ones. The fact that Rawls does not ascribe this motivation directly to parties in the original position, but rather treats it as an empirical fact about the parties that they then consider as self-interested agents, suggests that this principle does not sit easily with the instrumental reason that characterizes the parties in the original position.

However, the central issue with regard to the Aristotelian Principle is the purpose and truth of this motivational principle in the context of Rawls's overall theory. If the Aristotelian Principle were true, it would make sense for the parties to the original position to distinguish between two conceptions of justice and accord priority to the civil liberties at a certain stage of economic development. It would make sense for Rawls's rational contractors to argue, as they do, that, when people are too impoverished to engage in cultural activities, it is rational for them to sacrifice their freedom for the sake of greater material wealth (the general conception of justice). But beyond a certain level of material well-being, Rawls argues, it is irrational for people to satisfy material interests over cultural activities (the special conception of justice). Rawls appeals to the Aristotelian Principle to arrive at the special conception's conclusion that people would give priority to the civil liberties—freedom of conscience, freedom of speech, freedom of religion, political participation—for they would not want to jeopardize their ability to engage in critical thought and discussion, political self-government, and spiritual development. But, as an empirical fact, Rawls's Aristotelian Principle is probably false. It is a sad fact that large numbers of people would rather read *Playboy* than *A Theory of Justice*, would rather be entertained than entertain themselves. But, as his theory is unable to appeal to the inherent superiority of some ways of life over others, some activities over others, Rawls is forced to import highly controversial, and probably false, motivational assumptions into his theory to avoid the implications of deriving his principles of justice from the wants and desires that people actually have.

In many respects, Rawls's Aristotelian Principle parallels Mill's distinction between the higher and lower pleasures.[39] Both theories are anti-perfectionist at the foundational level; both attempt to give importance to people's choices; and both seek to avoid the obvious corollary of their theories, namely that people may choose the baser pleasures and activities and that, within the context of their theories, they cannot make judgements about the content of people's choices. But whereas Rawls argues that the person engaged in simple activities feels that her life is dull and boring and wants to exercise her abilities to the fullest extent, Mill allows that the person pursuing the lower activities could be quite happy because 'unconscious of the imperfections' of her lifestyle,[40] but argues that the person who has experienced both forms of life finds the higher pleasures more desirable. That seems more plausible than Rawls's claim, but it proves only the superiority of the higher pleasures, not that the parties to the original position would base their principles on this conception of superiority. (They are rational in the sense that they seek to fulfil the desires that they have or are likely to have.) And this illustrates precisely the problem with granting such import-ance to autonomy defined in terms of choice as such, namely that, at the ordinary level, those things which people choose may not reveal the value of the object chosen, but may reflect the chooser's vulgar tastes or selfish desires; and, at the ultimate level, the choice criterion cannot apply, for, if everything is open to question, there is nothing on which to base the choice. In applying his hypothetical choice criterion from the standpoint of pure autonomous reason, Rawls is faced with two equally unpalatable alternatives: appealing to want-regarding consider-ations will not yield the kind of result that his liberal theory needs; and appealing to a particular ideal of the person does not provide the kind of foundation that liberalism requires.[41] Rawls wants to avoid the implications of a purely subjective cri-terion of value, with its reliance on individually relative wants and desires, but he refuses to consider the value of things apart from the fact that people choose them or want them or desire them, for that would introduce perfectionism into his theory. Rawls 'solves' this dilemma by setting up false distinctions to prevent the collapse of his objectively valuable list of primary goods into subjectively valuable goods, by employing the mis-leading language of quantity to obscure the need to appeal to a substantive conception of value to assign importance to the different liberties or priority among the principles of justice, and by masquerading ideals as empirical facts to arrive at the conclu-sions he wants to.

3. The Motivation Problem

Defining the Problem

In conceiving of morality in terms of a standpoint divorced of all particular and contingent aims and attributes, desires and ideals, Rawls opens up a wide gap between prudential and moral considerations, between the person as she is characterized in the original position and the person outside the original position, in full knowledge of her interests and aims and ends. This has important implications for his theory, specifically for explaining why we should be moral, why we should accept the principles of justice. To this motivation problem, Rawls's conception of morality as impartiality cannot provide a satisfactory solution.

The Rawlsian contract has difficulty in explaining the motivational force of the principles of justice for the person, because the instrumental rationality which Rawls employs in the initial situation does not justify its results outside the initial situation. From within the standpoint of the original position, the person accepts the principles of justice and the process of reasoning that leads up to them, for she agrees to the contract. The person tries to maximize her own self-interest within the constraints imposed by the original position, that is, while ignorant of many important features of herself. But, from the standpoint of the person once the veil of ignorance is lifted, the principles cannot be validated by self-interest. The person agreed to them, so to speak, when ignorant of crucial features of her own identity and may now find that the principles embody ideas antithetical to her deeply held moral convictions, contrary to what she considers her vital interests. Why should she accept the principles of justice?

One attempt by Rawls to link the two standpoints—that of the original position and that of the person once the veil of ignorance is lifted—is by requiring that the person in the original position agree only to those principles that she could adhere to in real life. That is, he stipulates that one constraint on choice in the original position is that any principles agreed to there must be honoured by the person outside the original position; therefore, the person should agree only to principles that she would accept once she is aware of all features of her identity. This is

the 'strains of commitment' requirement.[42] While this requirement recognizes that there must be some congruence between
the principles of justice and the person's particular desires and
interests and aims—in other words, that too great a gap between
them would make adherence to the principles of justice burden-
some and the society itself unstable—this solution is not compatible with the structure of Rawls's theory. Rawls's theory is a
common standpoint theory in the sense that all parties to the
original position are required to adopt the same standpoint and
agree to the principles of justice from that standpoint; whereas
the 'strains of commitment' requirement suggests a convergence
theory, a theory in which the parties to the contract agree from
their different standpoints to the same principles of justice.[43]
While the convergence (or full-knowledge) form of contractualist
agreement would undoubtedly overcome the motivation problem, because the parties would agree to the contract only if they
recognized it was in their rational self-interest, it is not consistent
with the contract among rational abstracted selves that is Rawls's
original position. How could the parties to the original position
possibly know whether what they agree to in ignorance of their
identity would unduly tax the strains of commitment? They could
only know that if they knew who they were, what their deepest
commitments and aims and beliefs were. And that is precisely
the knowledge denied to them in the original position.

Rawls's theory, like Gewirth's, needs some ground where the
two standpoints meet, some linkage between morality and self-
interest, between the standpoint of the original position and that
of the person once the veil of ignorance is lifted. Rawls needs
to explain why the person should accept the formal requirement
of universalizing her principles and goals, and act on the results
of prudence universalized. Why should the person consider
other people's desires and aims as equivalent to her own desires
and aims? Why should we adopt the view of ourselves as undifferentiated reason, abstracted from our particular features, mental content, and bodily and social situation? It is important to
the success of Rawls's theory that he is able to answer these
questions, for his principles of justice purport to be universal
principles, derived from an initial situation that is not confined
to or relative to a particular community, but one that is regulative
with respect to people's actions and moral ideals. To justify the

universality of Rawls's principles, this conception of oneself as an abstracted being has to be relevant to practical reason, has to be implied in some way in the person's everyday life. Only in this way can Rawls ensure that the abstract moral standpoint has universal applicability. Only by making the Rawlsian moral conception follow in some way from practical reason or autonomy or everyday life can Rawls justify the regulative role of the principles of justice to people with conceptions of the good that are not easily accommodated to it, to people who seek to embody their moral ideals in the political life and legislation of the society.

Rawls's Proposed Solution

Rawls attempts to bridge the gap between the real person in society and the abstracted noumenal self by postulating that each person has a capacity for a sense of justice. In fact, Rawls conceives of the person as having the capacity for both a conception of the good and a sense of justice: the former refers to the capacity to develop and live according to a plan of life which orders one's desires and interests and aims into a unifying whole, and which the person is committed to and seeks to fulfil;[44] the latter refers to the capacity for a desire to act justly and promote just institutions that are also regulative with respect to the person's plan of life or conception of the good.[45] It is significant that the sense of justice is not merely a vehicle to explain how a rationally self-interested person could come to act morally, although that is one of its functions, but that it must also regulate the person's central desires and interests and aims, which constitute her conception of the good. Just as Rawls's two principles of justice define the limits of the operation of self-interested (or negatively free) action, and just as the principles of justice are regulative with respect to differing conceptions of the good, so, at the level of the person, the sense of justice must have priority over the person's other desires and interests and aims. Rawls's distinction at the level of the person between her capacity for a conception of the good, which is seen in wholly self-interested or personal terms, and her capacity for a sense of justice is consistent with Rawls's conception of justice as the 'first virtue' of society,[46] and as justified in arbitrating among all other moral (and nonmoral) conceptions. Rawls's sense of justice must not be seen as merely one of the person's numerous desires and interests and aims, all of which are incorporated into her rational plan of life, but on a different level entirely, and so justified in defining the limits of the person's actions in pursuit of her plan of life.

In postulating the capacity for a sense of justice as a vehicle between self-interest and morality, Rawls seems to be presenting an account of moral motivation which departs in important ways from the account provided by Gewirth. Rawls's sense of justice does not explain the motivating power of justice in terms of the rational or cognitive recognition of the duties required by justice, but in terms of the response at the level of the person's feelings and emotions to the distress of others. In Gewirth's theory, the bridge between self-interest and morality is provided by reason's adoption of the impartial standpoint, which takes the form of a cognitive recognition that the claims that one makes on one's own behalf are made by other people on the same grounds. What is at the root of this theory is a conception of each person as equal to all others, i.e. a rational perception of the equality and, indeed, identity of all people. The problem with Gewirth's rationalist view is that there is nothing in the standpoint of self-interest which necessitates the adoption of this conception of the person, indeed no reason to adopt the moral point of view, and so, ultimately, moral action is left unexplained. Rawls recognizes, at least implicitly, that the cognitive understanding of someone else's claims or plight is not sufficient to explain why the person would be moved to moral action. Indeed, seeing the person's plight or claims as a reason presupposes the adoption of the moral standpoint; and this is what needs to be explained.

A similar difficulty attaches to some versions of sympathy theory. It is not sufficient to claim that people have the capacity for a sense of justice (or sympathy), for that does not explain the relation of the sense of justice to the self-interested standpoint. Merely being aware at a rational or cognitive level that someone is in distress will evoke a sympathetic response only if the person views suffering as something to be alleviated, as something she should aim to prevent, as will occur with the normal moral person. The mere cognitive perception that an injustice has been done or an unfairness perpetrated does not necessarily give rise to the sense of justice nor does it necessarily provide one with a reason to act. Indeed, it is precisely this reaction to the knowledge of suffering or injustice which separates the cruel or sadistic person from the indifferent or unperceptive. Someone who is cruel or sadistic knows at a cognitive level of someone's suffering or distress or of some injustice being done to that person; and what leads us to label her cruel or sadistic is that it does not move her to feel sympathy or provide her with a reason to alleviate the distress: on the contrary, the awareness that others suffer may provide her with a reason to contribute to the suffering or perpetrate some injustice. What this indicates is that the reaction of sympathy, far from being a natural or inevitable biological response to suffering, will occur only if the person is already moral; only, that is, if the person already accepts injustice or suffering as something to be regretted and prevented, if possible.[47] If sympathy theory is to *explain* moral action, and not merely presuppose the adoption of the moral standpoint, it must explain how the sympathetic understanding is related to the self-interested point of view. Similarly, Rawls's postulate of a sense of justice must explain its relation to self-interest, which it is conceived as regulating.

Rawls explains how the capacity for a sense of justice develops in three stages, and at each stage he outlines a psychological principle or law that corresponds to that level of development. The first stage, called by Rawls the 'Morality of Authority', roughly describes the stage of the child who is living under the loving authority of her parents. The psychological principle that corresponds to this stage is: 'given that family institutions are just, and that the parents love the child and manifestly express their love by caring for his good, then the child, recognizing their evident love of him, comes to love them.'[48] The second stage, called the 'Morality of Association', refers to a higher level of development, in which the person's interests and attachments are enlarged to encompass various associations and roles. The psychological law that corresponds to this level of development is: 'given that a person's capacity for fellow feeling has been realized by acquiring attachments in accordance with the first law, and given that a social arrangement is just and publicly known by all to be just, then this person develops ties of friendly feeling and trust toward others in the association as they with evident intention comply with their duties and obligations, and live up to the ideals of their station.'[49] In the final stage in the acquisition of the sense of justice, the person transcends all particular attachments and adheres to the rules of justice for their own sake. She recognizes the benefits to herself and those she cares for in the rules of justice and feels a duty to reciprocate such benefits by supporting these just institutions. Rawls formulates the psychological principle corresponding to the Morality of Principles (principles of justice) as follows: 'given that a person's capacity for fellow feeling has been realized by his forming attachments in accordance with the first two laws, and given that a society's institutions are just and are publicly known to be just, then this person acquires the corresponding sense of justice as he recognizes that he and those for whom he cares are the beneficiaries of these arrangements.'[50]

In the first two stages of the development of a sense of justice, the enlargement of the person's affections and reshaping of her interests and desires is crucial. Rawls does not conceive of justice as regulating the desires and interests of a purely egoistic, self-related individual, but thinks that the sense of justice can develop only if the person has already developed bonds or attachments to others and to ways of life beyond her self narrowly defined. In this respect, his theory departs from many other individualist theories: he does not try to relate the individual (defined independently of all moral relations to others) to morality by entailment (Gewirth) or self-interest (Gauthier) or even by pure sympathy alone. Rawls defines the person as already moral in the sense that she has natural attachments to others and feels a sense of responsibility arising from these, while failure to fulfil these responsibilities gives rise to the moral feeling of guilt. It is doubtful whether Rawls could plausibly have described the development of the sense of justice in any other way: to merely postulate the existence of the sense of justice presupposes the acceptance of morality but does not explain it; to describe it in terms of the person's rational recognition or perception of pain or suffering does not explain why the person feels sympathy rather than some other emotion, and so also presupposes the acceptance of morality. What Rawls must do is explain how the person comes to accept the moral point of view in a way that ties the acceptance of morality to the person's subjective motivational set. And the most plausible and natural way to do this is in terms of the development or enlargement of the person's desires and aims and interests. Thus, the first two stages of his account of the development of the sense of justice resemble the kind of account that could be given by a communitarian.[51]

However, Rawls is anxious to distinguish his account from a communitarian conception: he does not wish to make the sense of justice merely one of the person's desires or interests, for that relation of the sense of justice to the person would collapse Rawls's distinction between the sense of justice and conceptions of the good. To give priority to justice, to make justice distinct from conceptions of the good and not merely another attachment or desire of the person, Rawls cannot characterize the development of justice simply in terms of the enlargement of the person's affections or interests or aims. He must relate the development of these desires to justice in a way that preserves the independence of the sense of justice. Rawls does this by arguing that these feelings or attachments will develop only if the family is just, and if the institutions and associations in society are just and seen to be just, and if the general framework of society is just. This formulation makes the development of the sense of justice itself dependent on the justice of the institutions and arrangements of society.

The third and final stage in the acquisition of justice is attained when the person acts on principles because she 'understands the values they secure and the way in which they are to everyone's advantage'.[52] The sense of justice follows from the recognition of the justice of social arrangements and an understanding of how justice has promoted her good. The notion of reciprocity which grounds the sentiment of justice is to be understood as a cognitive awareness of the good or benefit that the person has derived from just institutions combined with a desire to return good for good. Of course, an egoistic individual would not have the virtue of reciprocity, would not feel a duty to return good for good or support institutions that have benefited her and others: it is crucial to the success of Rawls's argument here that the person is already a moral person. But while the development of the moral virtue of reciprocity requires the extension of the person's interests and attachments, Rawls does not want his theory of motivation to be affection-based: thus, he claims that this enlargement of attachment and the subsequent development of the virtue of reciprocity will occur only if the institutions and associations in which the person has been educated and to which she feels ties of attachment are *just* institutions.

Critique of Rawls's Solution

The central question raised by Rawls's argument is whether the *justice* of the institutions of moral development is indeed crucial to the development of the moral sentiments. In the case of the family, that is doubtful indeed: Many contemporary families are unequally structured: the conceptions of husband and wife and the responsibilities and duties which attach to these roles are profoundly unequal and particularly oppressive to women; but, despite this, moral sentiments do develop in such families and family members are frequently attached to one another. One implication of this observation is that families do not have to be just in order for children to develop such moral feelings as guilt, which arise from disobedience of parental authority, for example; and children do grow up to care for their parents and others and have a full range of (patriarchal) moral sentiments.

This suggests a fundamental problem with Rawls's argument, namely, that the standpoint of justice, which involves conceiving of each person as equal to all others, as defined by her equal moral personhood or capacity for autonomy, is radically opposed to the standpoint adopted by members of a family in relation to one of its members. What characterizes relations within a family is that each person is viewed concretely, as somebody's daughter or brother or father (with all the cultural baggage that these conceptions invoke), as being cruel or kind, clever or slow, cynical, earnest, or trustworthy, and that these traits are further embedded within the context of the person's particular aims or desires, all of which are constitutive of the person's character.

At the second stage of ethical development, which Rawls calls the 'Morality of Association', the person is described as developing attachments to particular associations, and learning roles in the context of these associations, such as that of good colleague or entrepreneur; and she develops moral feelings and attitudes within these associations. Rawls uses the example of the moral feeling of guilt which occurs when the person fails to live up to the duties of her role. Once again Rawls wants to claim that

central to the acquisition of these moral feelings is that the institutions or associations in which the person interacts are just and
that these feelings will develop only in conditions of justice.
But, again, this seems manifestly false. The person could come
to endorse the aims and ideals of these associations and develop
attachments to the people in them not because they are just
but because they are perceived as good, or honourable, or in
accordance with the Koran, or as embodying admirable virtues.
One could develop attachments to these associations, not
because they are just but because they are perceived to be good
or exciting or fulfilling.[53]

It seems that the associations described in the first two stages
of moral development, while indeed crucial to the acquisition
of moral feelings, do not embody justice as Rawls claims. As
a matter of empirical fact, many contemporary families and associations are characterized by relations of domination and subordination rather than justice, and Rawls seems to treat both
patriarchal families and hierarchically structured organizations
as agents of moral development. Moreover, the attachments
developed in these associations, which Rawls recognizes are crucial to the acquisition of moral feelings, presuppose a standpoint
according to which each person is viewed concretely, as having
particular beliefs and feelings and aims, and possessing some
virtues and vices. The standpoint of justice or impartiality is
the exact reverse of this, in that it requires the person to abstract
from these desires, beliefs, ideals, and conceptions and view
each person as equal to all others.

We could, of course, interpret Rawls as saying that in the just
society, families and small associations would embody justice
or impartiality; but then the difficulty arises of how the person
could possibly develop attachments within these smaller associations. It is difficult to conceive how one could become attached
to another if required to view her as absolutely and abstractly
equal to all others, and undifferentiated.

The most plausible part of Rawls's account of the development
of morality is the description, which he shares with communitarian theorists,[54] of how the person develops a particular conception of the good within particular families and associations.
However, his transition to the morality of principles through
the concept of reciprocity either depends on illicitly presuppos-

ing the primacy of justice or on an implausible account of how family and group attachments depend on the justice of these institutions.

Perhaps, however, Rawls does not intend us to understand the operation of reciprocity in either of these two ways, but, rather, as a recognition at a purely rational or cognitive level of the benefits conferred on all by justice. This is suggested by Rawls's claim, for example, that 'eventually one achieves a mastery of these principle [of justice] and understands the values they secure and the way in which they are to everyone's advantage'.[55] But the problem with this rationalist interpretation of the reciprocity principle is that the principles of justice may not be beneficial to all or even most individuals viewed concretely, with particular desires, aims, and beliefs. They would not be beneficial to a person with a deeply held conception of the good life that cannot be realized in a liberal polity, or a talented and wealthy individual who must distribute some of her resources to the least wealthy group according to the difference principle. The principles of justice are only beneficial to people conceived not as concrete particular individuals but as equal moral persons—in other words, as the abstract rational contractors of Rawls's original position. And this begs the question which Rawls's discussion was designed to overcome: why should we conceive of ourselves in that way? Why should we adopt the standpoint of the original position and act according to the principles which are its outcome?

The central move in Rawls's attempt to solve the motivation problem is his postulate of a sense of justice. This postulate is necessary because his conception of justice as impartiality attempts to divorce considerations of justice or morality from that of self-interest. Rawls has to provide a motive other than self-interest to explain why the person would act in accordance with (impartial) justice. By postulating a sense of justice which is regulative with respect to self-interest at the level of the person, Rawls identifies the relation of self-interest to morality, the private to the public, that his theory requires, but he does not explain it. And his accompanying story of the acquisition of the regulative sense of justice lacks plausibility.

Rawls's solution to the motivation problem has recently been resurrected by Brian Barry in *Theories of Justice*. Barry approaches this issue by examining Gewirth's argument that justice is logically entailed in the self-interested standpoint. Barry concedes that Gewirth's argument does not work but he thinks that the additional premisses necessary to make it work are so 'natural and reasonable that it is easy to take them for granted'.[56] The recognition that others are like ourselves in having needs, interests, and goals gives us a compelling reason to adopt the impartial point of view and consider whether we can move beyond our own perspective in the world and find a standpoint that brings our perspective into relation with that of others. This move to the impartial standpoint is possible, Barry argues, because of the existence in people of an 'irreducible moral motive', which he identifies as the desire to be able to defend one's actions in impartial terms. He argues that 'common experience attests' to the widespread existence of this motive.[57]

One idea running through Barry's discussion of the moral motive is that the willingness to act on reasons whose force can be appreciated from the impartial standpoint is what defines the *reasonable* person. The self-interested agent who considers things from the point of view of her own aims, interests, and desires may be rational in the sense of logically consistent, but she is also unreasonable. The argument that adopting the impartial standpoint is a function of reasonableness not only overcomes the motivation problem but also the integrity problem: it links the requirements of justice with the person's capacity of reason, and so makes moral action less external to the person. What Barry does not explain, however, is the relation of reasonableness to rationality. He has not explained how the bifurcation of practical reason into its moral and prudential branches is possible, or confronted any of the difficulties attached to this conception in explaining human action. And because the relation of the concept of reasonableness to human reason is not explained, it is unclear why we should think of it as an aspect of reason at all, rather than simply a category of moral appraisal.

Barry could, of course, try to circumvent this criticism by denying that there is an intrinsic relation between human reason and reasonableness. He could emphasize the human propensity to act on the basis of impersonal considerations, which is an 'irreducible motive' in the sense that it is an aspect neither of human reason nor of self-interest. However, the problem that we have identified re-emerges on this formulation in terms of Barry's failure to relate the moral motive to the standpoint of self-interest. In *Theories of Justice*, Barry emphasizes that people do as a matter of fact seek to act in ways that can be justified impartially to others,[58] and indeed that the distinctively moral motive has 'priority . . . over the claims of self-interest'.[59] This formulation raises problems about the role of self-interested action: it does not explain why, if people are moved to act by impartial considerations, the rules of justice are conceived as merely regulative with respect to the interactions of individuals, which are conceived as self-interested? Why not base *all* our actions on what can be justified impartially, with no place for self-interest?

Moreover, Barry's 'proof' that the deliberations of the impartial standpoint are capable of motivating in the mere fact that people *do* care about morality does not give the person a reason to form herself, or form others in her care, to be concerned about impartial justice. Pointing to the mere fact that ethical norms do regulate most people's actions is not good enough: he needs to give us a reason to cultivate such norms in ourselves and our children.

4. Conclusion: Individualism, Universalization, and the Integrity Problem

This brings us to a general consideration of the conception of moral reasoning that informs Rawls's argument in *A Theory of Justice*. In arguing for the constraints on the original position, Rawls seeks to arrive at a standpoint of absolute rational autonomy, stripped of all particular knowledge and all differentiating features. From this standpoint, the parties to the original position make choices with the intention of maximizing their self-interest; but because they do not know which self they are, they are forced by the conditions of the original position to universalize their rationally self-interested choices. Rawls conceives of the process of moral reasoning as very similar to that of prudential reasoning; but the objects of the two types of reasoning are radically opposed, for the object of prudential reasoning is the prudential reasoner herself, and the object of moral reasoning is everyone, including the reasoner, each one counting equally. This conception implies that moral reasoning just *is* universalized

prudence, and that a universalization requirement is sufficient
to render prudential judgements and principles moral.

In *The Liberal Theory of Justice*, Brian Barry argues that there
is a fallacy in inferring from the fact that something is beneficial
to individuals to the conclusion that it would be beneficial to
all if these goods were distributed or available to all.[60] What
Rawls's method of reasoning ignores is that there are costs
involved in the social distributions of the primary goods which
are not apparent when these goods are considered prudentially,
from the point of view of the benefits to the agent in having
them. At the individual level, it is possible to possess great wealth
but not to make use of it; it is up to the individual whether
or not she chooses to exercise her primary goods. This fact makes
it plausible for Rawls to argue that individuals would want more
rather than less of the primary goods; this is the rationale behind
his assumption that individuals in the original position would
maximize their own interest, as measured by the primary goods.

However, at the social level, it is not at all clear that it is rational
or morally desirable to seek maximum wealth: it may be more
rational to opt for a society which is wealthy enough to provide
good basic services, such as health care, but not so affluent that
the costs associated with the production and consumption of
such wealth (routinization of work, pollution) outweigh the benefits. Similarly, from the standpoint of the individual, it makes
sense to choose maximum liberty, for there are no costs associated with having more rather than less liberty. But, at the social
level, there are costs involved in granting everyone maximum
liberty. It is not just that one's liberty is limited by the exercise
of others' liberties, but that the society that grants extensive liberties to its members may be less homogeneous, or less stable,
or less effective in dealing with crime or public contagions such
as AIDS. The scope of liberty that is desirable in a society does
not depend on the benefits of liberty to the individual person,
considered in abstraction from the society, but on the importance
one attaches to liberty and to those things, such as social order,
that may suffer in a liberal society. The kind of society that we
want cannot be decided by assuming that the kind of reasoning
employed at the individual, prudential level can be applied, by a
universalization requirement, to society. To decide on principles
to govern the structure of society, one has to consider what

the society as a whole would be like if that principle were operational, and whether that way of life, that kind of society, would be desirable. But that decision can be made only from the vantage-point of a reasoner with full knowledge of her values, with a particular moral perspective, because striking a balance between, say, the individual good of greater affluence and the collective goods of clean air, fresh water, and less urban congestion is a decision that involves moral values in the broadest sense. It cannot be made from the blank vacuum that is Rawls's Archimedean point.

In conceiving of the moral standpoint as divorced from all particular and contingent aims and attributes, desires and ideals, Rawls does not just deny to himself the possibility of making a moral choice between two types of societies, considered as societies rather than as a plurality of prudential agents or as a framework for 'mutual advantage'.[61] He also opens up a wide gap between the prudential and moral points of view and so cannot explain why the person should accept the principles of justice. The motivation problem arises in Rawls's theory because he defines self-interest and morality as radically opposed in their object: he conceives of the person's fundamental aims, interests, desires, and ideals as bound up with the person's self-interested self, which must be abstracted from the person to attain the moral point of view. Morality is achieved by the universalization of these particular aims, interests, principles; by sundering the content of one's goals and interests from their object, as a result of conceiving of the self as merely one person among others. The motivation problem is linked, then, to Rawls's conception of the person, which is similar to Gewirth's conception in so far as there is a division in the self between the self-interested self whose actions proceed from the person's particular aims, desires, and interests, and the moral self who seeks to universalize these aims and interests in conformity with a rational requirement of universalization. On this conception, there is no limit to the claims of morality and no unity in the self, for every action, every principle can be seen from both standpoints, and the two standpoints imply conflicting principles because the objects of the two standpoints are opposed.

Rawls seems to recognize that his unintegrated conception of the person and the motivation problem to which it gives rise poses difficulties for his theory. His appeal to the circumstances of justice is an attempt to make justice relevant to the person in the real, empirical world; unfortunately, it does not explain why people would adopt this conception of justice, why they would conceive of themselves in the abstract way required by the impartial standpoint. The last pages of his book raise and try to respond to the problems of justification and motivation. In the last paragraph of *A Theory of Justice*, he asks: 'why should we take any interest in it [the original position], moral or otherwise?' And he responds: 'Recall the answer: the conditions embodied in the description of this situation are ones that we do in fact accept.'[62] But this will not do. Reflective equilibrium will not support the universality of Rawls's principles of justice, for it is relative to a particular community (the secular Western world), which shares Rawls's conception of morality. The justificatory method of reflective equilibrium can only work in a system of shared values, because it presupposes moral attitudes and intuitions and preconceptions. It can justify a theory by showing its coherence to people within a particular tradition, but it cannot justify Rawls's theory to people who hold a quite different conception of morality and of moral justification, and who question the very thing that Rawls is trying to defend, namely the priority of the rules of justice over conceptions of the good. Thus, we can see that Rawls's theory is ultimately self-defeating: he needs an independent standpoint, an Archimedean point, to justify his claim to the primacy of justice, but to attain the independent standpoint he must abstract so much from the person that it renders the standpoint itself an optional one, a matter of preference. The standpoint can be denied by the same people who disagreed with Rawls's moral theory in the first place, who questioned his division of morality into the right and the good, and so necessitated his search for the Archimedean point.

NOTES

1. Rawls, *A Theory of Justice*, 4.
2. Ibid. 126–7.
3. Some proponents of mutual advantage theory attempt to avoid

these implications by introducing a premiss of the equality of power of individuals. Hobbes argued that people are fundamentally equal in the sense that no individual is so strong or so powerful that she is invulnerable to attack by others. Thomas Hobbes, *Leviathan*, ed. C. B. Macpherson (London: Penguin, 1968), 183. A similar idea is expressed by Rawls's description of the circumstances of justice (*A Theory of Justice*, 126–7).

4. Rawls, *A Theory of Justice*, 140–1.

5. Ibid. 24–5.

6. This conception is not peculiar to Rawls's version of liberal theory. Ackerman and Dworkin also argue that excluding justificatory appeal to particular conceptions of the good in politics is a way of treating people impartially. Bruce Ackerman, *Social Justice in the Liberal State* (New Haven, Conn.: Yale University Press, 1980) 54–8; R. M. Dworkin, 'What is Equality?', *Philosophy and Public Affairs*, 10/3, 10/4 (Summer and Fall 1981).

7. See Kai Neilson, 'The Choice between Perfectionism and Rawlsian Contractarianism', *Interpretation*, 6/2 (May 1977), 132–9.

8. Rawls, *A Theory of Justice*, 120.

9. W. B. Gallie, 'Essentially Contested Concepts', *Proceedings of the Aristotelian Society*, 56 (1955–6).

10. John Rawls, 'Fairness to Goodness', *Philosophical Review*, 84/4 (Oct. 1975), 537.

11. Rawls, *A Theory of Justice*, 72.

12. Robert Nozick, *Anarchy, State and Utopia* (New York: Basic Books, 1974), 224–7; Michael Zuckert, 'Justice Deserted: A Critique of Rawls' A Theory of Justice', *Polity*, 13/3 (Spring 1981), 477; and Michael Sandel, *Liberalism and the Limits of Justice* (Cambridge: Cambridge University Press, 1982), 77–85.

13. Of course, on Rawls's view, if there are competitions based on the possession of some feature which is a matter of arbitrary luck, such as a beauty contest, then the most beautiful entrant should win. The point Rawls wishes to stress is that justice doesn't require the establishment of beauty competitions. But what Nozick, Sandel, and Zuckert correctly point out is that, on Rawls's view, if you could redistribute beautiful physical assets, justice requires that you should.

14. See Sandel, *Liberalism and the Limits of Justice*; and Milton Fisk, 'History and Reason in Rawls' Moral Theory', in *Reading Rawls*, ed. Norman Daniels (Oxford: Basil Blackwell, 1975), 53–80.

15. This underlies Rawls's distinction between interests *in* a self and interests *of* a self (*A Theory of Justice*, 127).

16. An additional problem with basing his theory of justice and rights

on the capacity for autonomy is that it introduces a certain incoherence into his earlier arguments for the difference principle and for the exclusion of moral ideals. In resting the attribution of rights to the person on her capacity for autonomy, Rawls bases rights on something which is undeserved. No one deserves to be a moral agent rather than, say, an insect. Moreover, Rawls's claim that autonomous choice is of central significance in moral life is in tension with his earlier argument that a person's moral ideals should be excluded from the original position because they are contingent on the society one happens to be born in. Surely, Rawls is committed to the view that conceptions of the good cannot be morally arbitrary in the same sense as one's race or gender, for the person can subject her moral ideals to the power of autonomous reflection and reject them or justify them and so become committed to them. They are expressions of moral personhood. See William A. Galston, 'Moral Personality and Liberal Theory: John Rawls's Dewey Lectures', *Political Theory*, 10/4 (Nov. 1982), 507 and 501.

17. Thomas Nagel, 'Rawls on Justice', in *Reading Rawls*, ed. Norman Daniels (Oxford: Basil Blackwell, 1975) 9–10.
18. Rawls, *A Theory of Justice*, 147–8.
19. Ibid.
20. Ibid. 143.
21. Ibid. 62.
22. Ibid.
23. Ibid.
24. Ibid. 440.
25. Ibid.
26. Brian M. Barry, *The Liberal Theory of Justice* (Oxford: Clarendon Press, 1973), 20–6.
27. John Stuart Mill, *Utilitarianism and Other Writings*, ed. Mary Warnock (New York: Meridian, 1974), 135–6.
28. This account of Rawls's list of primary goods is supported by Rawls's recent interpretations of his theory. In recent articles, Rawls admits that his list of primary goods is derived from a particular conception of the person: 'primary goods are singled out by asking which things are generally necessary ... to enable human beings to realize and exercise their moral powers'. Rawls, 'Kantian Constructivism in Moral Theory', *Journal of Philosophy*, vol. 77/9 (Sept. 1980), 526.
29. See H. L. A. Hart, 'Rawls on Liberty and its Priority', in *Reading Rawls*, ed. Norman Daniels (Oxford: Basil Blackwell, 1975), 230–52.
30. Rawls, *A Theory of Justice*, 302.
31. Ibid. 203.

32. Ibid.
33. Ibid. 204.
34. Ibid.
35. Ibid. 202.
36. Ibid. 205.
37. Ibid. 44–5.
38. Ibid. 426.
39. This similarity between Rawls and J. S. Mill is pointed out by Barry, *Liberal Theory of Justice*, 30.
40. Mill, *Utilitarianism and Other Writings*, 260.
41. This is the argument of Chapter 5, 'Contextual Arguments for Liberalism'.
42. Rawls, *A Theory of Justice*, 176.
43. This distinction is from Thomas Nagel, 'Moral Conflict and Political Legitimacy', 218.
44. Rawls, *A Theory of Justice*, 408 ff. and 433 ff.
45. Ibid. 456.
46. Ibid. 3.
47. Bernard Williams, *Ethics and the Limits of Philosophy*, 91.
48. Rawls, *A Theory of Justice*, 490.
49. Ibid.
50. Ibid. 491.
51. See e.g. *The Ethics of Aristotle: The Nicomachean Ethics*, trans. J. A. K. Thomson (London: Penguin, 1955), 91–2 (Bk. II, ch. i, 1103a14–1103b25); Peter Berger, 'On the Obsolescence of the Concept of Honour', in *Liberalism and its Critics*, ed. Michael Sandel (Oxford: Basil Blackwell, 1984), 156; Michael Oakeshott, 'Political Education', in ibid. 226–9. This conception of moral education is also implicit in Taylor's, MacIntyre's, and Sandel's accounts of the relation of the individual to the community (or tradition). See Alasdair MacIntyre, *Whose Justice? Which Rationality?* (London: Duckworth, 1988), 354; Charles Taylor, 'Self-Interpreting Animals', in *Human Agency and Language: Philosophical Papers, I* (Cambridge: Cambridge University Press, 1985), 61–5; Sandel, *Liberalism and the Limits of Justice*, 149.
52. Rawls, *A Theory of Justice*, 473.
53. The goal of promoting justice does not seem sufficient to explain the existence of many of the associations used as examples by Rawls, e.g. associations of sportsmen, educational associations, companions (*A Theory of Justice*, 468).
54. See e.g. James D. Wallace, *Virtues and Vices* (Ithaca, NY: Cornell University Press, 1978), 52–4; Charles Taylor, *Hegel* (Cambridge: Cambridge University Press, 1975), 376–83; Stuart Hampshire,

Thought and Action, new edn. (London: Chatto & Windus, 1982), 236–41; Alasdair MacIntyre, *After Virtue: A Study in Moral Theory* (London: Duckworth, 1985), 33–4, 149–54.

55. Rawls, *A Theory of Justice*, 473.
56. Brian Barry, *Theories of Justice* (London: Harvester-Wheatsheaf, 1989), 288.
57. Ibid. 284.
58. Ibid.
59. Ibid. 289.
60. Barry, *Liberal Theory of Justice*, 116–27.
61. Rawls, *A Theory of Justice*, 4.
62. Ibid. 587.

4

Gauthier and the Full-Knowledge Contract

IN the previous two chapters, we identified the shortcomings of impartial theories of justice through an examination of Gewirth's argument in *Reason and Morality* and Rawls's *A Theory of Justice*. This chapter examines the conception of justice as mutual advantage through David Gauthier's argument for this conception in his book *Morals by Agreement*.

The central aim of Gauthier's *Morals by Agreement* is to generate principles of justice from the starting-point of the individual agent as self-interested utility-maximizer. Like both Gewirth's and Rawls's liberal theories, Gauthier's argument begins from the conception of an individual who is independent of all moral relations to others. The individual's particular ethical conception is viewed from the standpoint of the theory as a purely subjective or personal desire. This division between the personal and public realms is implicit in Gauthier's starting-point in a conception of an individual who is independent of all moral relations. The principles of justice are given justificatory priority over all other ethical conceptions because they are derived from an argument which takes as its starting-point only what is essential to the person; while all other moral theories are viewed as personal or subjective, because based on contingent attributes of the person.

In Gauthier's view, not only does this starting-point in individual self-interest give his theory greater justificatory force, but it is also one of the liberalizing aspects of his theory. Here he cites the point forcefully made by feminist theory that personal or communal ties can keep a person committed to relations which do not serve her interests.[1] Gauthier claims that his theory represents an advance over affection-based theories, for what it justifies as moral is precisely what is in each person's rational self-interest, and the bonds which it endorses, i.e. the bonds which develop in accordance with the principles of justice, are ties of 'free affectivity', in contrast to the unfree ties of affectivity which bind people to ways of life in which their interests are subjugated.

Gauthier's conception also claims to overcome the problems that we have seen bedevil both Gewirth's and Rawls's theories. We have seen that Gewirth's theory fails to derive principles of justice by entailment from the standpoint of individual self-interest but must implicitly invoke the moral point of view—through the appeal to impartiality—to make the theory work. Kantian theories such as Nagel's *The Possibility of Altruism* and Gewirth's *Reason and Morality* conceive of reason not as an instrumental maximizing power but as a universalizing, theoretical capacity. The problem with this universalist conception of reason is that it already includes within it the moral standpoint: this conception of reason is defined partly in terms of the adoption of the impartial conception of each person as identical to all others; thus, the question which the theory purports to answer, 'Why should I be moral?', re-emerges at a deeper level in the form, 'Why should I conceive of myself this way?'[2] By contrast, if Gauthier's more radical deduction project is successful, he will have refuted the moral sceptic: by demonstrating that justice is self-interestedly rational, he can claim that his principles are justified by reason and that they apply to everyone who enters into relations of mutual benefit with another.

Because he conceives of morality as a subset of individual self-interest, Gauthier does not need to presuppose a sense of justice or moral motive to explain moral action, nor need he appeal to a process of moral education and socialization within communities which shapes the individual's desires and beliefs in accordance with a specific substantive ethical conception. In this respect, Gauthier can claim that his theory is superior to Rawls's theory. We have seen that Rawls's contractarianism fails to overcome the motivation and integrity problems because the Rawlsian contract is among abstract selves, ignorant of many features of their identity. The conception of the person that underlies the original position is too slim a conception to overcome the central problems that plagued Gewirth's theory; indeed, the conception strongly resembles the rational moral self of Gewirth's very Kantian theory. For example, since, on Rawls's theory, agents are denied knowledge of certain crucial features of their identity, there is a compliance problem for those agents who find that their conceptions of the good—i.e. the beliefs and projects and values that they are most committed to—are not compatible with Rawls's liberal principles, or for those who find that they are not in the least-advantaged group and are required by the difference principle to transfer some of their resources to this group. This is a problem for Rawls because he accepts, as does Gauthier, that the parties to the original position are moved to act in the first instance by self-interest, but he cannot explain compliance to the agreement in self-interested terms once the parties know which self they are. By contrast, Gauthier's contractarianism, while hypothetical, is conceived as a contract among people with full knowledge of their identities: the people who agree to constrain their utility-maximization in accordance with morals in Gauthier's theory are 'real, determinate individuals, distinguished by their capacities, situations and concerns'.[3] This represents a considerable advance over Rawls's conception, for, if morality can be shown to be in the rational self-interest of each person, there would be no difficulty in explaining the motivating force of morality, and no division at the level of the person between self-interest and morality, desire and reason. In *Morals by Agreement*, Gauthier's agents, in full knowledge of their preferences, beliefs and desires, simply maximize their utility, and in the process find that they need to co-operate with others and that the dynamics of co-operation make it rational in self-interested terms to constrain their utility-maximization. By considering in this way the principles and constraints which it would be rational for co-operating self-interested agents to adopt, Gauthier claims to be able to deduce a system of moral constraints and principles.

After sketching the main outlines of Gauthier's argument, this chapter focuses on two central problems which Gauthier's theory must overcome: the Compliance Problem, which Gauthier claims to solve by demonstrating the (self-interested) rationality of complying with the agreements one makes; and the Bargaining Problem, which Gauthier also claims to solve by his argument for a specific, uniquely rational solution to bargaining problems. It then turns its attention to Gauthier's overall conception of morality, specifically his exclusion of affections from the moral sphere, and his chapter on the Archimedean Point, which attempts to validate the principles that would be agreed to for self-interested reasons from an impartial (moral) standpoint. Throughout this discussion, it will be emphasized that it is the starting-point in rational self-interest that makes Gauthier's theory so ambitious and therefore worthy of attention; but ultimately it is that starting-point which is its failing. This chapter argues that it is not possible to demonstrate the individual rationality of the moral life, and that Gauthier's attempt to derive morality from considerations of self-interest is important ultimately because its failure is instructive. The point of weakness of Gauthier's argument illustrates clearly the nature of the gap between self-interest and morality and why any attempt to derive morality from this starting-point is doomed to failure.

1. OUTLINE OF GAUTHIER'S ARGUMENT

Gauthier's argument does not unfold in a steady sequence from natural interaction to the fully just co-operative interaction of moral beings but begins instead within the market, which itself presupposes the acceptance of moral constraints (against force and fraud), and then moves backward to Gauthier's version of the state of nature and its initial moralization through the acceptance of the Lockian proviso. Chapters V to VII contain the heart of *Morals by Agreement*, for there Gauthier explains how morality is in each person's rational self-interest. In the latter part of the book, Gauthier tests the results of his derivation from an Archimedean point which embodies impartiality and so demonstrates that what his agents have self-interested reason to do can indeed be called moral, and then concludes in the last two chapters with a description of the transformation of mutually unconcerned, rational utility-maximizers into moral persons. At the heart of Gauthier's derivation are his arguments that the principle of Minimax Relative Concession is the uniquely rational solution to Bargaining Problems; his solution to the Motivation Problem, which involves demonstrating the rationality of co-operation; then, of adhering to the terms of co-operation; and, finally, his argument that only certain (fair) terms of co-operation are rational. At each stage of the argument Gauthier must show that the moral conclusion he seeks to derive is both collectively and individually rational: collectively rational because it produces an optimal state of affairs; and individually rational because it is in each individual's interest.

By conceiving of justice as instrumental to self-interest, indeed as emerging or coming into play initially in co-operative behaviour for mutual advantage, Gauthier limits the scope of his principles of justice. Justice is not something owed to each person simply in virtue of certain features which he or she possesses as a human person, as it is on the Kantian conception; rather, justice applies only to those who contribute to producing a co-operative surplus. Gauthier makes this point by beginning his derivation from the conception of an idealized, competitive market which he regards as a 'morally free zone' in the sense that constraints on individual utility-maximization are not necessary.[4] Gauthier's idealized market is a device which enables each individual to maximize his or her utility in harmony with the utility-maximization of others. The first step of Gauthier's argument centres around the existence of externalities in actual markets which make straightforward utility-maximization sub-optimal. In a market characterized by externalities, as all actual markets are, what is rational for the individual—to maximize her utility—is not collectively rational, for it results in a sub-optimal state. Gauthier argues that, to avoid the logic of the prisoner's dilemma which is embedded in market externalities, individuals would constrain their utility-maximization in order to achieve an optimal state of affairs. The identification of rationality with individual utility-maximization must be modified in view of the sub-optimal state that it produces in prisoner's dilemma situations. In such dilemmas, individual utility-maximization makes all the parties worse off than they would be if they agreed to and complied with a mutually beneficial co-operative strategy. One solution to a prisoner's dilemma would be for the parties to change their preferences. The dilemma would not arise if the co-operators had preferences of a certain content, such as preferences to behave honourably or preferences for the well-being of other people. On this solution, the person's well-being would be so identified with that of her fellows, or with a certain conception of herself, that maximizing her utility would not involve disregarding the interests of others. The individual would of course seek to realize her aims and desires, but these would not be wholly self-referential and without regard for the type of actions she does and the person that she is. However, Gauthier seeks to show that moral action is in one's interest, regardless of the content of one's desires and aims. He seeks, in other words, a formal, not a substantive, solution to prisoner's dilemmas.[5]

Gauthier argues that it is necessary to change our conception of rationality to one that is more appropriate to co-operative interaction. In situations where co-operation is not involved, it makes sense to straightforwardly maximize one's utility; but in co-operative interaction it is rational—and he means here that it is individually and collectively rational—for individuals to constrain the pursuit of utility-maximization. He has already shown that it is collectively rational to co-operate, for it is only through co-operation that individuals can achieve an optimal state whereby all do as well as possible without making anyone else worse off. But he has not yet demonstrated that it is individually rational to co-operate. Here Gauthier must respond to Hobbes's Foole who recognizes that it is one thing to agree to co-operate and quite another to comply with the terms of the agreement. The Foole argues that it is rational to agree to enter into bargains with others, for then the person can hope to achieve the benefits of co-operation but not be restricted to the terms of the agreement if another course of action offers greater utility.[6]

Gauthier responds to the compliance problem articulated by the Foole by severing the direct connection between the rationality of action and maximum benefit. He argues that the question is not whether it is rational to comply or not to comply with a bargain in each particular case (straightforward maximization) but whether it is rational to dispose oneself to compliance with one's agreements (constrained maximization). His argument for the rationality of the disposition to comply with mutually beneficial though not necessarily utility-maximizing agreements focuses on the dynamics of interaction and in particular on the fact that the probability of interacting co-operatively with others is partly dependent on one's dispositions. People enter into agreements for advantage, and advantage can be secured only by interacting with people who will uphold their agreements. Gauthier argues that people are neither transparent nor opaque with respect to their dispositions: he describes them as 'translucent', by which he means that people can frequently ascertain the dispositions of others, though not, of course, with complete accuracy. Because constrained maximizers will bargain only with those they assume are also constrained maximizers, straightforward maximizers have fewer opportunities of co-operative beneficial interaction compared with constrained maximizers. Of course, constrained maximizers do risk defection and exploitation by unconstrained maximizers in those cases where they fail to recognize their true disposition and so enter into agreements with them. But Gauthier points out that the more constrained maximizers there are in the population the greater the risks a constrained maximizer can accept of failed co-operation in interacting with a straightforward maximizer. Subject to the conditions (*a*) that there is a fairly high probability that one will be recognized for what one is, and (*b*) that there is a threshold number of constrained maximizers in the population, Gauthier concludes that it is rational to dispose oneself to compliance and so make oneself attractive to other constrained maximizers for the purposes of mutually beneficial co-operative enterprises.

At this stage, Gauthier claims to have demonstrated only the rationality of complying with agreements, but not that the agreements need to be fair. He equates fairness with his principle of Minimax Relative Concession which, he argues, is the uniquely rational solution to bargaining problems.[7] The idea behind this solution is that it is rational to minimize or make as small as possible the greatest or maximum relative concession that any party to the agreement has to make (hence, the principle of Minimax Relative Concession). Gauthier argues that the solution reflects the actual bargaining process, because it is based on the idea that it would be irrational for any party to concede more than necessary; and that it is intuitively fair because it divides the fruits of co-operation with equal concessions from the maximum claims.

In his argument for the rationality of complying with agreements that are fair and nearly optimal, i.e. that satisfy the Minimax Relative Concession principle from a fair initial position, Gauthier distinguishes between narrow compliance, or compliance with fair agreements only, and broad compliance, or compliance with any mutually beneficial agreement one makes. Gauthier has two arguments for the rationality of narrow compliance. The first is an extension of his argument against Hobbes's Foole. Gauthier points out that the value of co-operation is quite low for those who are given less than fair shares. This means that if co-operation is to be rational for the person with less than fair shares, that person must be very certain of the disposition of the person(s) with whom she is interacting. The idea here is that the risk of failed co-operation must be very low because the value of co-operation is very low. In practice, Gauthier thinks that this will mean that it will not be rational for the person to agree to less than fair shares because the value of co-operation is so small relative to the risks. The second argument for the rationality of narrow compliance is that in many situations the person who is disposed to comply with agreements that are mutually beneficial, even if unfair, will lose, because others will take advantage of this disposition and make available to her only co-operative opportunities with minimal benefit.

In the final stage of Gauthier's derivation, he seeks to show that it is rational to bargain only from fair starting-points. This is important to his aim of deriving morality from self-interest because the moral relevance of his conclusion would be jeopardized if the products of fraud and coercion were considered part of the bargainer's factor endowments, i.e. what the person brings to the bargaining table. Gauthier's first argument is that bargains from unfair starting-points are inherently unstable, a claim which he illustrates through a hypothetical reconstruction of a contract between Masters and Slaves. His central argument, however, is that it would be irrational to bargain with people who have benefited from fraud and coercion in the state of nature. It is rational to discourage predation in the state of nature by denying predators the benefits of co-operative activity. And because it is individually rational for the victims of predation to discourage predation and so prevent their future victimization, it becomes individually rational to refrain from preying on others, because that activity is not utility-maximizing in the long term. The benefits of predation are presumably outweighed by the costs of being excluded from beneficial co-operative agreements in the future.

Gauthier's derivation of morality from self-interested rationality claims, then, to overcome the two central problems confronting rational-choice contractarian theories: (1) the Bargaining Problem, and (2) the Motivation (or Compliance) Problem. The Bargaining Problem is the problem of deriving substantive moral principles from a bargain for mutual advantage. Gauthier must show that rational agents, with full knowledge of their preferences and beliefs and situation, would reach agreement on a set of constraints on utility-maximization. The Motivation, or Compliance, Problem is the problem of demonstrating, not the rationality of making such agreements, but of complying with them. This problem arises because it is sometimes more advantageous in utility-maximizing terms to make agreements and defect from them than to make and comply with the agreements or not make them at all. This problem is a variation on the problem of the moral sceptic, who asks, 'Why should I be moral?'

2. GAUTHIER'S RESOLUTION OF THE MOTIVATION PROBLEM

The validity of Gauthier's resolution of the motivation problem rests on the validity of each step of his derivation of morality from utility-maximizing reasons. Specifically, it rests on the argument for the individual and collective rationality of constrained maximization and the irrationality of straightforward maximization, for narrow compliance in contrast to broad compliance, and for the rationality of bargaining from a fair initial position.

His argument for the collective rationality of constrained maximization and narrow compliance presents few difficulties, for, at both stages, the conclusion Gauthier wants to derive is the optimal one. His argument that it is self-interestedly rational for the individual to be moral is less obvious and straightforward. At each stage of his derivation, Gauthier employs strategic rationality arguments to demonstrate that moral action, i.e. action leading to optimal outcomes, is in each individual's interest. One of the assumptions Gauthier relies on is the translucency of individual dispositions. This is the claim that individuals can detect the dispositions of others, not, of course, with complete certainty but with a very high degree of accuracy.

We first encountered this assumption in Gauthier's argument for constrained maximization. There Gauthier argued that it is self-interestedly rational for individuals to adopt dispositions to keep the agreements that they make, because this will give them greater opportunities for beneficial co-operative interaction with other constrained maximizers. If there is a sufficient number of constrained maximizers in the population and a fairly high probability that the individual will be detected for what she is, constrained maximization is rational. Gauthier's threshold condition presents difficulties for his argument, however, because he does not explain how it is possible to reach the point at which sufficient numbers of people become constrained maximizers in the first place. It is irrational to become a constrained maximizer (CM) if most people are straightforward maximizers (SMs): the constrained maximizer would not benefit by interacting with other CMs since, *ex hypothesi*, there are none or very few, and interaction with SMs may result in defection and exploitation. Given these premisses, it is difficult to explain how the threshold number of CMs would emerge in the first place.

The other condition—that there is a high chance that one's disposition will be accurately recognized—is also problematic. The rationality of inducing in oneself a disposition toward constrained maximization makes sense because Gauthier assumes that one's true disposition will be detected most of the time. He writes: 'Suppose a population evenly divided between constrained and straightforward maximizers. If the constrained maximizers are able to co-operate successfully in two-thirds of their encounters, and to avoid being exploited by straightforward maximizers in four-fifths of their encounters, then constrained maximizers may expect to do better than their fellows.'[8] This is a crucial assumption, for if there were only a low probability of being detected, it would be rational for straightforward maximizers to pretend to be constrained maximizers and so benefit from co-operation but not keep agreements when it was not utility-maximizing to do so. Yet this crucial assumption is presented with very little argument: indeed, the only argument is for the translucence of dispositions, by which Gauthier means that people do have some insight into the characters and dispositions of others, but he provides no argument in support of his claim that people can detect the dispositions of others with such a high degree of accuracy. It seems unlikely that Gauthier is right in ascribing a high probability to accurate detection, especially when we consider that constrained maximizers pretend to be straightforward maximizers in interaction with straightforward maximizers in order to avoid exploitation, and straightforward maximizers try to disguise their disposition from constrained maximizers in order to effect an agreement with them. The situation he envisages seems positively comical, with Gauthier's agents pretending to be the opposite of what they are, adopting different disguises depending on the person(s) they are interacting with. Gauthier's high estimate of accurate detection seems even more implausible when we recall that the only difference between straightforward and constrained maximizers is their different conceptions of rationality. Both straightforward and constrained maximizers are self-interested; the only difference between them is that they have different conceptions of what self-interest involves in co-operative interaction. Given that this is the only ground for distinguishing between them, it is difficult to imagine how a person would know whether the person she is bargaining with is a SM or a CM. How could one know prior to interaction what form of self-interest the self-interested other has induced in him or her self?

Gauthier's argument for the rationality of narrow compliance is similar to his argument for constrained maximization in so far as it also depends on the translucency assumption. This is the argument that broad compliance is irrational because others will recognize this disposition and react strategically to it by offering the broad complier less than fair shares. Here Gauthier assumes that people can distinguish between self-interested rational agents who comply with any agreements that they make and self-interested rational agents who comply with fair agreements only. Presumably, they can detect which is which even when the broad complier tries to disguise her disposition when she thinks she is interacting with potential exploiters. More seriously, the threshold assumption that Gauthier required in his argument for constrained maximization undermines his argument here for narrow compliance. Gauthier's argument against broad compliance (and for the rationality of narrow compliance) is that people will recognize the disposition to broad compliance and attempt to exploit it. But who are the exploiters? If two broad compliers reach an agreement and one gets more than fair shares and the other less than her fair share, this does not show the irrationality of broad compliance as a disposition. They have both benefited, though one has benefited more than the other. Narrow compliers will not exploit broad compliers, for narrow compliers will agree to fair bargains only and so will not attempt to extract more than their fair share.[9] The only group that broad compliers need to worry about is the straightforward maximizers, and straightforward maximizers are not a threat to broad compliers alone; narrow compliers too risk exploitation by this group. Given a threshold population of constrained maximizers, which is necessary for Gauthier's argument to work anyway, broad compliers will interact in most cases with other broad compliers or with narrow compliers. Under these conditions, they will flourish and perhaps even do better than narrow compliers since they are open to more opportunities for beneficial interaction.

Finally, Gauthier argues for the rationality of bargaining from fair starting positions only. His argument is that it is rational to exclude former predators from beneficial bargaining and so deter predation in the state of nature. One of the difficulties with this argument is that it ignores the fact that successful predators may be exactly the people one needs to bargain with: it may be necessary or self-interestedly rational to bargain with them in order to gain access to the land and goods and raw material in their possession. A more serious problem is that this argument, like Gauthier's constrained maximization argument, depends on a threshold number of narrow compliers in the population, but cannot explain how this population of narrow compliers could have arisen in the first place. The deterrence strategy is effective only if there are a sufficient number of narrow compliers who refuse to bargain with former predators. But below that threshold it is individually rational to bargain with the predators since (*a*) one may gain in the bargain, and (*b*) refusing to bargain will not have the desired effect of deterring predation anyway.

Gauthier's Implicit Communitarian Appeal

At crucial stages of his argument for the rationality of morality, Gauthier appeals to the condition that there must be threshold numbers of people with the same disposition to act in the same way. Synchronized action, if not collective action, is necessary to make immoral action irrational (not in one's interest). And the translucency assumption is necessary for this synchronization to be possible. Gauthier is successful in showing that it is irrational for the individual self-seeker to maximize her utility on the sly, attempting to reap the benefits of co-operation while making others pay the costs involved in deterring predation or keeping fair agreements, *if* others can detect the person for what she is, and act together, or in synchronization, in ways that will make it rational for her to comply with fair agreements. But in the present human condition, where people can deceive and be deceived, and where threshold numbers of people with similar dispositions do not just occur as if by magic, Gauthier's resolution of individual rationality (self-interest) with what is collectively rational (morality) simply collapses.

It is instructive that Gauthier's argument requires that a collection of people act in the same way—for example, that there is a threshold number of constrained maximizers or narrow compliers in the population—but is unable to explain how that threshold could have arisen in the first place. Moral action can be shown to be individually rational only by making very strong assumptions about the accuracy of detecting the dispositions of others and the existence of a threshold number of people with the same disposition. That Gauthier cannot show that morality is individually rational in the absence of such peer pressure, and in the absence of the assumption that people have unique insight into each other's minds and character, is demonstrated by his inability to explain how the threshold numbers of constrained maximizers or narrow compliers could have emerged. His argument fails to demonstrate that morality is a subset of self-interest, for there is a significant, indeed a glaring, gap between self-interest and morality at the heart of his theory. Gauthier's discussion of the prisoner's dilemma shows that acting on self-interest is collectively self-defeating, for if all act from this motive, they may be worse off in self-interested terms. But it does not follow from this that it is better in self-interested terms to be moral: Gauthier cannot demonstrate that morality is in each individual's interest: he cannot explain from his starting-point in individual self-interest how the threshold number of narrow compliers could have arisen in the first place. Those who make up the threshold number of narrow compliers must have arrived there, become moral, not through self-interested calculation but through the adoption of the collective standpoint. They must have ceased to think in terms of self-interest and identified themselves with the interests of the whole, of the collective body. And this is precisely the substantive solution to the prisoner's dilemma which Gauthier rejects. This is the recognition of the truth that morality is not always self-interestedly rational: morality involves the adoption of the interests of the whole as one's own interests. Once this has been achieved, once people have adopted the standpoint of the 'we' rather than the 'I' and identified themselves with their moral community, they can then act collectively to make it difficult for straightforward utility-maximizers to exploit them. Gauthier tries to avoid this truth by substituting for a direct appeal to collective action the assumption that there are threshold numbers of people with the same disposition, but this assumption begs the question of how this threshold emerged originally, and his derivation of morality from self-interest quickly unravels. Nevertheless, the failure of Gauthier's resolution of the motivation problem is itself important, because it represents another failed attempt to derive morality from self-interest and so suggests that the true explanation and justification of moral motivation would concentrate not on its individual self-interested rationality but on the adoption of the collective standpoint.

3. Gauthier's Resolution of the Bargaining Problem

The Principle of Minimax Relative Concession

Even if Gauthier has not succeeded in solving the Motivation Problem, his claim that there is some fair and rational principle of distributing the surplus from co-operative interaction requires consideration, for, if his argument is successful, this would represent a considerable achievement in itself.

Because Gauthier conceives of morality as part of rational-choice theory, it is crucial that there is a rational solution to the problem of how to divide the surplus resulting from co-operation, and that this solution can make a claim to being fair and impartial. By conceiving of his theory as part of rational-choice theory, as grounded in reason, Gauthier can claim for his principle the justificatory leverage to assess alternative principles and practices, to condemn those affection- or kin-based theories or societies that do not operate in the rational self-interest of each individual, or those sub-optimal states which result from uncoordinated individual strategies.

The principle of Minimax Relative Concession (MRC) is put forward by Gauthier as the principle which rational contractors would select to define the terms of co-operation. It is addressed solely to the issue of the division of the fruits of beneficial social co-operation in those situations where co-operation is necessary to avoid the sub-optimal state which results in prisoner's dilemma-type situations. It is not, that is, a principle of rectificatory justice but only comes into operation when the market fails to produce the optimal outcome.

It is evident that Gauthier's theory requires a solution to the bargaining problem which can claim to be rational to mutually unconcerned utility-maximizing agents and to be fair. But it is not necessary that the principle be the Minimax Relative Concession principle, although Gauthier thinks that the MRC solution is *the* rational solution, and argues vigorously on behalf of this principle. His central argument in favour of the MRC solution is that it captures the nature of the bargaining process. Gauthier's principle requires that the rational contractors make equal concessions from their maximum claim and this gives a meaningful role to the maximum claim, which, in turn, is sensitive to the agent's contribution to producing the co-operative surplus, and to the concessions that the parties make in the process of reaching agreements. This mirrors real bargaining processes, Gauthier argues, where the initial claims advanced by utility-maximizers are the largest claims they can possibly make, and concessions are necessary if the contractor is to be included in the agreement.

Although Gauthier's argument in favour of the MRC principle as the rational solution to bargaining procedures is plausible, it does not seem conclusive. Jean Hampton, in her review essay of Gauthier's book,[10] argues convincingly in favour of another solution to bargaining problems, the Principle of Proportionality, which requires that the fruits of co-operation be divided, not with equal concessions from maximum claims, as Gauthier's MRC solution requires, but in proportion to each person's contribution to the production of the surplus. The most damaging aspect of Hampton's argument from the point of view of Gauthier's theory as a whole is her demonstration that the MRC principle would benefit small contributors more than large contributors, while her Principle of Proportionality would benefit large contributors more than small ones.[11] This leads her to suggest that utility-maximizers who are in a position to contribute fairly large sums to joint ventures would support the Proportionality Principle, while smaller contributors would favour the MRC principle. It is also plausible to suppose that others, mindful that their co-operation is only instrumental to utility-maximization, would argue for an equal distribution of utilities as a method of dividing the co-operative surplus, if that principle promises greater benefits to them.

We have seen that it is absolutely essential to the success of Gauthier's project that the bargaining problem has a rational solution. It is crucial, as Hampton points out, for the contractarian project as a distinctive methodology to demonstrate that its substantive principles would be rationally agreed to, and not merely to use contractarian language as a mask for the organization of intuitions that we already hold. But it is particularly crucial to Gauthier's project that the contractors arrive at a rational method of dividing the fruits of co-operation: if the terms of co-operation are themselves essentially contested, with each principle supported by those maximizers who calculate that this principle would serve their interests best, it would be impossible for Gauthier to derive moral principles from rationality alone.

The Lockian Proviso

But even if we accept Gauthier's claims for the Minimax Relative Concession principle, there remains the problem of establishing a determinate initial position from which bargaining can proceed. The MRC principle presupposes the existence of a co-operative surplus, and that in turn presupposes an initial distribution of powers or rights. This base line is established through Gauthier's argument for the rationality of bargaining from fair initial positions only.

Gauthier's first argument is that bargains from unfair initial positions will be unstable, and that the only stable agreements, i.e. the only agreements worth making, will be ones that proceed from a fair initial position. He illustrates this with a hypothetical example of a slave society that abandons the practice of slavery through a mutually beneficial agreement whereby the masters renounce coercion and so are spared the costs of coercing, and the slaves agree to serve the masters voluntarily and are spared the costs of being coerced. Such an agreement is unstable, in Gauthier's view, because, in the absence of coercion, the slaves have no reason to accept their unfairly small share of the benefits of co-operation. The agreement is unstable: the slaves revolt, demanding their fair share; and the resulting distribution of the surplus ends up satisfying the Minimax Relative Concession principle as it would operate from a fair initial situation. Gauthier extrapolates from this example to conclude that fair agreements reach a stable outcome, and that agreements from unfair starting-points are unstable because irrational, and irrational because they involve unproductive transfers. The crucial claim in this argument is the irrationality of complying with agreements involving unproductive transfers. An unproductive transfer, Gauthier writes, 'brings no new goods into being and involves no exchange of existing goods; it simply redistributes some existing goods from one person to another. Thus it involves a utility cost for which no benefit is received and a utility gain for which no service is provided.'[12] Unproductive transfers are involved in all agreements from unfair bargaining positions, where costs are paid without corresponding benefit. Because unproductive transfers are costly for the party that makes that transfer, they can be rational or utility-maximizing only if coercively exacted. No one would voluntarily agree to such a transfer, Gauthier argues, because of its cost to them.

Here one might argue against Gauthier that whether an unproductive transfer is utility-maximizing or not depends on the cost of not making that transfer. Agreeing to a bargain involving unproductive transfers may be rational if there are no better opportunities available. This is the implication of J. M. Buchanan's theory of bargaining.[13] On Buchanan's view, the rationality of making unproductive transfers depends on the opportunity costs of not making that transfer. Buchanan characterizes voluntary compliance to existing agreements as resulting from imagining how one would fare if the natural distribution of advantages which exists underneath social relationships and institutions were realized. Buchanan appeals to an implicit threat point in his analysis of bargaining situations. It is present in the idea that, in bargaining, people consider the non-agreement point as the initial position and voluntarily comply with agreements because they imaginatively appeal to the natural distribution that is implicit in or underneath social relationships and institutions. This analysis is also accepted by Rawls in *A Theory of Justice*, in his argument in favour of imposing the veil of ignorance on his rational contractors. Rawls argues that contracts in which the bargainers have full knowledge of their social positions would not model a moral conception: justice as mutual advantage becomes 'to each according to his threat advantage' and this, Rawls writes, 'is not a principle of justice'.[14]

Gauthier explicitly rejects Buchanan's description of the initial bargaining position as based on implicit threats because, he argues, the threat (the return to the natural distribution) is an 'unreal' one in the sense that it benefits no one.[15] It is irrational to make threats because it is irrational to keep them. It is irrational to make unproductive transfers in the absence of coercion; and threats by the beneficiaries of these transfers cannot be taken seriously because the non-agreement point that the threat appeals to is sub-optimal. Gauthier does not even consider the possibility that the former masters would threaten to reimpose coercion and retain their privileged status, presumably because such a state is sub-optimal. But what is at issue here is not whether coercion is sub-optimal, and therefore collectively irrational, but whether it is individually rational for the masters to threaten, and threaten with plausibility, to reintroduce coercion. Whether or not it is individually rational for the former masters depends on the costs of giving up some of their unfairly large share relative to the costs of coercion. If the cost involved in coercion is less than the cost of giving up some of their unfairly large share of the surplus, and the masters have retained their control of technology and power to make their threat effective if the need arises, they may decide that the threat-making strategy is rational. And the slaves, who are also rational, will know whether to take seriously this threat because they too can calculate the costs in utility-maximizing terms of the two strategies. And if the threat is credible, the slaves, being rational, might decide that it is after all better to serve their former masters 'voluntarily' than to serve them and endure physical force. But this is a possibility that Gauthier does not consider and his analysis of bargaining does not allow for.

For those who are unconvinced by his argument that unproductive transfers are always irrational, Gauthier provides another argument for the rationality of bargaining from a fair initial position. This argument proceeds through a rejection of Buchanan's conception of the initial bargaining situation. Buchanan argues that, prior to the bargain, people engage in a suboptimal cycle of predatory and defensive activity in a quest to enhance their position at the bargaining table. Because defending against predation is costly, people are driven to reach an agreement to end it, but prior to the agreement they are anxious to secure as much as possible from preying on others. This is because the natural distribution of goods, including goods gained through plunder prior to the agreement, serves to identify persons for bargaining purposes. It is from this distribution of goods and advantages that bargaining proceeds. Gauthier, who seeks to establish Lockian conclusions of ownership of self and rights and possessions from the Hobbesian assumption of utility-maximizing rationality, must reject this Hobbesian conception of the utility-maximizer's state of nature. He wants to claim that rational agents would agree to bargain only if the initial bargaining situation meets the conditions of his version of the Lockian proviso. This leads Gauthier to the argument, considered earlier, that rational agents would seek to deter predatory activity in the state of nature and that they would do this by denying the former predators the fruits of co-operation. This would render predation in the state of nature irrational, because the benefits of predation would be outweighed by the costs of being excluded from beneficial co-operative agreements in the future.

These two arguments lead Gauthier to his desired conclusion, namely that rational agents would bargain only from a position in which no one has interacted with another in a way that makes the other worse off. The person prior to coercive interaction is taken as the base point in relation to which individual welfare (measured in terms of units of utility) is defined as better or worse. This is Gauthier's version of Locke's proviso that the person in interaction can exercise rights to her body and powers and acquire rights in objects through labour as long as she leaves 'enough and as good' for others.[16] Gauthier argues that the idea of not taking advantage of others is the central idea animating Locke's proviso. He expresses the same idea in his version of the proviso, which gives each person rights to herself and her powers and the acquisition of property subject to the constraint that in exercising these rights the person does not harm others. Of course, Gauthier concedes that a system of exclusive control will benefit people differentially and may result in denying opportunities and advancement to some, but Gauthier thinks that the system as a whole increases efficiency, provides security, and makes available more opportunities. His proviso is a weak one which prohibits parasitism and free ridership, or, to put it positively, requires each person to internalize all costs arising from her pursuit of utility-maximization. This is a corollary of Gauthier's argument that unproductive transfers are always irrational. The Lockian proviso implies a whole theory of the sovereignty of the self and powers and appropriation of labour. Gauthier acknowledges that Locke, whom he is following here, does not explain adequately the status and basis of the laws of nature (these rights), so he improves on Locke by offering what he calls a 'secular understanding of rights'.[17] He admits that his theory of morals by agreement does not derive rights in the usual sense: the rights to one's person and property are not derived from a contract based on shared understandings or on the convergence of rational understanding and acceptance of a theory of individual rights. Gauthier writes, 'Rights provide the starting-point for and not the outcome of agreement. They are what each person brings to the bargaining table, not what she takes from it. Market and co-operative practices presuppose individual rights.'[18]

In other words, the basic substantive principles of Gauthier's moral theory—the Lockian proviso constraining appropriation, and, implicit in the proviso, the rights to one's person and power and property within these constraints—are not generated by his argument but presupposed in his starting place in the market.

The market presupposes rights to one's person and property; at the minimum, it presupposes constraints on force and fraud. Gauthier calls the market 'morally free' in the sense that in idealized markets the individual does not need to engage in co-operation with others. It is *not* morally free in the sense that there are no constraints on the pursuit of self-interest; on the contrary, the market would break down if people acted completely self-interestedly, i.e. without regard for the rules which define the market. But the fact that Gauthier's principles are presupposed in his starting-point does not render his theory viciously circular and so raise the question of the validity of his principles and rights. Gauthier could have begun from his conception of human rationality as individual utility-maximization, and demonstrated that the market and co-operative arrangements are expressions of this; and that rights are presuppositions of these arrangements.

But if Gauthier does not require the starting-point of the market to derive his conclusions, why does he proceed in such an indirect way? Why doesn't Gauthier begin his discussion from the real starting-point of his argument and analyse what is necessary to or implied in utility-maximization, and in this way demonstrate that both the market and co-operative interaction are necessary? The reason is that the substantive principles that are the outcome of his argument would be altered in ways that Gauthier would not welcome if he began his argument at the beginning. Gauthier's principle of Minimax Relative Concession only comes into play in cases where externalities arise from straightforward utility-maximization, either negative externalities such as pollution or positive externalities which take the form of public goods such as lighthouses. But the greatest public good of them all, at least for a proponent of the market such as Gauthier, is surely the restraint on force and fraud that makes the market itself possible. This suggests that the MRC principle should be applied to the co-operative surplus that arises from market arrangements, that the existence of a market should be the subject of a bargain. This conclusion is supported also by the consideration that, although the market, like all public goods, is beneficial to the society as a whole, and so collectively rational,[19] it benefits individuals differentially, and some individuals may benefit more from another distributive arrangement.

Here one might object that it is silly and counter-intuitive to require that the co-operative surplus resulting from the existence of the market be distributed according to the MRC principle, for, in order for the market to function properly, the market principles of supply and demand and the profit incentive must be respected. But what this objection points to is a serious incoherence in Gauthier's account: if, on the one hand, we apply the MRC principle to all public goods, we undermine one of the public goods (the market); but if we treat the market as a given, if we treat the constraints on force and fraud as outside the argument of *Morals by Agreement*, we have left unexplained how the most basic moral principles, and an important public good, could have arisen.

One way of reacting to this argument would be to question the MRC principle on the grounds that we have here an example where applying the bargaining solution to a public good (the market) would not be rational. In his essay, 'Social Contract Theory's Fanciest Flight',[20] David Braybrooke points out that applying the MRC principle to the market, as the formal structure of Gauthier's argument requires, provides grounds for substantial redistribution of resources, but Braybrooke does not consider whether this would undermine the operation of the market.[21] But the implications of this argument may be more radical for Gauthier's theory than this: it suggests grounds for rejecting Gauthier's whole method of proceeding, and specifically the requirements of demonstrating the individual and collective rationality of all public goods. This problem arises in Gauthier's theory because his version of contractarianism requires—as Locke's, for example, did not—optimization over all public goods, and this is embodied in a hypothetical contract in which the parties agree to the terms of the bargain. Locke did not propose a distributive principle to facilitate optimization, as does Gauthier, but considered the market as a corollary of natural laws laid down by God.[22] By contrast, Gauthier, with his seemingly more radical deduction project, and his stated aim of deriving the principles of morality from reason alone, must treat the market as not itself the subject of a bargain, and so violate the neutrality of his deduction, i.e. its derivation from pure reason. And this suggests that Gauthier does not escape the criticism that he himself makes of Rawls's theory, namely that Rawls does not demonstrate the rationality of his principles, because he unjustifiably constrains the choice situation. On this interpretation of Gauthier's theory, he too constrains the choice situation in *Morals by Agreement* by presupposing that choice take place within the context of the market; and he adopts a particular (market or economic) conception of the person, which, like Rawls's conception, is radically individualistic, in that the person is conceived of as not interested in the interests of others.

4. GAUTHIER'S CONCEPTION OF JUSTICE AS MUTUAL ADVANTAGE

This brings us at last to a consideration of Gauthier's overall conception of justice as mutual advantage. Gauthier begins his theory from the conception of mutually unconcerned, utility-maximizing individuals and regards as justified only those principles that rationally self-interested maximizers would agree on. But in conceiving of morality as justified by a hypothetical bargain for mutual advantage, and so as based on a conception of persons as mutually uninterested utility-maximizers, Gauthier may be undermining the very basis of his moral theory. What makes respecting the constraints of morality a rational strategy from the point of view of rationally self-interested individuals is the relative weakness of each person. Morals by agreement is possible because each person requires the co-operation of others to maximize her utility, and in order to gain the confidence of other co-operators she must constrain her utility-maximization. But in the absence of the circumstances of justice, and, specifically, in the absence of the assumption of the equal weakness of all persons, there is no reason to accept the constraints of morality on utility-maximizing behaviour. This is Glaucon's argument against Socrates in the *Republic*.[23] An obvious extension of this argument is that, if morality is regarded as merely instrumental to the achievement of one's self-interested aims, as a necessary constraint in circumstances where individuals cannot secure what they want in any other way, genuine adherence to morality is not possible. If a person or group of people discover that she or they are particularly talented or intelligent or powerful or secure *vis-à-vis* other people, they would have no reason to abide by moral principles. Rational self-interest, which initially seemed so secure a foundation for moral principles, may in fact not be strong enough, for when 'reason and justice . . . part company',[24] as Gauthier admits is possible, justice has no hold on the mutually unconcerned maximizer.

Gauthier is naturally anxious to deny that his theory provides such a tenuous hold on individuals. He is not satisfied with showing that morality is individually rational if certain (contingent) circumstances obtain: he seeks to make morality a motivating reason for the individual even in the absence of these conditions. Thus Gauthier argues that, although he conceives of people for the purposes of his principles of justice as essentially non-tuists, he recognizes that the motivational structure of real people is much richer than this in that it encompasses the person's affective desires and feelings, her concerns and commitments to others. Gauthier argues that, although his principles are justified in terms of self-interest, there is nothing to preclude them from engaging the person's affections, so that the person comes to be committed to upholding the principles of justice.

Although Gauthier requires a version of sympathy theory to overcome the motivation problem when acting justly is not self-interestedly rational, he does not want to make affective commitment to justice one of the foundations of his theory. And so, like Rawls, he implausibly supposes that the possibility of affective commitment to morality, of real commitment to specific people or ways of life, is dependent on the prior existence of just relations.[25] But the precise relation between justice and particular attachments, between self-interested reason and affective relations to others, is never explained. And it is difficult to envisage how the person could come to be centrally concerned with the interests of the other as such, as in a love relation, while, at the same time, organizing her relations with that person in terms of a conception of herself as mutually unconcerned maximizer. For even if the relation was initially one of mutual advantage, as the relation developed into one of love, or even friendship, the lovers, or friends, would naturally organize their relations in accordance with this: they would see their relationship not as one in which both benefit as individuals but as one in which each conceives of her interests as identified with the interests of the beloved. The relation would indeed be one of mutual benefit in some sense of that term, but the lovers would benefit by the relation not as individuals, for they would not conceive of themselves in that way, but because they were lovers and identified their interests with the interests of the other.

The difficulty posed for Gauthier's argument by the relation that he envisages between utility-maximizing reason and the person's commitment to particular people or ways of life can also be conceived in terms of the separation of reason and motive in Gauthier's theory. One of the most striking aspects of Gauthier's theory is its repudiation of human affections as the basis of a justifiable moral conception. Gauthier's theory is justified in terms of rational self-interest: the moral principles that are the outcome of his theory are conceived of as those that would be endorsed by non-tuist maximizers, each considering only her own advantage. This conception of justice as mutual advantage excludes from the moral realm all those who have nothing to bargain with: 'Animals, the unborn, the congenitally handicapped and defective, fall beyond the pale of a morality tied to mutuality.'[26] This conception of morality presents considerable problems for his theory, not because rejecting much of conventional morality is counter-intuitive, for Gauthier could claim that conventional morality is irrational, but because the conception of the person at the base of his theory, as a self-interested utility-maximizer, ignores very essential aspects of the person, such as her deep commitments and affective responses and motives, and so sets up a division between the requirements of justice as mutual advantage and the person's subjective motivational set. In the real world, people frequently, perhaps even typically, act out of concern for particular others. They feel affection or friendship or love for a particular person and act in the interests of that person for no other reason than that they care about that person. But the motives on which people in the world act cannot be embodied in Gauthier's principles of justice, because the moral principles are derived by considering what rationally self-interested maximizers would agree to.

Annette C. Baier has argued against the conception of morality as derived from self-interested reason, pointing out that Gauthier's theory does not exclude only the categories that Gauthier lists, such as the congenitally defective, animals, the unborn, but also excludes human infants from the moral realm, because, being helpless, they are parasites on the rational, utility-maximizing adults.[27] On Gauthier's theory, there is no reason for rational self-interested maximizers to care for their young. Of course, it is to be hoped that the parents freely choose to care for their children, but there is no moral requirement on them to do so. Baier points out that most parents want to care for their children: most mothers, she writes, are 'involved in some very unfree maternal affectivity'.[28] This leads her to suggest that, in framing all reasons in terms of utility-maximizing non-tuism, Gauthier is not merely giving us bad reasons for what we do anyway but rejecting much of what we regard as central to morality, central to our moral conception of ourselves, and rejecting it because it cannot be generated from his implausible conception of the person. In his response to Baier's charges,[29] Gauthier suggests that his theory can indeed justify the care of helpless human infants in rationally self-interested terms: 'looking forward to the infirmity of old age, Joanna and Jonathan [the parents] are likely to view children as an investment, giving them the assurance of care when they will need it as the reward for their child-raising labours. This attitude is, after all, not uncharacteristic of persons in those parts of the world that lack pension plans or social security.'[30] But why should we suppose that the children would care for their parents when the parents are infirm, for this can hardly be a utility-maximizing strategy from the children's point of view? Thus, Gauthier's rejoinder succeeds in lending further support to Baier's claim that Gauthier's liberal morality, and others like it, 'is itself a parasite on what it claims to improve upon—it relies on and exploits the usually unfree affectivity of the mothers of surviving children, and the contributions of all those who help a child acquire and develop capacities as well as preferences . . . [and] who socialize us into autonomy'.[31]

Gauthier does not, of course, deny that our actual psychological make-up differs in important respects from the psychology that he attributes to his rational contractors, and he justifies the psychological premises of his theory on the grounds (*a*) that nothing in his argument precludes the possibility of the rational contractors developing affective attachments to the principles that they accept on self-interested grounds (indeed he thinks that the principles of justice facilitate this affective response); and (*b*) that grounding his principles in self-interested reason is a very secure foundation for his theory. But whatever we think of these arguments, there is no doubt that he pays a price for basing his principles on this conception of reason and the person: Gauthier's method of proceeding opens up a gap between people in the real world, who frequently act on the basis of concern for other (particular) people, and the essentially external relations between people embodied in Gauthier's principles of justice. And that separation between reason conceived as a utility-maximizing power and reason based on the contents of the person's subjective motivational set suggests something alluded to earlier, when we saw that Gauthier's theory depends on a specific, non-neutral conception of the person as mutually unconcerned utility-maximizer. It suggests that Gauthier's contract is not, after all, a contract that would be agreed to by all people, with full knowledge of their aims and beliefs, desires and interests, but a contract that would be acceptable only to people who conceive of themselves as rationally self-interested non-tuists. The division at the level of the person between reason and motive does not emerge only in those cases in which the person conceives of herself as essentially identified with certain relationships or commitments, and is given a justificatory rationale for morals that is based on an entirely different, and indeed incompatible conception of the person: rather, the division between reason and morals is only an instance of a dichotomy running through Gauthier's entire theory, between two different, mutually incompatible conceptions of self-interest.

Gauthier's theory claims superiority over Rawls's theory because it successfully overcomes the motivation problem: Gauthier makes explicit that his contract is a contract among people with full knowledge of their situation and aims and identities, and that the principles which are the outcome of the hypothetical full-knowledge contract are ones that it is self-interestedly rational for such people to agree to and comply with, and so he has no difficulty in explaining what Rawls could not explain satisfactorily, namely why people act morally. The conception of self-interest suggested by his official version of his contract is a purely formal conception, in which people act to promote their interests, to maximize their utilities, but he makes no assumptions about the substantive content of their interests or what kind of aims and ends and beliefs such selves might have.

But this official conception of self-interest is not employed consistently by Gauthier: he frequently appeals to a quite different (substantive) conception of self-interest.

One of Gauthier's aims in *Morals by Agreement* is to provide a substantive moral theory which can serve as a standard by which other theories, other moralities can be tested as more or less rational or irrational. Gauthier subscribes to the feminist argument of the potential tyranny of affection- and kin-based theories. He accepts the feminist claim that there may be relationships and ways of life to which the person is committed, which do not serve her individual interests but keep her in a state of subjection. The core idea behind the feminist claim is that the formal conception of self-interest, which Gauthier employs to solve the motivation problem, has built into it a deep circularity: the beliefs and preferences, aims and interests, which shape the person's utility function, and the abilities and talents which are part of the factor endowment which the person brings to the bargaining table, are shaped in society and reflect the predominant beliefs and conceptions and opportunities in society. A bargain based on these utility-functions, or these factor endowments, would no doubt endorse something like the distribution of resources of the society in which the person is formed, but it is not clear what justificatory conclusions, if any, can be drawn from this. All we can know is that there is a fit between the individual and society, but there is no way to assess whether that is because society has shaped the person to fit it, has discouraged her from developing her more lucrative talents, encouraged her to find fulfilment in marriage and a family, or whether she endorses the society because she thinks that it answers to her needs and interests and understands herself here as an independent entity. If, on the one hand, we understand Gauthier's theory as a bargain based on a formal conception of self-interest, as a bargain among full-knowledge individuals, bringing whatever interests and aims and beliefs they have to bear on the bargain, then we can accept that Gauthier has solved the motivation problem, but only at the price of disempowering his theory of any justificatory force; but if, on the other hand, we understand Gauthier's theory as involving a more substantive conception of self-interest, then we re-empower his theory with justificatory clout, but at the price of rendering it unable to explain why agents, in the real world, would act morally. And so we see that Gauthier's theory has not, after all, advanced beyond Rawls's theory, for he too must abstract certain substantive features from his agents to attain a point of view with the justificatory force that makes his theory worth reading.

5. GAUTHIER'S ARCHIMEDEAN POINT

Because, on Gauthier's conception, morality is a subset of self-interested rationality, he requires some standard to validate his principles as *moral* principles. He needs to show that his principles are rational and that they are moral: thus, he requires a conception of rationality which is independent of his moral theory to demonstrate the former claim; and a conception of morality independent of his conception of reason to substantiate the latter claim. His conception of rationality is that of instrumental, utility-maximizing reason; his conception of morality is similar to that of Rawls and Gewirth, for he accepts their view that the hallmark of morality is impartiality. In order to demonstrate that the principles that would be chosen by self-interested utility-maximizing agents are also moral principles, Gauthier must show that they are impartial.

Gauthier claims that his principles are superior as moral principles to the principles endorsed by other contractarian theorists such as Harsanyi and Rawls, because they more completely embody impartiality between persons.[32] This line of argument runs parallel to, but does not replace, the argument we have already considered, which occupies chapters V to VII, that these principles would be chosen and complied with by mutually uninterested utility-maximizing agents. Gauthier outlines his conception of the impartial or moral point of view in terms of an Archimedean agent who tries to maximize the utilities of each person, and so reaches a point of convergence, or optimal point, at which the utilities of any agent cannot be maximized further without making another agent worse off. This simulates actual bargaining situations, in which each person tries to maximize her utility. There is no difference between the process adopted by the Archimedean agent, who identifies each person with her abilities and talents, beliefs and conceptions, and seeks to give to each person the maximum share possible, and Gauthier's description of the actual bargaining process, in which bargainers are identified by these same features and are assumed to be motivated by utility-maximization. But Gauthier is not content merely with showing that the principles which are the outcome of his theory are also endorsed from an impartial point of view on a certain understanding of impartiality: he also argues that his understanding of impartiality is superior to Rawls's conception, for Rawls denies the importance of our individuality in conceiving of our abilities and talents and beliefs as social creations and so excludes them from the original position. Gauthier's claim that his theory respects the importance of our individuality seems to suggest that, on his view, people identify themselves with their beliefs and conceptions and abilities and that treating these aspects of the person as socially created violates our sense of self.

But on this conception of the Archimedean point, which parallels the formal conception of self-interest, there remains the problem of circularity to which feminist theory has pointed. Indeed, this problem is suggested by Gauthier's own conception of justification, according to which principles and institutions and practices are justified only if they serve individual interests. This leads naturally to the question of whether the institutions and practices of the society are themselves in the interests of those living under them. To overcome the problem of circularity—that is, to be able to assess the justice of the society as a whole—Gauthier must consider the effects that the institutions of society have on the formation of the individual. And so Gauthier is led to argue that the Archimedean agent is concerned not merely with what each can get from a bargain in which she is unproblematically identified with her capacities and talents, beliefs and aims, but with how well each would develop in that society compared with other possible societies.

The principles chosen from the Archimedean point must therefore provide that each person's expected share of the fruits of social inter-action be related, not to what he actually contributes, since his actual contribution may reflect the contingent permissions and prohibitions found in any social structure, but to the contribution he would make in that social structure most favorable to the actualization of his capacities and character traits, and to the fulfillment of his preferences, provided that this structure is a feasible alternative meeting the other requirements of Archimedean choice.[33]

In this passage, Gauthier is no longer concerned with the principles which should govern interaction between determinate individuals, as they are in society, but with the principles governing the society in which the individuals develop. And in accepting Rawls's notion that justice applies in the first instance to the social framework, Gauthier is moved to accept Rawls's slim conception of the person as identified with an asocial core.[34] But just as Gauthier's shift from a formal to a substantive conception of self-interest undermined his claim to have solved the motivation problem, so here his re-description of the Archimedean point makes apparent that Gauthier's conception does not after all represent an advance over Rawls's. A moment's reflection will make clear that the principles that would be endorsed by people prior to all socialization may not be acceptable to people with certain substantive aims and desires and beliefs. Thus, the integrity problem and the motivation problem re-emerge in Gauthier's theory, and they do so because the conception of justification that Gauthier and Rawls accept, and their quest for a vantage-point from which to assess different theories, different societies, leads inescapably to it. To avoid the issue would be to accept a deeply circular and question-begging theory. Thus, we see that Gauthier's theory is plagued by the same problems as Rawls's and Gewirth's theories, and is deeply ambiguous in presenting two different and incompatible conceptions of self-interest, and two different, incompatible versions of the Archimedean point.

NOTES

1. David Gauthier, *Morals by Agreement* (Oxford: Clarendon Press, 1986), 11.
2. This criticism is made by Gauthier, ibid. 3.
3. Ibid. 9.
4. Ibid. 84.
5. Joseph Mendola makes this point in his 'Gauthier's Morals by

Agreement and Two Kinds of Rationality', *Ethics*, 97/4 (July 1987), 767.

6. Gauthier, *Morals by Agreement*, 160–1.

7. Ibid. 144–5.

8. Ibid. 177.

9. I am assuming here that narrow compliance involves a disposition to make and comply with fair bargains only. But, as Jody S. Kraus and Jules L. Coleman, 'Morality and the Theory of Rational Choice', *Ethics*, 97/4 (July 1987), point out, there is a crucial ambiguity in Gauthier's description of narrow compliance. It is not clear whether narrow compliance involves only the disposition to comply with fair agreements, but involves no disposition with regard to making agreements, or whether it involves the disposition to make and comply with fair agreements. Even if we assume that the former interpretation is correct, Gauthier does not escape difficulty: this complicates any attempt at detection records and makes Gauthier's translucency assumption even more implausible.

10. Jean Hampton, 'Can We Agree on Morals?', *Canadian Journal of Philosophy*, 18/2 (June 1988), 334–8.

11. Gauthier, *Morals by Agreement*, 337.

12. Ibid. 197.

13. J. M. Buchanan, *The Limits of Liberty: Between Anarchy and Leviathan* (Chicago: The University of Chicago Press, 1975), 23–6.

14. Rawls, *A Theory of Justice*, 134.

15. Gauthier, *Morals by Agreement*, 196.

16. Ibid. 202.

17. Ibid. 222.

18. Ibid.

19. I am adopting here Gauthier's very positive interpretation of the benefits of a market.

20. David Braybrooke, 'Social Contract Theory's Fanciest Flight', *Ethics*, 97/4 (July 1987).

21. Ibid. 759–60.

22. From ibid. 758.

23. Cited by Gauthier, *Morals by Agreement*, 306–7.

24. Ibid. 313.

25. Ibid. 312–13.

26. Ibid. 268.

27. Annette C. Baier, 'Pilgrim's Progress', *Canadian Journal of Philosophy*, 18/2 (June 1988), 315–30.

28. Ibid. 326.

29. David Gauthier, 'Moral Artifice', *Canadian Journal of Philosophy*, 18/2 (June 1988).

30. Ibid. 405.
31. Baier, 'Pilgrim's Progress', 328.
32. Gauthier, *Morals by Agreement*, 238–9, 249–50.
33. Ibid. 264.
34. Hampton, 'Can We Agree on Morals?', 351.

PART II

Revisionist Liberal Theories

5

Contextual Arguments for Liberalism

THUS far, this book has questioned the coherence and plausibility of the theories of justice as impartiality and justice as mutual advantage. This chapter examines an argument, put forward by Rawls, in his recent essays, and by Charles Larmore in *Patterns of Moral Complexity* (1987), which justifies liberal political principles in contextual terms. The attraction of this justificatory argument is that it is not subject to the flaws pointed out here and to the criticisms advanced by communitarian theorists. This chapter argues that there is an important ambiguity in this defence of liberal political principles and that ultimately liberal principles cannot be sustained by contextual foundations.

The best-known liberal exponent of contextual foundations is John Rawls, who, responding to criticisms made by communitarians such as Sandel that his theory of justice presupposes an implausible Kantian metaphysics, now emphasizes the contextual character of his theory. He claims that his theory of justice was not intended as a universalist theory, applicable to all people in all types of societies, but to be the most reasonable political conception for modern democratic societies. He has abandoned his earlier claim that the principles of justice are justified in terms of an Archimedean point and now conceives of them as expressions of a particular conception of moral personhood that we accept.[1] He argues that his theory should not be understood as presupposing an implausible metaphysical conception of the person as identified with her capacity for rational autonomy but as a purely political conception, which is justified on the grounds that it is appropriate for modern democratic societies.

This interpretation of *A Theory of Justice* is consistent with certain elements of that work, particularly with Rawls's description of the process of reflective equilibrium, but does not sit easily with Rawls's claims to have provided his theory with an Archimedean point or his characterization of the principles of justice as 'the principles that free and rational persons concerned to further their own interests would accept in an initial position of equality' with no further qualifications.[2] But the issue here is not whether Rawls has been misinterpreted or has changed his position: what is clear in either case is that the text of *A Theory of Justice* certainly supports the universalist, rationalist interpretation that many find in it; and that it is important to assess Rawls's repudiation of universalist claims for his theory, and his emphasis instead on the situated character of his theory within a particular type of society.

What Rawls seems to have done is to blunt the force of the communitarian or pragmatist attack by embracing it and justifying his political liberalism in its terms. He now accepts Sandel's point that liberal theory rests on a specific conception of the person and even that this conception is, as Sandel claimed, a very slim conception of the self as pure rational agency, but he avoids the metaphysical thesis that Sandel attributes to him by arguing that the principles are purely political and independent of any particular controversial philosophical or religious doctrine. 'What justifies a conception of justice', he writes, 'is not its being true to an order antecedent and given to us, but its congruence with our deeper understanding of ourselves and our aspirations, and our realization that, given our history and the tradition embedded in our public life, it is the most reasonable doctrine for us.'[3] He agrees with Sandel that the conception of the person embedded in his theory is identified with the possession of the capacity of autonomy and that the original position is a 'nonhistorical . . . device of representation',[4] a device to characterize people as free and equal beings, timeless in the sense that all their contextually relative beliefs and conceptions and commitments have been systematically excluded. But, he argues, the principles derived from this abstract conception of the person have implications for people in contemporary democratic society, because this conception of the person is an appropriate conception for people to adopt in the circumstances of modern democratic society. Indeed, Rawls now argues that the task of political theory is to articulate a conception of justice which will provide a basis for agreement and so contribute to the creation of social unity, and he represents his principles of justice as giving form to the intuitive conceptions appropriate for or implicit in Western industrialized democracies and as justified by the support they receive from an 'overlapping consensus' of people in these societies.

This attempt to ground liberal political principles in a contextual argument has important implications for the argument of this book. In Part I it was claimed that liberalism's doctrine of the priority of the right over the good forces the advocates of liberalism to search for an Archimedean point which will justify their theory in arbitrating among various substantive ethical conceptions. Specifically, the doctrine led them to take as the starting-point of ethical theory the individual agent, understood independently of all moral relations to others, and to represent as justified the principles which would be agreed to or rationally acknowledged by such an agent. The basic thrust of Part I was that it is not possible to derive a substantive moral or political theory from a conception of the person so defined, and that theories which attempt to argue in this way are fatally flawed. But if it is indeed plausible and coherent to ground political liberalism in the empirical conditions that obtain in modern societies, then the argument of the preceding section will have been refuted. It could of course be correct that the theories examined there—Gewirth's, Rawls's, and Gauthier's—are flawed in important ways, but the general conclusion drawn from that examination will have been refuted if Rawls and Larmore are successful in grounding liberalism in a contextualist argument.

Unfortunately, however, the relation between contemporary democratic society and the abstract political conception of the self as essentially free and equal remains obscure and underdeveloped in Rawls's recent essays. In fact, Rawls's treatment of this relation is more suggestive than clearly articulated: he frequently hints at a close relation between the two but fails to make explicit the precise nature of that relation. Even more troubling is that what he does say in this regard points to two different conceptions of the relation between the political and private selves, two different theories of the relation of self-interest to morality, and, corresponding to this, two different sources for the 'fundamental intuitions' on which Rawls's theory is constructed. The

ambiguity over the precise status of Rawls's fundamental intuitive convictions, which are the starting-point of his constructive
method, infects the whole theory. The relation between the political and private conceptions of the person, between self-interest
and morality, changes depending on how the very linchpins
of his theory are conceived. And because Rawls's theory leaves
itself open to two radically different, mutually incompatible
answers to the question of how political consensus or convergence is possible—one, a communitarian conception, the other,
a self-interested (*modus vivendi*) one—both will be examined; but
I shall argue that neither is able to avoid being either extremely
counter-intuitive or incoherent or both; and that this jeopardizes
the success of Rawls's response to his communitarian critics.[5]

1. The Communitarian Interpretation

The central question to which all the other ambiguities and tensions in Rawls's revised theory are related is, how is consensus
possible at all in societies characterized by deep moral disunity?
On what basis would people agree to Rawls's particular principles of justice in deeply divided societies such as Rawls
describes?

One way of explaining the possibility of overlapping consensus
on particular principles is in terms of the principles expressing
or representing the shared beliefs and ideals and conceptions
which underlie modern democratic society. The principles command the allegiance of their adherents, not by their rational basis
but because they articulate or express beliefs and conceptions
and ideas that they already hold. Thus Rawls writes in his essay
'Justice as Fairness: Political not Metaphysical' that the basic
intuitive ideas of his theory are '*embedded* in the political institutions of a constitutional democratic regime'.[6] On this view,
theory proceeds by examining the culture of modern society—its
institutions, traditions, ideals, and public life—and formulates
these underlying ideas into a coherent conception of political
justice on which all are likely to agree. The original position
is not conceived as a justificatory method at all but as a heuristic
device to attain greater self-understanding, a device to enable
people to comprehend the principles which underlie their society

and which form the bases of the rules of justice and co-operation. And this is precisely how Rawls characterizes the original position in his recent essays: it is, he writes, a 'device of representation' which, by situating the parties in positions of freedom and equality, articulates the most fundamental intuitive conceptions, of the freedom and equality of persons, in our society.

In *A Theory of Justice* Rawls did not elaborate on the source of the 'moral intuitions' that form the material on which his method of reflective equilibrium works but treated them instead as mere brute facts about people.[7] It is doubtful, however, that he regarded them as inborn, since he was aware that the 'intuitions' that people have regarding ethical matters tend to vary from society to society.[8] If we interpret the moral intuitions as themselves generated within the society—as fixed points of understanding that are transmitted through the moral education of the members of society and are fundamental to their comprehension of each other and the world—then we can indeed understand the theory of justice as an elaborate articulation of communally held beliefs. On this interpretation, the principles of justice are justified by an overlapping consensus in society, which itself represents the deep theory of the good held by members of the society. This is expressed most clearly in Rawls's 1987 essay 'The Idea of an Overlapping Consensus', where Rawls argues that what is needed as a basis of justification is a regulative political conception of justice that can 'articulate and order in a principled way [the] basic political values . . . of a democratic society'.[9] Thus, while justification consists in the first instance in the theory's ability to secure overlapping consensus or agreement on its principles, that consensus is rooted at a deeper level in the fact that the theory expresses, in a principled way, the deep-rooted convictions of the society in question.

The Extent of Consensus and the Moral Diversity Assumption

Although Rawls seems to accept that a core of agreement in society on certain fundamental intuitive conceptions is necessary to arrive at a political conception which can secure consensus, he rejects the view that a political conception of justice can be reached by merely applying a substantive or fully worked-out moral theory to the political sphere. This claim is made on empirical grounds: in Rawls's opinion, contemporary democratic society is characterized by such a variety of different full moral conceptions that agreement on a single moral theory is impossible. In order to combine Rawls's communitarian grounding for his political principles with the liberal doctrine that excludes substantive moral conceptions from the political sphere, Rawls appeals to the assumption of moral diversity. He argues that agreement can be obtained only on a few fundamental conceptions and that any attempt to embody a full moral conception in the political framework of society would be so divisive as to risk a breakdown in the consensus which makes political cooperation possible.

What this formulation does not explain, however, is how fundamental intuitive ideas as abstract as freedom and equality can be given concrete expression without raising the spectre of disagreement on the political principles themselves. It is conceivable that people holding a variety of ethical conceptions could agree that any adequate political theory would respect the freedom of persons and endorse the principle of equality. At the most general level of argument, liberal egalitarians, radical feminists, Hegelian Idealists, and libertarian liberals could all agree on the central importance of freedom both in their respective theories and for a theory of justice. But their understanding of freedom, the interpretation that each gives to the concept of freedom, varies widely. Whereas the feminist argues that unfreedom can result from ties of personal affectivity, from affection- or kin-based relations which do not operate in the best interests of the person concerned, the libertarian liberal counts only external constraints such as coercion as an obstacle to individual freedom. Egalitarian liberals such as Rawls in *A Theory of Justice* accept the importance of equality in situating free persons and take seriously the implications of inequalities in power or starting-points for the exercise of liberty, but do not go so far as to accept either that poverty or ignorance as such constitutes an obstacle to freedom, or the feminist critique of the public–private dichotomy. And Hegelian Idealists such as Bradley would deny both the feminist claim that affective family ties constitute an obstacle to freedom, and the negative liberal position that freedom consists in the exercise of choice as such. Right-Hegelians typically conceive of freedom as realized through being able to identify with the ways of life of the person's community. Each one of these differences concerning what counts as an obstacle to freedom reflects a different conception or interpretation of freedom itself, and these differences are bound to emerge in any attempt to secure agreement on a determinate political conception of freedom.

The same pattern emerges in terms of the concept of equality. Once again, it is perfectly conceivable that people holding widely divergent moral views would agree in upholding a principle of equality, understood in a sufficiently general way. For example, libertarian liberals may endorse the principle of equality in the distribution of rights but deny that any substantive distributive conclusions follow from this: although everyone has an equal right to liberty, it is perfectly acceptable from this point of view for widely unequal distributions of goods to result from the exercise of those rights. By contrast, egalitarian liberals would not only apply the principle of equality to the distribution of purely formal rights but would also justify a certain amount of redistribution to secure the conditions of equal freedom. Feminists may operate with an even more substantive conception of equality, which involves the transformation of existing relations of power and dominance, while Hegelians accept an equality principle only at the purely formal level of treating like cases alike. It seems evident that, although agreement could be reached on very abstract intuitive convictions, this consensus would evaporate once the process of arriving at a more determinate conception or representation of these principles was under way. This conclusion is hardly surprising, for an abstract concept such as freedom or equality is typically given shape or form within the context of an overall ethical conception or world-view, and people holding divergent moral theories would interpret differently such abstract conceptions as freedom and equality. But if this is the case, then it seems that isolating a few shared intuitive conceptions which underlie social practices and institutions and giving form to them by constructing a theory or representation of these conceptions would not be sufficient to secure consensus on a determinate theory of justice. It seems that consensus on a political theory is possible only if people share not just a few fundamental intuitive convictions but a broadly similar world-view which enables them to interpret abstract conceptions such as freedom and equality in similar ways. Unfortunately, however, Rawls cannot accept this conclusion, for it renders the political conception of justice derivative from a full-blown ethical conception, and so undermines his justification for the liberal exclusion of substantive ethical conceptions from the political sphere.[10]

According to the argument just outlined, Rawls's characterization of modern society as possessing a deep tension between pluralism and unity cannot be sustained: consensus on a political theory presupposes a shared ethical conception; agreement cannot be secured when the abstract intuitive convictions are given determinate shape unless the parties to the agreement share a similar world-view or overall ethical conception. Rawls attempts to overcome this objection by appealing to the idea of theory as a heuristic device, as itself altering the balance of reasons in favour of one theory over others, and so possessing the persuasive power to win over adherents. Of course, giving the inchoate intuitive convictions a principled form in itself excludes any theories that are contradictory or incoherent: the theorist is required to adjust or modify or reject principles which, though initially attractive, are found to have unacceptable or contradictory implications, and to adjust or modify the scope of principles if applying them in a particular area would be counter-intuitive. But these formal requirements could be met by many moderately reflective full ethical conceptions: they could be met by feminism or Hegelianism or Nozickian liberalism just as adequately as by Rawls's more egalitarian version of liberalism. We should therefore reformulate the question we are considering to read: how is agreement on a political conception possible among people who hold widely divergent but reasonably coherent and plausible (to them) moral theories?

Rawls anticipates this problem: 'The public political culture may be of two minds even at a very deep level,' he writes. 'Indeed, this must be so with such an enduring controversy as that concerning the most appropriate institutional forms to realize the values of liberty and equality.'[11] And his response to the problem he has just posed is: 'This suggests that if we are to succeed in finding a basis of public agreement, we must find a new way of organizing familiar ideas and principles into a conception of political justice so that the claims in conflict, as previously understood, are seen in another light. A political conception need not be an original creation but may only articulate familiar intuitive ideas and principles so that they can be recognized as fitting together in a somewhat different way than before.'[12] But this response is not adequate to the seriousness of the objection just outlined. It is based on the vague hope that the political conception of justice will dissolve the deep disagreements that characterize contemporary democratic society by presenting its principles 'in a new light'. And this amounts either (*a*) to the admission that it is impossible to arrive at consensus on a political conception of justice in a society riddled by deep moral disagreements, and so to an implicit acknowledgement that contemporary society must be unified not only in accepting a few fundamental convictions but on a whole range of ethical issues; or (*b*) to an appeal to a Platonic apprehension of the appropriate expression of freedom or equality, in which case Rawls's revised theory is not ultimately based on communitarian or contextual foundations at all but on an unexplained and inexplicable intuitive perception of political truth.

The Incoherence of Communitarian Foundations and Liberal Political Principles

The relation of the individual to society suggested by Rawls's communitarian foundations is that of a person immersed in the society, a person whose central aims and conceptions, beliefs and values, are formed in community with others and are an expression of this shared or communal identity. By envisaging the hypothetical contract or original position, not as serving a justificatory function as in *A Theory of Justice*, but as a heuristic device designed merely to represent the abstract conceptions that underlie modern society's institutions and practices, Rawls suggests that the direction of justification is from the society to the theory. It seems from Rawls's ultimate appeal to pre-existing, communal conceptions and practices that ethical or political theory's central aim is to articulate more clearly the beliefs underlying the society, to give expression to shared conceptions of what is reasonable or unreasonable, or what constitutes a justification, and so secure consensus in society. But the substantive conception that he articulates from this communal basis suggests precisely the opposite relation of the individual to society. Rawls extracts from the shared practices of contemporary societies a conception of a person free of all bonds to others and all communally relative beliefs, as autonomously shaping the conditions of her existence and the shape and direction of her life.[13] This is suggested by Rawls's claim that the 'fundamental intuitive conceptions' of the freedom and equality of persons are the building-blocks of his political theory.

This conception is not, of course, confined to Rawls's theory: the conception of the person as autonomous chooser, as essentially free and equal, underlies the paradigmatic liberal conception of contractual ethics and contractual politics. In contract theory, legitimacy is conceived of as deriving from the choices or agreement or consensus of individuals; and this derives from a more fundamental conception of individuals as directing their own lives, not only in the immediate personal sphere but in choosing the mores they will live by, and the political or institutional structure of their society. But, if this is merely constructed from a communal reservoir of shared beliefs and practices and values, as in Rawls's contextualist theory, its status must be that of an elaborate myth. On the two-stage theory presented by Rawls, in which political or ethical principles are justified in the first instance by consensus or agreement, which in turn is derived from the shared traditions or conceptions that the principles express, the society is presented as *in fact* bound together by its shared conceptions and beliefs and way of life, although what the members of the community share, what they have acquired in the course of their induction into the way of life of their society, is a conception of themselves as creating their society, as choosing their way of life in abstraction from all communally relative beliefs. But the recognition that this conception is itself relative to particular communities, and dependent for its survival and content and legitimacy on being embodied in communal practices, involves a denial of the substantive content of the community's self-conception. From the philosophical, as distinct from the participant, perspective, the conception of the person and her relation to society must be regarded as an elaborate fiction, the acceptance of which requires a denial of the (real) source of its legitimacy in the way of life of a particular community.

The incoherence of communitarian foundations and liberal political or moral principles may be suggested to anyone who recalls that liberalism initially conceived of itself as opposed to tradition, as wiping away the centuries of obedience to irrational super-stition and deferential subordination to traditional authority by applying the power of reason to social and ethical questions. Grounding liberal values in an appeal to shared values in a com-munity is thus fundamentally antithetical to liberalism's original understanding of itself. Grounding political principles designed to protect the autonomy of individuals in terms of their embodi-ment in communal institutions and practices—in terms of their fundamental role in contemporary democratic society, which is then reflected in the 'intuitions' of the people educated in this society—undermines the autonomy of the person which it is intended to support.

This tension has been emphasized by those feminist theories which have argued that the person's affective commitments or kin-based relations or ways of life could keep one in a state of subjection, committed to relationships and ways of life which do not serve her individual interests.[14] Such a person may accept a menial or subordinate or low-paying job or position because she has been encouraged to find fulfilment vicariously, through the success of her family and children, not through her own achievement or the full exercise of her own abilities. From the point of view of the abstract chooser who is ignorant of all particu-lar relations, beliefs, values, and commitments, the woman is self-sacrificing and the social relations and institutions which she accepts are exploitative. What Rawls in *A Theory of Justice*[15] correctly perceived is that choice or agreement based on the beliefs or values that the person possesses merely because she has been taught them does not carry any justificatory force. There is undoubtedly a fit between society and individual, but on this account it is because the society has shaped the person to fit it, has taught her to think in certain ways and believe and value certain things.

The position of the woman brought up in a sexist society is analogous to the people who accept the liberal conception of the person and liberal political principles because they are edu-cated in a liberal society. Their agreement, their consent carries no justificatory force as agreement or consent, but is merely a reflection of their education within the society. By taking these

conceptions as the fixed points from which theoretical construction proceeds, but not themselves the product of autonomous
self-creation, Rawls develops a theory which endorses principles
designed to protect individual autonomy but which is ultimately
grounded in a conception of the person as fundamentally unautonomous because unable to move beyond her particular community's most fundamental beliefs. The irony in these theories
is that their support for the value of individual autonomy is itself
grounded in an unautonomous, or unchosen, commitment to
certain conceptions which people simply 'have', and for which
Rawls does not offer any rationale or justification.[16]

This conclusion is not merely ironic but fatal for this liberal
justificatory argument. For constitutive of the conception of the
autonomous, self-defining individual is the requirement that
these individuals are transparent to themselves. The person can
be autonomous only through rising above the ignorance and
superstitions engendered by obedience to tradition or inner neur-
oses and achieving full self-consciousness in choices and relations to others. But if Rawls's agents attain to the liberal ideal
of reflective disengagement from the practices and values and
conceptions which they once accepted, they would see the liberal
conception as itself a fraud, as another irrational superstition.
And so ultimately the liberal conception of the self-defining individual is transformed into irrational subjective self-assertiveness.
And from this perspective there is no reason to choose anything
at all, neither liberal principles nor authoritarian ones.

2. THE *MODUS VIVENDI* INTERPRETATION

There is another, perhaps even more plausible interpretation
of the basis of Rawls's overlapping consensus which focuses,
not on those passages which emphasize the fundamental intuitive convictions underlying society and which thereby suggest
the possibility of a communitarian justification of the principles
of justice, but on Rawls's claim that contemporary democratic
society is characterized by a 'plurality of opposing and incom-
mensurable conceptions' of the good.[17] In the account of Rawls's
theory given above, his theory is assimilated to communitarian
theory by concentrating on his account of the process of reflective

equilibrium and the deep or underlying basis of agreement in contemporary democratic society. The problem with that interpretation of his theory, quite apart from being incoherent and unsupportable, is that it is incompatible with Rawls's public–private distinction, and with his claim that his theory is a purely political conception, and not a moral theory applied to the political sphere. The *modus vivendi* interpretation of Rawls's theory offered here supports this distinction and is compatible with Rawls's frequent references to the deep moral disunity in contemporary democratic society, but it is not easy to reconcile with Rawls's appeal to the fundamental intuitive convictions which suggest a communitarian interpretation of the foundation of his principles of justice.

A central tenet of Rawls's theory, both in *A Theory of Justice* and in his more recent essays, examined here, and, some would argue,[18] of liberalism in general, is the view that the state should not appeal to any particular conception of the good to justify its principles or policies. In *A Theory of Justice*, Rawls maintains his doctrine that particular conceptions of the good should be denied a justificatory role in the political arena, while at the same time justifying his principles of justice by arguing that the list of primary goods, on which the selection of the principles of justice is based, is not derived from a particular, fully worked-out moral theory, but is an all-purpose means to the fulfilment of any conception of the good.[19] From a standpoint independent of all particular ethical conceptions, rival moral theories can be viewed as lacking justificatory force: they are mere human conventions on a par with other (non-moral) conventions to which people happen to be committed. To justify his principles of justice in their role as political arbiter, that is, in deciding as either permissible or impermissible all actions and so implicitly all moral theories, Rawls needs to ground his principles in a strong justificatory argument similar to the one he invoked in *A Theory of Justice*, but without the ahistoric, rationalist, Kantian suggestions of that work.[20] He needs, in other words, to articulate a *contextual* grounding for his principles that will make his theory sufficiently distinct from rival moral theories to justify it in adjudicating among them. The strategy he adopts in his recent essays is to justify his liberal political principles in their role of adjudicator on the same grounds that he employed in *A Theory of Justice*, namely that they are neutral among all other moral or philosophical theories. This neutrality is in turn justified, not in an ahistoric Kantian conception, as in *A Theory of Justice*, but as a reasonable response to the moral disunity of contemporary democratic society. It is justified as a strategy for achieving co-operation in the face of a plurality of incompatible conceptions of the good.

Rawls argues that the diversity of moral and philosophical theories affirmed in contemporary democratic societies makes it practically impossible for any general moral conception to provide a basis for overlapping consensus on political principles.[21] The conceptions and beliefs that people have are important in determining the kinds of principles appropriate for their society, not because the principles are *based* on the conceptions that people hold, as on the communitarian interpretation of Rawls's theory, but because what principles are appropriate for a particular society depends on the particular circumstances, and included among the circumstances of justice are the degree of unity (or disunity) in beliefs and the kinds of beliefs held by people in society. On this interpretation of the contextual nature of his theory, the principles that would be agreed to are conceived of as appropriate in the context of the particular society, but do not possess validity beyond the bounds of the society in question. The agreement or consensus that justifies the principles of justice is based on the pragmatic recognition of these circumstances by the people giving their consent, and, particularly, the recognition that agreement on a single moral conception is not possible. In the light of this, each person is conceived of as withdrawing from political consideration his or her particular moral theory, his or her particular conception of the good, and confining her attention to principles which could form the basis of agreement or consensus.

Lurking in the background of this more Hobbesian defence of Rawls's principles is the threat of the autocratic use of state power. It seems to be a presupposition of Rawls's theory here that all parties to the agreement regard this as threatening, regardless of which group might wield state power. Rawls argues that the extent of moral disunity in society requires that a pragmatic distinction be drawn between the public and private realms: in the public realm are those principles to which all could agree as a basis for adjudicating interaction between people; while included in the private sphere is each person's particular conception of the good life, i.e. the aims and desires, values and beliefs that give meaning to each person's life.

This conception of the contextual basis of liberal political principles has also been advanced, but in greater detail, by Charles Larmore in his book *Patterns of Moral Complexity*, which Rawls explicitly endorses in a recent essay.[22] Larmore begins his argument with the claim that central to liberalism is the conception of a state neutral among conceptions of the good,[23] and he attempts to justify the separation of public and private realms that liberalism involves by appealing to the impossibility of achieving agreement in society on a single substantive moral conception. It is a premiss of both Larmore's and Rawls's *modus vivendi* argument that different people fundamentally disagree not only on the purposes and aims that they seek to pursue but also on the purposes that ought to be pursued. Since, on this view, conceptions of the good in contemporary society are bound to diverge, Larmore reasons that it is necessary that the political sphere provide some grounds for adjudicating among them, and the best way to do this is by not basing liberal principles on any particular conception. The political principles are primarily a mechanism for accommodation among competing moral conceptions, and what makes them successful, what makes accommodation and, ultimately, political stability possible, is that these political principles are derived from a basis neutral among all these contending principles.

Abstraction and the Public–Private Dichotomy

Both Rawls and Larmore require the person to respond to the circumstances of justice, and, particularly, to the moral disunity that characterizes modern society, by abstracting from her contested moral and philosophical beliefs in the effort to reach agreement on political principles. Thus the tension in their theory between division and unity, between a society characterized by deep divisions and yet sufficiently unified to attain consensus on a single set of political principles, is resolved by conceiving of the person as divided between her personal and political aspects. Both Rawls and Larmore argue that their requirement that the person abstract from her controversial moral and philosophical conceptions does not entail the view that the person's beliefs and values are unimportant or not constitutive of the person. They are anxious to deny the claim forcefully made by Bernard Williams in his essay 'Persons, Character and Morality', and, in a different way, by Michael Sandel in his critique of the liberal conception of the disengaged self, that liberalism does not take seriously the commitment of the person to her ends and aims.[24] Sandel and Williams argue that, in viewing these as merely chosen and so at a distance from the self, liberalism assimilates the person's fundamental commitments and values to mere preferences, treating them as subjective and so both as an inappropriate basis for political principles and as unimportant relative to the overriding claims of the principles of justice. Larmore writes in response to the line of criticism:

In order to take up a neutral position by abstracting from our substantial conception of the good life, we are not . . . repudiating that conception or lessening our attachment to it. We have not adopted a general posture of neutrality or detachment toward our idea of what makes life worth living. That idea may remain so close to us, so 'constitutive' . . . of what we understand to be of ultimate significance, that we would be unwilling to accept in imagination our lives without it.[25]

Rawls echoes these sentiments:

Citizens may have, and normally do have at any given time, affections, devotions and loyalties that they believe they would not, and indeed could and should not, stand apart from and objectively evaluate from the point of view of their purely rational good. They may regard it as simply unthinkable to view themselves apart from certain religious, philosophical and moral convictions, or from certain enduring attachments and loyalties. These convictions and attachments . . . help to organize and give shape to a person's way of life, what one sees oneself as doing and trying to accomplish in one's social world. We think that if we were suddenly without these particular convictions and attachments we would be disoriented and unable to carry on. In fact, there would be, we might think, no point in carrying on.[26]

By stressing the central importance to the person of her values and attachments and commitments, Rawls and Larmore deflect the criticism that the liberal conception does not view them as 'constitutive' of the self. Ironically, however, their affirmation of the importance of the person's aims and beliefs and values to her also serves to highlight the tension created in the person by the necessity of abstracting from her fundamental beliefs and ideals and values in the quest to reach political principles on which all or many are likely to agree. It suggests not only a dichotomy between the personal and political aspects of the person, but the unsatisfactoriness, from the subjective point of view, of a situation in which the principles which govern the institutional framework of one's society do not express one's moral conception, one's most fundamental beliefs concerning what is good or right or objectively valid.

Fundamental to the *modus vivendi* conception, then, is the public–private dichotomy: at the private, moral level, people are conceived of as holding widely varying conceptions of the good to which they are deeply committed; while, at the political level, aware of the lack of means to organize society in accordance with the good and of the need to co-operate, they agree to co-operate on liberal principles of justice. From the point of view of the co-operating agents, the liberal principles are principles of expediency, grounded in the need to co-operate in the face of disagreement over full moral conceptions. Thus, the feminist has her own particular conception of what is good or right or just, but, recognizing that she cannot gain the agreement of other members of society on feminist principles, she accepts the principles of justice as a basis for co-operation. Similarly, the Christian fundamentalist has her own ethical conception which she regards as justified in being embodied in the political or institutional structure, but, recognizing that Christianity could not possibly serve as a basis for consensus on political principles, she confines her religious and moral views to her personal life, and does not seek to enshrine Christian principles in the constitutional or legal structure of society. For both the Christian and the feminist, liberal principles represent a necessary compromise with reality, not an ideal. The ideal situation would be the recognition of the truth of Christianity or of feminism by a sufficient number of people in society to make possible the organization of society in accordance with the good. Failing that, she accepts liberal principles on the expedient grounds that co-operation is necessary and these principles make co-operation possible. For the committed feminist or Christian, the liberal principles agreed to are not *moral* principles but principles of expedience, instrumental to the achievement of stability and co-operation. And since the basis of their agreement to the principles of justice is expedience, it follows that there can be no reason to adhere to the principles when they are inexpedient or not in one's interest. When the constellation of moral conceptions prevalent in society changes and Christianity, say, becomes dominant, there is no reason to respect the liberal principles and every reason to seek to entrench Christian principles in the institutional framework of the society.

The problem with the *modus vivendi* foundation is not its conception of justice as secured by a convergence of self or group interests, for, if one could show, as Gauthier attempts to do,[27] that action in accordance with the principles of justice is in each individual's interest, the principles of justice would be provided with an extremely secure foundation because entrenched in each person's subjective motivational set. The problem is that Rawls's and Larmore's principles are a compromise by all parties, given their inability to secure the situation that each most favours. Justice, on this conception, is supported by a *modus vivendi* in which each group adheres to the constraints only in order to secure its own good, its own advantage in the circumstances, but each lacks an independent moral commitment to the constraining principles of justice. This formulation characterizes the person as acutely divided between her political and personal aspects. It requires the person—who may hold a moral theory which she believes is true or objectively valid—to adhere to a political conception which does not recognize or support (what she regards as) the objective truth and which is not itself justified in moral terms. Thus, it gives rise to a motivation problem in situations in which there is some possibility of embodying one's moral principles in the political sphere in place of the principles of justice.

The Argument from Rational Conversation

The conclusion drawn here—that the *modus vivendi* justification of liberalism is unstable and unattractive—has recently been vigorously denied by Larmore in his *Patterns of Moral Complexity*. Larmore attempts to avoid the conclusion that the *modus vivendi* justification is inherently unstable by re-describing what is involved in the conception of the person as divided between her personal and political aspects. Larmore argues that the confinement of certain contested beliefs and conceptions and values to the personal sphere does not create a radical and unnatural division in the person: in fact, the procedure is embedded in the very concept of a rational conversation. Here Larmore draws on Habermas's argument that putting forward claims for which we believe we have good reason implies the concept of an ideally rational conversation; it implies, that is, a conversation under ideal conditions such that the reasons we advance would command the assent of others. Larmore regards this Habermasian conception as 'the lever by which people can be pried into accepting the commitment to rational norms of conversation that underlies the argument for political neutrality'.[28] He appeals to the notion of a rational conversation, not to draw substantive (liberal) principles from such a conception—indeed, he concedes that that is not possible[29]—but to demonstrate that the norms of rational conversation are implicit in everyday discursive argument. The norm embodied in the notion of rational conversation which Larmore requires for his argument is: 'When disagreement arises [among interlocutors], those wishing to continue the conversation should withdraw to neutral ground, in order either to resolve the dispute or if that cannot be done rationally, to bypass it.'[30] This leads Larmore to claim that, in cases of substantial disagreement, the rational strategy is to 'devise political principles that are themselves neutral, that do not require for their justification the ideas of the good in dispute'.[31] Since the retreat to neutral grounds follows from the commitment to rational conversation, which is claimed to be implicit in the very idea of giving reasons for one's beliefs, Larmore concludes that abstraction from disputed issues or beliefs or concepts does not create an unnatural and undesirable division in the person but is part of the process of justifying one's beliefs and actions to others.

As presented thus far, Larmore's argument does not constitute an adequate response to the objection raised concerning the instability and unattractiveness of the *modus vivendi* conception. It may be, as Larmore claims, a rational strategy on the part of interlocutors committed to their conversation to abstract from the controversial issues that divide them and proceed from a common or shared understanding. Indeed, this procedure is wholly consistent with a communitarian conception of the grounds of values or beliefs or principles. The deeper question that must be answered is why the people are engaged in the conversation in the first place. The communitarian would interpret the interlocutors as moved by a desire to explore a shared problem or common understanding and would claim that adopting the strategy of abstracting from their controversial beliefs and conceptions indicates that the desire to continue the conversation is stronger than the desire to terminate the conversation. If the person finds the other uninteresting or completely alien, she would not engage in the conversation at all. On a communitarian interpretation, what keeps the interlocutors conversing, and what is the basis of the principles or conclusions arrived at, is their shared understanding or shared conception of the subject in question. But this communitarian interpretation of the dynamics of a conversation is not open to Larmore, for he seeks to ground his liberal principles in a conception neutral among conceptions of the good. He is not describing strategies for arriving at a deep theory of the good, a shared or communal understanding of political principles, but a neutral justification of them.

This brings us to the second step of Larmore's argument. He has argued that the interlocutors' strategy of abstracting from their contested beliefs and conceptions is derivative from or conditional on a prior desire to continue the conversation; and he must ensure that the grounds of this desire, the reason for initiating the conversation, is neutral among conceptions of the good. Larmore initially suggests, rather weakly, that sympathy could move people to engage in a conversation;[32] but this is unsatisfactory for his purposes because sympathy presupposes shared bonds, a shared sense of identity, but does not explain it. He also considers a desire for civil peace as a motive for initiating a conversation, but this too seems inadequate for his purposes, for it does not explain why we would converse with those who are powerless to threaten our civil peace.[33] This brings Larmore to the motive which he thinks is central to explaining the interlocutors' commitment to the conversation: this is the wish to show everyone equal respect.

In one sense of the term, to treat someone with equal respect means to treat her as one treats others unless there is a sufficient reason not to do so.[34] This minimal or formal sense of the term is neutral with respect to divergent conceptions of the good. But this sense, Larmore admits, is 'far too weak' for his purposes;[35] no commitment to specifically liberal, or indeed any substantive principle follows from this. Larmore understands equal respect for persons as involving treating them not as mere objects of our will but as owed an explanation for actions of ours that affect them. This attitude towards others holds regardless of the views they express: we adopt the attitude of equal respect, Larmore writes, because 'we recognize other persons as being capable of coherently developing beliefs from within their own perspective'.[36] It is the recognition of their *capacity* for autonomy, their capacity for developing their own particular views on the world, that leads to the obligation of equal respect.

The non-neutrality of Larmore's liberal theory can be seen in terms of the person who has convictions or beliefs so overwhelming that she cannot, or will not, abstract from them and see herself in the general terms that Larmore's argument requires. There may be people who hold another person or another way of life in such contempt, and perhaps justifiable contempt, that they cannot regard that person or that way of life as just another instance of a general type, such as seeker after her ideal of the good life. Such people are not irrational: indeed, they may be very able to justify their beliefs and conceptions to other people, but they are unwilling to abstract from their concrete particular identity in the way Larmore's argument requires. Such people could accept Larmore's argument concerning the rationality of abstraction, but would claim that such abstraction can proceed only as long as both parties to the conversation wish to continue it. And the motive Larmore provides to explain why the person would continue the conversation—the desire to show equal respect—is not a motive for them but presupposes the acceptance of the liberal conception of morality and of the person.

Larmore recognizes that the desire to show equal respect is not universal, but he does not think this seriously threatens his theory. He writes:

some views of the good life—some especially virulent forms of racism, for example—must reject the obligation of equal respect in order to remain consistent. But . . . I do not believe that this forms a significant limit to the neutrality of my argument. Liberals need not have an argument to convince people of this sort, only safeguards for preventing them from acquiring political power. After all, such people seem little interested in rational argument.[37]

Of course, the obligation to show equal respect, to treat others as ends, not as means, would be rejected not only by racists but by all who refuse to abstract from their determinate beliefs and conceptions and commitments and view themselves in the generic terms required by Rawls's and Larmore's argument. And this *does* pose a serious problem for their theory. Recall that the justificatory ground of their theory, at least in the first instance, is the ability to command consensus or agreement on their principles. And this is rooted in the belief that principles or institutions are justifiable only if they secure, or can secure, the allegiance of those governed by them. However, the commitment to consent cannot prevent the liberal from imposing liberal principles on the racist or other illiberal people. To survive at all as a political theory, liberalism must prevent actions which cause harm or infringe the autonomy of others whatever the justification for their action. But on what grounds can liberal theorists justify the imposition of liberal principles on others? For the imposition is itself a denial of the very thing liberalism stands for, namely the right of each person to determine for herself the shape of her life and the conditions of her existence, including the political principles under which she lives. Larmore argues against this that consent from 'such people' as the racist and, presumably, other illiberal people is not necessary because they 'seem little interested in rational argument'. The implication is that, if they were rational, they would be committed to a rational conversation and, so, in modern circumstances, to a process of abstraction which leads to the conception of each person as offering reasons justifiable from her own perspective. The problem with this argument is that, while there are many grounds on which we may object to racists, the claim that they are not committed to rational argument in the sense of having reasons for their beliefs is not one of them. It is certainly convenient for Larmore to portray racism and other illiberal attitudes as the product of blind irrational forces in control of the racist, but the truth is that most racists are able to give reasons for their racism.

They do not view a certain race or nationality as in itself worthy of admiration or contempt: race is generally viewed as a sign for something else, for some quality possessed by the members of the race which is viewed as admirable or contemptible. If racism is to be confronted effectively, it is by responding to the beliefs that the racist holds, not by offering convenient but mistaken caricatures of it.

Moreover, it is misleading to portray liberalism as 'largely neutral' except when confronted with 'virulent forms of racism'. Larmore's theory is also fundamentally antithetical to any hierarchical conception. He concedes that the desire to treat everyone with equal respect is not a motive in most societies: hierarchical or aristocratic societies certainly never hold this as an ideal. Nevertheless, Larmore denies that his liberal political theory is not neutral with respect to hierarchical theories:

I do not mean to suggest that a commitment to equal respect has been a perennial feature of human culture. . . . I wish to insist only that it is *compatible* with a very great variety of ideals of the good life, including those that were dominant at times when, as a matter of fact, the norm of equal respect was not so widely shared. For example, the belief that some particular hereditary class produces those most fit to rule does not exclude equal respect, for one could feel obliged (as some such aristocrats were) to justify this belief to the other classes.[38]

But Larmore's argument here is clearly fallacious. It is true that the aristocrat may feel inclined to justify her beliefs or views to the lower classes, but this would not commit her to an interminable conversation about her own aristocratic fitness to rule in an effort to gain the consent of those she regards as unfit to rule. A properly aristocratic conception of fitness to rule is not consistent with a conception of the equal worth of persons: the aristocrat's fitness to rule is not a technical question, related to fitting particular jobs to particular talents, but is inherent in aristocratic birth. It is not a matter that requires the consent of those classes of people who are unfit to rule; and it would be inconsistent to converse with the lower classes merely out of respect for their capacity for autonomy, since this capacity is granted no respect in the aristocratic political conception.

Larmore's liberal political theory is not, as he claims, a conception neutral among a large range of political or ethical theories,

but requires or presupposes the acceptance of the liberal conception of the person as identified with her capacity for autonomy.
But if liberalism cannot claim to be derived in a way which is
neutral among the competing conceptions of the good prevalent
in contemporary society, how does it justify coercing those who
do not accept liberalism to live according to its principles? This
is a particular problem for liberalism because it is committed
to the view that institutions or principles are legitimate only if
they secure the consent of those subject to them. The argument
from rational conversation attempts to link the acceptance of
neutral grounds and so of liberal principles (which Larmore
claims are derived from neutral grounds) to the concept of rationality. This confines valid consent or rational consent to those
who accept the liberal starting-point. But the argument from
rational conversation fails: Larmore cannot show that not accepting the liberal starting-point is irrational. And this means that
it is unjustifiable to confine valid consent to those who accept
the liberal doctrine of equal respect for persons and the liberal
conception of morality. To confine valid consent to those who
accept liberal assumptions is on all fours with the communist
who claims that her theory is legitimate because acceptable to
those who are not blinded by false consciousness (and is unable
to give a non-circular explanation of what this is) or the fascist
who claims legitimacy for her theory because grounded in an
unargued-for hierarchical conception of morality and society.[39]
Liberalism may be somewhat more lenient in the range of actions
permitted under its principles, but the justification of liberalism
is no different in form from the justification of these other ethical
conceptions.

3. Communitarianism (Again!)

Larmore is able to avoid the unattractive implications of the *modus
vivendi* justification of liberalism only by smuggling into his
theory a communitarian element. It is only by implicitly appealing to shared beliefs or values or conceptions in the idea of a conversation that Larmore is able to avoid the conclusion that the *modus
vivendi* justification is an unattractive and unstable version
of liberalism. Rawls, by contrast, while at times suggesting

that his liberal political theory represents a *modus vivendi* among competing ethical theories, never endorses such a conception. Rawls needs to emphasize the radical disagreement and diversity in society in order to exclude the possibility that political principles would be based on a substantive ethical doctrine held in the society. However, he does not want to go too far in this direction and represent his political conception as a mere *modus vivendi*, with all the social instability and personal division that this conception entails. But how, in a society characterized by radical moral disagreement and diversity, could there be a political consensus based on something other than the convergence of prudential self-interest? Rawls, it seems, must avoid both horns of this dilemma: he must emphasize the diversity in contemporary society to justify the exclusion of conceptions of the good from the political sphere; but too great an emphasis on moral disunity seems to suggest either that agreement is not possible or that it is possible only as a prudential *modus vivendi* among competing ethical conceptions.

Rawls's solution is to represent his political conception as the product of agreement based on the convergence of diverse *moral* conceptions. This solution avoids the instability inherent in the *modus vivendi* justification by conceiving of each person as agreeing to the principles of justice on *moral* grounds, without jeopardizing the liberal exclusion of substantive ethical theories from the political sphere. The solution rests on a characterization of contemporary democratic societies as riddled with a tension between unity and diversity: there is just enough unity to make agreement on political principles possible, but not enough unity to secure agreement on substantive ethical questions. But is this characterization of the relation of ethics to politics in contemporary society plausible? Is it possible that radically diverse moral conceptions would converge on the same political principles? The only example Rawls has to support his conception is agreement among Kantian liberals, Millian liberals, and religious believers who accept the principle of religious toleration.[40] Rawls correctly claims that proponents of these three ethical theories may find his principles of justice acceptable on moral grounds; but what is wholly implausible is the characterization of these conceptions as diverse. At the moral level, where Rawls claims diversity reigns, there is a remarkable degree of unity: all three conceptions are individualist; all three accept the value of liberty, of a private sphere in which the person is free to exercise choice over her life; in short, all three share broadly liberal moral values!

Just as Larmore appealed to shared moral beliefs and shared conceptions to avoid the objection that agreement based on prudential self-interest is unstable, so Rawls must base his principles on shared moral beliefs and values if the 'overlapping consensus' is to be stable. Although Rawls talks the language of moral diversity and disunity, what does the work in his theory, what makes possible stable consensus on his liberal political principles, is the (prior) acceptance of liberal ethical beliefs and values. Consensus on Rawls's political principles is possible ultimately because there is a deep consensus or unity in society on an individualist conception of ethics, on the importance of individual liberty, on a conception of the person as identified with her capacity for autonomy. The problem is that the communitarian foundations that Rawls and Larmore implicitly appeal to do not support their liberal political theory. They invoke a conception of justification at odds with their liberal conception of choice as such conferring legitimacy on social practices and institutions. The communitarian appeal to a deep ethical conception underlying the society is at odds, too, with the liberal public–private dichotomy. But providing liberal principles with the kind of justification, the Archimedean point, which is necessary to support the exclusion of moral conceptions from the political sphere, and which is compatible with the liberal conception of individual choice or autonomy conferring legitimacy on social practices, was the project of *A Theory of Justice*. The contextualist foundation Rawls appeals to in his more recent essays is less controversial, less exciting, but more defensible. However, the justificatory appeal to shared values and to shared ways of life that it involves suggests a different political conception from the one offered by liberalism. It suggests a political theory justified because of the expression of communal practices; and it suggests a conception of political discourse as involving the creation of unity, of consensus, from the articulation of diverse beliefs and values, rather than the banishment of all contested beliefs, and all discussion of the good for human beings, from the political sphere.

NOTES

1. Rawls, 'Kantian Constructivism in Moral Theory', 532.
2. Rawls, *A Theory of Justice*, 11.
3. Rawls, 'Kantian Constructivism in Moral Theory', 519.
4. John Rawls, 'Justice as Fairness: Political not Metaphysical', *Philosophy and Public Affairs*, 14/3 (Summer 1985), 236.
5. See Jean Hampton, 'Should Political Philosophy Be Done Without Metaphysics?', *Ethics*, 99/4 (July 1989), 798. She also argues that Rawls's recent essays leave themselves open to two mutually incompatible interpretations. She approaches the discussion of Rawls's theory by focusing on the *modus vivendi* interpretation, which she considers to be a version of Hobbesian theory. The 'delicate balance between diversity and agreement' involved in Rawls's recent defence of his principles of justice is also noted by Joseph Raz, 'Facing Diversity: The Case of Epistemic Abstinence', *Philosophy and Public Affairs*, 19 (1990), 7. However, Raz does not discuss this tension but is more concerned to criticize Rawls's requirement that citizens not consider the truth or validity of their beliefs in reaching agreement on principles of justice.
6. Rawls, 'Justice as Fairness', 225; italics mine.
7. See Rawls, *A Theory of Justice*, 120–1.
8. This is the argument for excluding them from the original position. See Rawls, 'Fairness to Goodness', 537.
9. John Rawls, 'The Idea of an Overlapping Consensus', *Oxford Journal of Legal Studies*, 7/1 (Spring 1987), 6.
10. Rawls explicitly endorses justificatory neutrality or what he sometimes calls neutrality of procedure. Of course, Rawls accepts that his liberal theory is not neutral with respect to consequences, but he argues that it is derived in a way that is neutral among, or does not appeal to, substantive ethical conceptions. See Rawls, 'The Priority of Right and Ideas of the Good', *Philosophy and Public Affairs*, 17/4 (Fall 1988), 263.
11. Rawls, 'Justice as Fairness', 228–9.
12. Ibid. 229.
13. It may be objected that I am here positing a very strong conception of the value of personal autonomy which Rawls does not endorse. It is true that Rawls claims to be agnostic on questions of value in these recent essays. See Rawls, 'Justice as Fairness', 245–6. However, he also claims that we have a higher-order interest in 'realiz-[ing] and exercis[ing] [our] capacity to form, revise and rationally to pursue a conception of the good', which seems to be based on

a conception of the value of personal autonomy. Rawls, 'Kantian Constructivism in Moral Theory', 525.

14. This feminist point is made persuasively by Annette C. Baier, 'Pilgrim's Progress', 330; David Gauthier, *Morals by Agreement*, 102; and Marilyn Friedman, 'Feminism and Modern Friendship: Dislocating the Community', *Ethics*, 99/1 (Jan. 1989), 281.

15. This is implicit in Rawls's procedure to apply the principle of justice to the social framework only.

16. This point is also made by Joseph Raz, 'Facing Diversity', 19. He writes: 'It is difficult to see how the popularity of a (putative) ideal bears on its validity.' Later (20), he points out that the acceptance of the principles of justice in Rawls's later essays is not achieved 'under conditions which amount to a free and informed consent to them'.

17. Rawls, 'Justice as Fairness', 249.

18. Charles E. Larmore, *Patterns of Moral Complexity* (Cambridge: Cambridge University Press, 1987), 43-5.

19. Rawls, *A Theory of Justice*, 93.

20. Rawls's claim in *A Theory of Justice* that his list of primary goods are all-purpose means to the fulfilment of any ends was met with the objection, persuasively put forward by Thomas Nagel, that Rawls's primary goods are not neutral among different ethical conceptions or plans of life, because not equally valuable to the pursuit of all plans of life. See Nagel, 'Rawls on Justice', 228-9. This point is taken up in a different way by Michael Sandel in *Liberalism and the Limits of Justice*, 42. He argues that the primary goods only make sense in terms of a (deep) Kantian moral theory which lays emphasis on the autonomy of persons.

21. Rawls, 'Justice as Fairness', 225.

22. Rawls, 'The Priority of Right and Ideas of the Good', 263.

23. Larmore, *Patterns of Moral Complexity*, 69.

24. Bernard Williams, 'Persons, Character and Morality', in *Moral Luck* (Cambridge: Cambridge University Press, 1981), 4-5; Sandel, *Liberalism and the Limits of Justice*, 61-4.

25. Larmore, *Patterns of Moral Complexity*, 74.

26. Rawls, 'Justice as Fairness', 241.

27. Gauthier, *Morals by Agreement*.

28. Larmore, *Patterns of Moral Complexity*, 56.

29. Ibid. 61.

30. Ibid. 59.

31. Ibid.

32. Ibid. 59-60.

33. Ibid. 60.

34. Ibid. 61.
35. Ibid.
36. Ibid. 63.
37. Ibid. 66.
38. Ibid. (his emphasis).
39. N. J. H. Dent, 'The Tensions in Liberalism', *Philosophical Quarterly*, 38/153 (Oct. 1988), 481–5.
40. Rawls, 'The Idea of an Overlapping Consensus', 18.

6

Perfectionist Arguments for Liberalism

JUST as Rawls in his recent essays bases his theory of justice on certain fundamental intuitive conceptions, so Will Kymlicka, in *Liberalism, Community and Culture*, and Joseph Raz, in *The Morality of Freedom*, articulate a new type of justificatory argument for liberal political principles, which, they claim, is not subject to the problems that communitarians associate with liberalism. Kymlicka is explicit in presenting a formulation of liberalism based, not on what liberals have said in the past, but on what they could say in response to the communitarian critique of liberalism. Joseph Raz also claims that his version of liberal theory is able to overcome the difficulties which face other formulations of liberalism.[1] They argue that liberal political principles can be justified as an important component of living a life of value.

One often-repeated criticism of liberal theory, advanced by communitarians such as Unger and feminist critics such as Jaggar, is that liberalism is based on scepticism.[2] Raz and Kymlicka claim that their formulation of liberal theory is not open to this objection. Kymlicka writes: 'Liberty is important not because we ... can't know about our good, but precisely so that we can come to know our good.'[3]

Many of the arguments in the earlier chapters of this book are aimed at showing that liberalism cannot sustain its claim to justificatory neutrality, that it does presuppose a particular ideal of the good. This is also a central argument in Michael J. Sandel's critique of Rawls's *A Theory of Justice* and Charles Taylor's essays on liberalism.[4] Raz and Kymlicka seem to accept this contention, but they turn it to the advantage of liberalism by embracing it and grounding liberalism in terms of the good life. But the arguments put forward in Part I of this book, and the arguments of important critics of liberalism such as Taylor and Sandel, are not confined to refuting the liberal claim to neutrality: that argument is combined with the argument that the conception of the person, the conception of the good on which liberalism is based, is woefully inadequate.

The conception of the person which is presupposed in both Gewirth's and Rawls's versions of liberalism leaves their theories vulnerable to some of the types of criticisms which plagued Kant's moral theory. Its critics claim that liberalism is an impoverished conception, deeply and mistakenly individualistic, unable to give real importance to the community or to communal values. It is unable to give a proper place to the community because the conception of the person that is at its heart ignores the role that society plays in shaping the person and forming her identity. The person is seen as in essence apart from society, identified only with a transcendental autonomous capacity. And because the identification of the person with the capacity for autonomy involves the abstraction from the person of her determinate characteristics, there is a serious gap or dichotomy between the conception of the person on which the theory is based and particular embodied human beings in the real, empirical world. This leads directly to another major problem facing liberal theory, namely the motivation problem, the theory's inability to explain why anyone would act in accordance with the principles of liberalism. In deontological liberal theory, all the springs of action—all the desires and beliefs and goals on which the person bases her actions—have been abstracted from the person to arrive at the conception on which the theory is based.

Both Raz's and Kymlicka's recent formulations of liberal theory can be read as attempts to answer these objections: they both claim that it is wrong to conceive of liberalism as fundamentally individualistic or abstract; and they prove their point by justifying liberal political principles in terms of a conception of a flourishing life, which also includes other (substantive) values. Raz argues that his perfectionist-liberal theory escapes the charge of being individualistic because collective goods and communal values are constitutive of his objective conception of the good life.[5] Kymlicka claims that 'liberalism couldn't be based on ... [abstract individualism]. If abstract individualism [was] ... the fundamental premise [of liberalism], there'd be no reason to ...

suppose that people are being made worse off by being denied the social conditions necessary to freely and rationally question their commitments.'[6] Raz also emphasizes that his conception of the person is not a purely formal, abstract conception: he combines his conception of well-being, an important component of which is autonomy, with substantive values, thereby giving importance both to individual subjective freedom and to objective values.

To answer the critics of liberalism, while preserving liberal principles, Raz and Kymlicka must accommodate the (formal) value of autonomy within the framework of an objective list theory of well-being, which includes substantive values. The value of autonomy (and hence of liberal political principles) is conceived by Raz and Kymlicka as grounded in the importance of having a good life. This is explicit in Kymlicka's version of liberalism: he argues that 'our essential interest [is] in leading a life that is good'[7] and that traditional liberal principles, such as religious freedom, freedom of the press, and artistic freedom, are 'preconditions'[8] of the fulfilment of this fundamental interest. On this formulation, autonomy is an important component of the good life, but it is not the only value: this is clear from Kymlicka's claim that autonomy is essential to the discovery of what is of value.[9] Raz also seems to endorse an objective list theory of well-being or human flourishing, according to which the possession of certain things makes one's life go better than their absence. This is suggested by Raz's references to some aims and projects as being more valuable than others from an impersonal or objective point of view.[10] Goods which are typically included in objective list theories of well-being are such things as ethical virtue, mutual love between two adults, caring for one's child(ren), appreciation of aesthetic beauty, rational activity, and the development of one's talents or abilities.[11] On this formulation of liberal theory, personal autonomy is conceived as valuable because an essential constituent of valuable action: 'autonomy', Raz writes, 'is valuable only if it is directed at the good.'[12] Kymlicka, too, argues that autonomy is valuable because necessary to the discovery and realization of what is of value.[13]

On Raz's and Kymlicka's formulation of liberal theory, personal autonomy is conceived as valuable because an essential constituent in objectively valuable actions. The goals, projects, and relationships that the person has chosen or otherwise acquired are viewed as contributing to her well-being only if they are objectively valuable forms of life.[14] Autonomy is an essential element of the good life, though it only contributes to well-being if the form of life the person has chosen or is committed to embodies substantive objective values.[15]

The central aim of this chapter is to question this reconciliation of the formal value of autonomy and a theory of substantive values. It is precisely because the ideal of personal autonomy is a formal conception, concerned with the *way* in which the person conducts her life and acquires her values, goals, and commitments, while other values on the objective list theory of well-being are substantive values, concerned with the *content* of the person's goals, ideals, and values, that there is always the possibility that the two may come apart, that the person may freely choose to adopt ways of life which are contrary to the ideal.

This is a problem for this formulation of liberal theory because liberal political principles (principles designed to protect autonomy) receive their value from their role in objectively valuable action. Rawls's recent defence of liberal principles, by contrast, involves an acceptance of liberal neutrality. Rawls claims that his principles of justice are *political* principles, arrived at in a way that is neutral among contested ethical theories and so justified in assuming the role of adjudicator among diverse ethical conceptions.

This chapter is concerned to assess Raz's and Kymlicka's claim that political liberalism can be justified in terms of a non-neutral conception of the good life. This will involve an examination of the internal value argument and the revisability argument, both of which are designed to give priority to autonomy when it conflicts with other (substantive) values. It will then examine Raz's and Kymlicka's treatment of concrete cases in which liberal values conflict with other substantive objective values, which are embodied in community. Finally, this chapter will assess the success of this liberal response to the communitarian critique, particularly its attempt to embrace the value of community.

1. THE ARGUMENT FROM INTERNAL VALUES

Perhaps because Kymlicka presents his formulation of liberal theory as consistent with the central presuppositions of liberalism, he does not acknowledge the liberal fear that grounding liberal principles in terms of our essential interest in living a good life will bind the conception of autonomy too closely to moral action or the ethical life. Nevertheless, he must be aware of the possible tension between (*a*) his recognition that some lives are better or more valuable than others, and (*b*) the liberal commitment to respecting each person's choices with regard to her life, because he advances two arguments designed to give priority to autonomy, conceived in negative freedom terms.

Kymlicka's first argument is based on the idea that many values can only be realized internally. Objective values, such as love or friendship or beauty, cannot merely be dispensed to people, X units for each person: the person must *feel* love or affection to realize the objective value of a fulfilling relationship, or appreciate art to realize the objective value of beauty. Well-being cannot be defined in abstraction from the person's central desires and interests: it is important that the person feel a subjective commitment to these values in order to live a good life.

This point is also made by Raz in a different way, through elaborating his conception of well-being. Raz argues that the success of the projects and goals that the person has chosen and is committed to is an important component of well-being. But well-being can only be attained by the person whose life it is: a successful life, Raz writes, is 'a life well spent . . . a life of achievement, of handicaps overcome, talents wisely used, of good judgment in the conduct of one's affairs, of warm and trusting relations with family and friends' and so on.[16] These values can only be realized by the person whose life it is: at best, society can provide a framework within which people can choose from among these objective values.[17]

The argument that many values can only be realized internally is used to defend this version of liberal theory against the charge that it could justify coercive perfectionism. 'No life goes better by being led from the outside according to values the person doesn't endorse,' Kymlicka writes,[18] and he supports this with the familiar liberal example of a person who goes through the external motions of praying but who lacks religious faith.

However, the argument that coercion is counter-productive does not address the main case for coercive perfectionism. Those who seek to suppress someone's way of life because it is wrong or evil or devoid of value are not typically concerned with making the wrong-doer's life more valuable. They are concerned with eliminating corrupt influences in the community. As Brian Barry has argued in the context of coercive practices aimed at enforcing uniformity of religious practice, the concern is not with converting existing heretics but with preventing the spread of the heresy, and, especially, with ensuring that future generations adhere to the true faith. He points out that 'the effectiveness of coercion in producing genuine belief over the course of a few generations is beyond question': many of the contemporary adherents of Islam, and many Catholics and Protestants in Europe, are descended from people who originally adopted it at the point of a sword.[19]

It is difficult to see how Kymlicka can respond to this argument, given that he accepts that the community is important in shaping people's lives, and especially given that he accepts that some ways of life are more valuable than others and that the ultimate justification for political and ethical principles is their contribution to living a life of value.

2. The Argument from Revisability

Kymlicka's second argument focuses on the possibility that we may be wrong about what is truly valuable. He argues that it is necessary to support (liberal) principles and practices which are not based on any particular conception of the good, in case we later discover that these beliefs are mistaken. Kymlicka claims that this is not a sceptical argument: indeed, it is precisely because our essential interest is in leading a good life that it is so important that we support a social framework which is conducive to the discovery of what is of value.

Central to his argument is a distinction between mere beliefs (about true value) and true value, which is designed to support the liberal private–public distinction. Kymlicka argues that our beliefs about value should be treated as mere beliefs: they should be confined to the personal realm and should not serve as the basis of public policy or to justify political institutions. Now, if this is not a sceptical argument (because it does not deny the reality of the good), it comes very close. It focuses on human uncertainty about our moral ideals or conceptions of the good, on the fact that we cannot be sure ours is the best conception and so we ought not to act as though it were. Hence, we ought to treat our conception of the good as mere belief, and mere belief should not serve as the basis of public policy.

The main problem with this argument is the unexplained differential treatment of public and private decisions. When people make decisions, whether private or public, they act on the basis of their beliefs—beliefs about true value, about what is good for them or their community, or about what will give them happiness. If people believe something, they believe it to be true; this is the objective component that Kymlicka emphasizes to refute the charge of scepticism; and people also frequently experience a degree of uncertainty or apprehension about their decisions, because they know they are fallible. This is true of both decisions concerning one's personal life and decisions about the political organization of one's community. For example, a person may be wholly committed to her relationship with her partner and firmly believe in the institution of marriage, but, recognizing the distinction between belief and truth, aware that love might fail. Is that a reason not to marry? It may be a reason, but it is not a strong one. People generally and reasonably do act on the basis of their strong beliefs and feelings and expectations, and they do so even with the awareness that they might revise their beliefs in the future and change their expectations. It is not unreasonable for a person to accept that marriage is a risky proposition and still believe in marriage. Similarly, it is not unreasonable for a person to base her political decisions on her considered moral beliefs even though she is aware that her present moral views might change in the future.

It is worth emphasizing the strength of the conclusion which Kymlicka seeks to elicit from the argument about revisability. This argument is *not* intended to support the view that our (present) values and considered beliefs should be appealed to in political decisions, but that there should be an opportunity for collectively revising them at some later time (which is an argument for democracy). That would parallel the typical attitude to marriage discussed above: we act on the basis of our present beliefs and feelings, even though we are aware that these may change, and if these change, we would have reason to dissolve the marriage. But Kymlicka is using the revisability argument to ground the liberal doctrine that beliefs about values should not be appealed to in the public realm, that they should be treated as mere beliefs, not as truths.

Both decisions concerning one's individual life and those concerning the organization of one's community involve an element of uncertainty and apprehension. This uncertainty about the wisdom of one's choice is frequently enhanced in the case of decisions which have serious consequences for the future, decisions which alter the context in which all later decisions will be made, and which make it difficult or even impossible to return to the earlier state. But all people *can* do is act on the basis of reasonable and considered beliefs in making decisions (whether private or public), and while it is unfortunate that mistakes might be made and opportunities forgone, that seems to be a fact of life. To argue for the suppression of one's beliefs in the public sphere does not follow from Kymlicka's point about the possibility that one may later revise one's beliefs. We do not require the person to suppress her beliefs and feelings and convictions just because there is the possibility that she may be wrong when making decisions about her own life; and Kymlicka does not provide an argument to justify his differential treatment of public and private decisions. Indeed, Kymlicka's argument here is decidedly odd, given that his case for liberal political principles is itself based only on a reasonable belief about the importance and value of protecting autonomy.

3. The Claim to Accommodate Community

Both Raz and Kymlicka regard their theories as recognizing the value of community, and, in both cases, this value is based on the essential contribution of the community to the good life. This is most clearly articulated by Raz, who develops a distinction between ultimate, intrinsic, and instrumental value. On his theory, human well-being, which is conceived as encompassing both the formal value of autonomy and (unspecified) substantive values, is of ultimate or non-derivative value. The importance of this distinction in Raz's theory is that he uses it to emphasize that certain conditions are necessary to the realization of the ideal of an autonomous life (which is of ultimate value).[20] Raz argues that it is 'constitutive' of an autonomous life that there is a sufficient range of acceptable options present; and because some of these options involve the existence of certain social practices, it follows that some social practices are intrinsic (collective) goods.[21] By viewing collective goods and communal values as constitutive of his objective conception of the good life, Raz can claim to have responded to those communitarians who argued that liberalism is fundamentally individualistic, unable to accommodate the value of community and communal values within it.[22]

Kymlicka also puts forward an argument for the value of community which is strikingly similar to Raz's: he argues that community is valuable because a necessary condition of well-being (a central component of which is autonomy). Kymlicka approaches the question of whether liberalism can accommodate the value of community in his theory by presenting a liberal argument for the protection of minority cultures. In his view, members of minority cultural groups, such as aboriginal people in Canada, are disadvantaged relative to members of the non-aboriginal majority because their cultural structure is threatened. '[A] rich and secure cultural structure [is necessary for] people ... [to] ... become aware of the options available to them, and intelligently examine their value.'[23] The cultural structure is an important context for choice, which provides 'meaningful options' for members of the culture.[24] Protection of threatened cultures is justified on the grounds that it is necessary to secure conditions for native people which are equal to those enjoyed by members of the majority population. In Raz's terminology, a culture which provides 'meaningful' options for its members is 'constitutive' of Kymlicka's conception of the good life because it is a necessary ingredient in the realization of the autonomous life.

One weakness in this argument is that, although both Raz and Kymlicka argue that a range of (acceptable) options or secure cultural structure (providing 'meaningful' choice) is 'constitutive' of an autonomous life, they do not show that any particular good or type of culture is necessary for personal autonomy, and it is just as reasonable to conclude from their argument that no present culture or collective good is valuable.

To arrive at a stronger conclusion, which will be able to respond effectively to the communitarian charge, Raz and Kymlicka must show that communal goods are part of the objective conception of the good life (not merely compatible with it); that they are necessary elements of an adequate range of acceptable options. This could be achieved by articulating a more determinate conception of human nature and then linking this view of the nature of the person with the provision of communal goods, which are necessary if the options available are to be 'acceptable' or to provide a 'rich' context of 'meaningful' choices in which autonomy can be exercised. Neither Raz nor Kymlicka attempt this, and it is easy to see why: that formulation tends to bind closely the realization of autonomy with a certain conception of the good life, and so jeopardize their quest to derive a negative liberal political conception from the foundation of the good life.

The possible tension between the formal value of autonomy and those substantive values which are also essential to the good life emerges in Raz's and Kymlicka's theories in their discussion of the relationship between (1) liberal political principles, and (2) giving value to community.

We have seen that, in Kymlicka's theory, the cultural community is conceived as valuable because it provides an important context for choice: it is an essential element in the realization of autonomy (which is an important component of the good life). But what Kymlicka fails to address adequately is the possibility that the minority culture will fail to embody substantive values which are also necessary to the good life, or that there is a serious problem for his theory when the culture endorses practices which repress the exercise of individual autonomy, which both Raz and Kymlicka argue is of value.

Kymlicka attempts to avoid this issue when he puts forward his argument in support of minority aboriginal cultures in Canada. The tension between (*a*) the truth that a cultural framework is a necessary pre-condition to the development of individual autonomy and (*b*) the possibility that the specific content of the particular culture will be repressive, is at the heart of the difficulty in the old Canadian *Indian Act* regarding the differential treatment of native men and native women. According to the *Indian Act*, a native woman who marries a non-native man loses her aboriginal status, while a native man who marries a non-native woman not only retains his status, but aboriginal status is conferred on his wife as well. Interestingly, Kymlicka does not discuss this issue in terms of the patriarchal character of native society (this provision of the *Indian Act* was supported by native groups such as the National Indian Brotherhood in 1973, when it was challenged in court by two native women[25]). If he had discussed this in terms of the values upheld in native communities, he might have been led to discuss the *limits* of the liberal support for cultural communities. He might have had to indicate how the value which liberals attach to community fits with the value of autonomy and the (unspecified) values which comprise his ideal of the good life. Unfortunately, Kymlicka does not discuss this issue in these terms at all. He contends that this provision of the old Canadian *Indian Act* is instrumental to preventing over-population on native reserves:

these problems [the penalization of certain marriage choices and the sexist discrimination of the Act] arise unnecessarily, for they result from the fact that reservation lands are not just inalienable, but non-expandable. An expanding population may need to occupy expanding territory, but Indians don't usually try to establish communities outside their present reserved lands, partly because they lack the resources to do so (since they lack their fair share), but also, and more importantly, because they'd have no way of protecting the new communities from plans to develop that and nearby land in such a way as would lead to unwanted assimilation. However, I see no reason why the government shouldn't, when overpopulation threatens existing reservations, aid in the establishment and protecting of new communities.[26]

Even if it is true that this provision is necessary to prevent over-population, as Kymlicka argues, that does not account for the fact that it is applied in a discriminatory way. It does not address the central issue which Kymlicka needs to address, namely what is the relation of the value of culture to other values? Should cultures be protected even when their substantive content is contrary to the other values in his theory?

We do get some indication of Kymlicka's view of the relation between the value of community and other values in his theory in his discussion of American Indian communities, such as the Pueblo, which enforce uniformity of religious practice on the grounds that this is necessary to protect their distinctive culture from assimilationist pressures. Kymlicka concedes that, 'in the eyes of many Pueblo, violation of religious norms is viewed as literally threatening the survival of the entire community'.[27] But he dismisses this belief: 'the Pueblo would continue to exist with an organized Protestant minority as it now exists without one,' he writes.[28] He arrives at this conclusion without examining the specifics of the Pueblo culture, or the role that their religion plays in preserving Pueblo distinctiveness. Those Pueblo who wish to restrict religious freedom do so, Kymlicka claims, not because of genuine and justified assimilationist concerns, but because they 'dislike . . . the dissident practice'.[29] And, in a particularly revealing admission, Kymlicka notes that he *cannot* 'support . . . the intolerant . . . character of a cultural community', for that would 'undermine . . . the very reason we had to support cultural membership—that it allows for meaningful individual choice'.[30]

In Kymlicka's theory, then, community is valuable only if it allows for meaningful choice, only in so far as it supports a framework in which individual autonomy can be exercised, which includes other values which are also necessary to the good life. Community has no independent value of its own. What is really doing the work in Kymlicka's theory—i.e. what determines which community conceptions are acceptable and which are not—are traditional *liberal* principles, which protect individual autonomy, understood in negative freedom terms. It is hard to see how this theory can credibly claim to meet the objections of communitarians, who criticize liberalism on the grounds (*a*) that it gives value only to the exercise of autonomy, and not to substantive values which are also important aspects of the good life,[31] and (*b*) that it is unable to give importance to the value of the community, which is also important to human flourishing.

4. The Coherence of Raz's and Kymlicka's Theories?

On Raz's and Kymlicka's formulation of liberalism, autonomy is conceived as valuable because an important component of the good life. This formulation of the value of autonomy suggests that the role of autonomy is circumscribed or limited by substantive values, such as the value of community, and other ethical considerations.[32] Though both Raz and Kymlicka hint suggestively at such a conception, and describe their theories as if they embody such a resolution of formal and substantive values, neither shows how this resolution could be achieved. Kymlicka's discussion of the relationship between the value which his theory places on aboriginal culture and on individual autonomy does not suggest a resolution of value. Rather, his theory accords primacy to the value of individual autonomy: the cultural community is conceived as valuable only in so far as it supports the development of individual autonomy, and is compatible with that value. Raz, by contrast, does not discuss in concrete terms the threat that the political embodiment of a substantive conception of value poses for free choice, because he never elaborates his conception of objective value. And yet, Raz has ample opportunities to sketch the role in his theory of the formal value of autonomy or free choice within a substantive conception of value.

The only ideal specified by either Raz or Kymlicka is that of an autonomous person; and deriving their political theories from that abstract conception does not overcome the derivation problem raised by the critics of Kantian liberalism.[33] The ideal of the autonomous person does not itself indicate what social practices and institutions should be supported or what rights people have. Though both Raz and Kymlicka point to the need to provide 'a sufficient range of options',[34] a context for 'meaningful' choice[35] within which the members of the society can exercise autonomy, the notion of autonomy does not itself suggest what would count as a meaningful choice or a sufficient range. Both Raz and Kymlicka would deny that the matter is a purely quantitative one, that all options are equally valuable and the only problem is providing a fairly large number to choose from. Raz is explicit on this: he agrees with John Rawls and R. M. Dworkin[36] that it is absurd to attach the same importance to all liberties or all choices. Freedom of speech and religion are protected by rights grounded in freedom, but not all options that increase the number and variety of choices are protected by rights. Although Raz and Kymlicka agree with all this, and both uphold the validity of objective substantive values, neither specifies his conception of substantive values or elaborates their foundation in a more determinate conception of the person. Both avoid the obvious tension that that undertaking would make evident—i.e. the tension between the formal nature of the value of autonomy and the substantive conception of value that it requires—even when, as in Raz's theory, it means that he must misleadingly treat the question of what counts as an 'adequate' range of options as a quantitative one.[37]

However, this tension surfaces in terms of the type of options that must be available in a society organized to promote the good life. Both Raz and Kymlicka contend that autonomy requires not only that there is more than one option, *but also that the options are acceptable*,[38] and provide a framework for *meaningful* choice,[39] and this seems to invoke a substantive conception of value. There is no way to derive a criterion of the acceptability of options from a conception in which value attaches to the activity of choosing as such. They need a conception of value prior to choice in order to assess whether the choice itself is made autonomously, in the sense of being a choice among acceptable options. Although in principle this should not pose a problem for this formulation of liberalism, because both Raz and Kymlicka believe that there are objective values independent of choice, they do not indicate how they define what options would count as acceptable. And it is difficult to see how, in developing their theory of objective value and applying it to the conditions for autonomy, either Raz or Kymlicka could avoid moving away from the liberal conception of autonomy which ensures a sphere of unimpeded action, and conceive of autonomy as closely bound up with choosing the good.

The problems discussed so far can be traced to a fundamental incoherence in this formulation of liberalism. On the one hand, Raz characterizes autonomy as valuable independently of content, as valuable in itself,[40] and this seems to suggest that the exercise of autonomy is compatible with making worthless choices. Yet, on the other hand, Raz also maintains that autonomy is possible only through choosing objectively worthwhile options.[41] And this latter claim seems to suggest that its value derives from the choice of objectively valuable options.

This incoherence is evident in Kymlicka's theory, too, which claims to derive the value of autonomy from its role in the good life, but which then treats autonomy as the fundamental value in his theory, as the basis on which all other values (embodied in cultures) are assessed. But why, if autonomy is *not* primary at the foundational level, is it given primacy at the *political* level? The answer is not to be found in the internal value argument or the revisability argument, for they do not support the primacy that Raz and Kymlicka accord to the value of autonomy.

One suspects that conceiving of choice or autonomy as limited by ethical considerations, by substantive conceptions of value, would jeopardize the liberal political conception that Raz and Kymlicka seek to elicit from their argument. And this suggests that Raz's and Kymlicka's foundations in terms of the good life do not, after all, support completely their political liberalism. Indeed, it seems that they must ignore their foundational argument when its implications threaten to jeopardize the liberal character of their political principles.[42]

5. CONCLUSION

Although Raz's and Kymlicka's quest to derive liberal political principles from the ideal of a good life ultimately fails, the arguments that they advance and the problems that beset them are both interesting and instructive. The failure of their argument seems to confirm the suspicion that an individualist conception of the person (as either abstract agency or self-interested non-tuist[43]) is peculiarly appropriate to ground liberal political principles. And it reinforces the thesis that political liberalism is fundamentally individualistic, by exposing the depth of its commitment to an individualist conception of the relation of the individual to society.

More importantly, these theories point in the direction in which an adequate ethical theory must move. Their appeal to the concept of well-being, or the good life, rather than self-interest, as fundamental to individual action goes some way to overcoming the dichotomy between self-interest and morality that is set up by the liberal conception of the person as self-interested (non-moral) individual agent.[44] In conceiving of well-being or the good life as the fundamental ethical category, Raz and Kymlicka invoke a conception of the person as both a particular individual, concerned in a special or direct way with the success and direction of her own life, and yet formed in a society, realizing her own individuality within, and relative to, a particular social context and particular biological nature. It suggests a political theory which can accommodate the value of individual autonomy, but not at the price of scepticism regarding other (substantive) values, which may also be necessary to live well. Unfortunately, in their derivation of specifically liberal political principles, both Raz and Kymlicka abandon or ignore much of that framework and never make clear the precise content or derivation of their theory of objective values. Their project, then, does point to the need for a theory which articulates a determinate conception of human flourishing, which will provide a reconciliation of formal and substantive values, of subjective freedom and a theory of objective goods.

NOTES

1. Kymlicka, *Liberalism, Community, and Culture*; Joseph Raz, *The Morality of Freedom* (Oxford: Clarendon Press, 1986).
2. Roberto M. Unger, *Knowledge and Politics* (New York: Free Press, 1975), 66–7; Alison Jaggar, *Feminist Politics and Human Nature* (Totowa, NJ: Rowman & Allenheld, 1983), 194.
3. Kymlicka, *Liberalism, Community, and Culture*, 18.
4. Sandel, *Liberalism and the Limits of Justice*, 49–53; Charles Taylor, *Human Agency and Language: Philosophical Papers, I* (Cambridge: Cambridge University Press, 1985), 5, 29–33.
5. Joseph Raz, *The Morality of Freedom* (Oxford: Clarendon Press, 1986), 216.
6. Kymlicka, *Liberalism, Community, and Culture*, 18.
7. Ibid. 13.
8. Ibid. 12.
9. Ibid. 11.

10. Raz, *Morality of Freedom*, 299.
11. Derek Parfit, *Reasons and Persons* (Oxford: Oxford University Press, 1986), 499; James Griffin, *Well-Being: Its Meaning, Measurement, and Moral Importance* (Oxford: Clarendon Press, 1986), 107.
12. Raz, *Morality of Freedom*, 381.
13. Kymlicka, *Liberalism, Community, and Culture*, 18.
14. Raz, *Morality of Freedom*, 319.
15. This is implicit in Kymlicka's theory, in his endorsement of the internal value argument. Notice that he does *not* say that autonomy confers value on things. That would have been inconsistent with his grounding in terms of the good life, which also includes substantive objective values.
16. Raz, *Morality of Freedom*, 306.
17. Ibid. 306–7, 387.
18. Kymlicka, *Liberalism, Community, and Culture*, 12.
19. Brian Barry, 'How Not to Defend Liberal Institutions', *British Journal of Political Science*, 20/1 (Jan. 1990), 5.
20. Raz's argument is in fact more complicated than this. He distinguishes between valuing the person's capacity for autonomy and valuing a life lived autonomously. He believes that his theory is perfectionist because the ultimate, i.e. non-derivative, value of personal autonomy is not posited in the person but is an achievement to be attained. He argues that a theory which conceives of value as attaching to the capacity for autonomy is fundamentally individualist, because the source of ultimate value resides in the individual, and it is in virtue of each person's possession of this capacity that each is deemed worthy of respect. By contrast, the central concern of Raz's 'perfectionist' theory is with the attainment of autonomy, and only derivatively with the capacity for autonomy.

    However, the distinction that Raz is relying on here is tenuous indeed. It is difficult to see how it is possible to value the capacity for autonomy without at the same time valuing its exercise, or vice versa. The capacity for autonomy is a potential which can be actualized, and the attainment of autonomy is the achievement of the full exercise of that potential. Individualist liberals do not in fact value only the capacity, and not its exercise. That would be compatible with imprisoning people or otherwise restricting their free action, as long as one does not harm their capacity for autonomy. At the same time, the achievement of autonomy can be conceived as valuable only if the capacity is regarded as valuable, as an aspect of the person which she should develop.
21. These goods are conceived as intrinsic goods rather than ultimate goods, because they are derived from the ultimate value of personal

autonomy. They are intrinsically rather than instrumentally valuable, because the range of acceptable goods from which the autonomous person chooses is part of what the exercise of personal autonomy consists in. And these intrinsic goods are public or collective in the sense that they are subject not to voluntary distribution by the individual but to collective or communal control. Raz, *Morality of Freedom*, 198–201.

22. Ibid. 206–7.
23. Kymlicka, *Liberalism, Community, and Culture*, 165.
24. Ibid. 166.
25. Michael Mandel, *The Charter of Rights and the Legalization of Politics in Canada* (Toronto: Wall & Thompson, 1989), 256.
26. Kymlicka, *Liberalism, Community, and Culture*, 195.
27. Ibid. 196.
28. Ibid.
29. Ibid.
30. Ibid. 197.
31. Sandel, *Liberalism and The Limits of Justice*, 168, 174.
32. Kymlicka, *Liberalism, Community, and Culture*, 18; Raz, *Morality of Freedom*, 381, 395.
33. Sandel, *Liberalism and The Limits of Justice*, 178; Williams, *Ethics and The Limits of Philosophy*, 61–9, 79–80.
34. Raz, *Morality of Freedom*, 373.
35. Kymlicka, *Liberalism, Community, and Culture*, 166.
36. Raz, *Morality of Freedom*, 6n.
37. Ibid. 373–4.
38. Ibid. 205.
39. Kymlicka, *Liberalism, Community, and Culture*, 166.
40. Raz, *Morality of Freedom*, 371.
41. Ibid. 411–12.
42. The problem with deriving principles from a substantive ethical conception is suggested by Jeremy Waldron's thesis in his essay 'A Right to Do Wrong', *Ethics*, 92/1 (Oct. 1981), 21–39.
43. These alternatives are suggested by Barry, *Theories of Justice*. He identifies two types of theories of justice: justice as mutual advantage and justice as impartiality. Underlying the conception of justice as impartiality is an abstract conception of the person, for this theory requires the person to abstract from all differences between persons and adopt an impartial perspective, in which all people are essentially alike (in virtue, usually, of their possession of autonomy or reason). Underlying justice as mutual advantage is the conception of the person as self-interested non-tuist.

44. This criticism of liberal theory is advanced by Michael Walzer, *Spheres of Justice: A Defense of Pluralism and Equality* (New York: Basic Books), 5; Williams, 69–70.

PART III

An Alternative Foundation

7

An Alternative Foundation for Political and Ethical Principles

THE integrity and motivation problems which bedevilled the versions of liberal theory considered thus far are symptoms of a deeper difficulty inherent in the structure of these theories. All the arguments examined in Part I begin from a conception of the person defined independently of all relations to others, either because they identify the person with her capacity for autonomy, thereby abstracting from the person all particular commitments and attachments to other people, or because they conceive of the person as essentially a non-tuist, uninterested in the interests of others, except perhaps as they affect her own interests, narrowly defined.[1] The individualist conception of the person is exemplified by Rawls's exclusion of the person's particular aims and attachments and socially relative conceptions from the original position; by Gewirth's identification of the person with pure rational agency; and by Gauthier's idealized conception of the person as non-tuist.

The central problem with this individualist starting-point is that the requirements of morality are viewed from this standpoint as external to the self, as alien commitments imposed from the outside. Thus, a central project of these theories is to make morality less external to the person and so explain why the person would be moved to act morally, or in accordance with the principles of justice. Both Gewirth and Gauthier attempt to integrate morality into the being of the person by conceiving of morality as a requirement of reason. Gewirth's conception of reason is broadly Kantian, concerned with logical principles of universalizability and non-contradiction, whereas Gauthier, who adopts an instrumental, maximizing conception of rationality, seeks to show that, in certain conditions, morality can be self-interestedly rational. We have seen that both arguments fail, and that Rawls's more complex arguments in *A Theory of Justice* and his recent essays are also unsuccessful. Rawls postulates a sense of justice which locates the motivating force of the principles of justice in the self; but his inability, on one interpretation (Chapter 3), to explain why the sense of justice would take a universal form suggests that ultimately he relies on a rationalist conception similar to Gewirth's; or, on another interpretation (Chapter 5), the sense of justice implicitly appeals to a commitment to a particular community, a particular morality, and so not only contradicts the individualism of Rawls's principles, but also leaves his theory without any foundation or justification beyond the fact that particular individuals are committed to it.

The project of justifying morality to the individual agent, viewed abstractly, is related to the quest for an Archimedean point, namely a standpoint from which ethical considerations can be accepted as decisive for each person, thus making morality binding on all agents. The arguments of Part I point to reasons to be sceptical about the success of this quest. It is not possible to attain to a vantage-point which is objective in the sense that it is neutral among all ethical or political conceptions, because the quest itself requires justification. The impartial standpoint can claim to be objective only in the sense that it is independent of all particular perspectives; indeed, it is very unlike any particular perspective, because embodying only universal features of all perspectives. The liberal moral standpoint acquires its objective character by filtering out any reasons which might be reasons for particular agents, by abstracting from personal identity and particular beliefs and commitments. This procedure is another manifestation of liberalism's tendency to define self-interest and morality, both understood formally, as independent of each other and initially unrelated, and is at the root of both the motivation and integrity problems. It raises the question, how can pure reason, developed from an abstract, impersonal standpoint, provide a motive for action in the absence of personal interest or desire? The integrity problem arises from the failure of the liberal moral point of view to give any moral importance to agent-relative reasons, that is, reasons for the agent arising out of the particular shape of her life. Certainly, the liberal theories considered earlier do give scope to subjective choice, but the space granted to choice does not necessarily coincide with the reasons, values, and commitments which define the subjective point of view. Rather, it coincides with the liberal public–private dichotomy, according to which the person can justifiably exercise control over her own (private) life, and the rules of justice apply in the public sphere to regulate relations between people. The liberals examined in Part I insist that the agent respect the spheres of freedom which attach, as it were, to each individual, as defined by liberal rights and rules of justice. But this requirement is unacceptable to the person whose deepest values and commitments are bound up with commitments to others or to a particular conception of a good society. Such an individual's life is radically unintegrated; she is unable to give expression to the things which she cares most about, and this denial is rooted in the interests of equal autonomy, which is defined from an impartial moral standpoint, wholly divorced from her own interests and beliefs and concerns.

What is required, then, is a conception of morality, not as identified with an impartial perspective, divorced from all particular perspectives, but as rooted in the conceptions and values of the people who are governed by moral principles. Rather than seek an Archimedean point from which different principles can be assessed and validated, it is more fruitful to begin from within a tradition, from within a morality which is embodied in the thoughts and actions, conventions and practices, of people within society. This is implied by the argument of Chapter 5, which concludes that the recent work of liberal theorists such as Rawls and Larmore avoids these problems only by implicitly appealing to shared conceptions and attachments in communities. Such a procedure ensures that the account of morality will be intelligible to the people subject to it. If a principle is not to be viewed as arbitrary and irrelevant, if it is to have any claim on their consideration at all, it must have *some* connection with what is taken to be important or relevant within the tradition in which they think and operate.

This concrete approach to ethics implies a conception of the person, not as abstracted from her community, from all ethical concerns or values, but as within a particular tradition, with particular interests, aims, and values. The person is conceived not as narrowly self-referential but as centrally committed to particular values or ways of life. This conception of the person denies from the outset the dichotomy between self-interest and morality, which is so central to individualist liberal theory, suggesting instead that an adequate conception of the person incorporates both a communal dimension and ethical considerations.

The rejection in Part I of the individualist quest for an Archimedean point does not leave as the only alternative a non-cognitivist conception of ethics. It may be thought that the failure of the individualist liberal theories to derive moral principles from a rationally secure starting-point leaves ethics without any objective foundations, and entails a return to a non-cognitivist conception, according to which all valuative judgements are an expression of our subjective desires while all factual judgements are determined by our powers of reason operating on the world. On this conception, judgements of intrinsic value are unconstrained by objective features of the world: they are a matter of our irrational subjective attitudes and will. But this non-cognitivist conception of ethics, which locates the source of valuative judgements in our desires or inclinations, does not necessarily follow from the failure of the Kantian quest. It does not necessarily follow from the failure to ground ethics in a rationally unassailable starting-point that moral or valuative principles must be a matter of mere desire. Rather, both conceptions are flawed because both view reason and desire as unconnected systems operating on the person. What is required is a conception of ethics as involving both reason and desire together, neither with priority, but each dependent on the other. And this involves the rejection of both the views (a) that desire *creates* value, and (b) that reason ascertains value independently of desire through a process of abstraction and inference (or through a 'faculty' of 'intuition').

The principal problem with non-cognitivist conceptions of ethics is that they are false to our sense that objective considerations matter, that what we value is dependent on our belief that something is (objectively) valuable, and that our evaluations are world-guided in that sense.[2] What is required, it seems, is a realist conception of ethics, in which the individual is viewed as responding to moral facts or situations in the world. But the realist conception which will be advanced here is not a form of moral intuitionism, according to which a realm of moral facts is postulated, and which the agent becomes directly, i.e. non-inferentially, aware of. The view defended here can be classified as a realist conception in so far as it rejects the metaphysical dualism between facts and values which is implicit in non-cognitive theories. Language is conceived of not as divided between impartial factual discourse on the one hand and emotive valuative discourse on the other, but as essentially expressive. The logical priority of thought over language, with language conceived of as merely instrumental to the communication of ideas, is rejected in favour of the more plausible view that thought is essentially embodied in language, analogous to the way in which art is without determinate form until it is embodied in an artistic medium.[3] The view that thought is necessarily embedded in language is supported by the consideration that there are no facts which are not mediated by language. And because all facts and all values are part of the seamless web of particular social and linguistic practices, there is no distinction *at the metaphysical level* between facts and values. Value concepts are acquired in the same way as other concepts: people who have been educated in the communal practices and ways of life simply recognize, non-inferentially, certain situations as situations of a particular kind; as ones in which courage, say, is called for, or generosity displayed.

One of the main implications of this conception for approaching ethical theory is the recognition that ethical reasoning begins from within a particular ethical conception. It is not possible to derive substantive principles from a standpoint which is neutral among particular conceptions of value, as the liberals examined in Part I maintained. One of the reasons why liberal theorists proceed in this way is to make their principles universal, to make the claims of morality binding on everyone by linking them with self-interest, which is thought to be unproblematic as a motive for action. But what is wrong with the liberal starting-point in self-interest is that any conception of self-interest precisely begs the question. It is only through induction in the social practices of her community that the person attains mastery of the concept of self-interest. The application of that concept to herself and others presupposes a particular conception of the person and the relation of the person to the objects or activities which are viewed as in one's interests and hence as valuable. Because the content of the concept is relative to a particular conception of the person, which is acquired through participation in social practices, it follows that what counts as in a person's interests is socially relative in the sense that it cannot be defined in a way which is neutral among broad valuative conceptions but is thoroughly implicated in a particular world-view. Once we recognize that the concept of self-interest is relative in the first instance to a particular linguistic community, the liberal justificatory project is brought into question. For underlying the liberal conception of a neutral starting-point is the belief that it is possible to reason from a vantage-point independent of social arrangements and conceptions, and objective in relation to the moral standards and values and beliefs of the reasoner. And it is this which cannot be sustained. It is not achieved in liberal theories: the conception of the person invoked by both its Kantian and utilitarian versions is historically and culturally specific, a product of the eighteenth and nineteenth centuries in which liberalism developed, and a reflection of the individualism characteristic of capitalist society. It is not achieved in the versions of liberal theory examined in Part I, because it is impossible to achieve. The ways in which we perceive the external world, and interact with it and with other people, and reason about it, are mediated by the language we speak in and think in, by the concepts and categories that we employ to make sense of the diversity of things that we encounter in the world.

To the extent that liberal theorists equate the moral point of view with the standpoint of impartiality among all particular substantive ethical conceptions, they leave their theories open to quite serious difficulties, such as the integrity problem and the motivation problem. And to the extent that they do arrive at determinate principles, they must presuppose a particular broad ethical outlook. For, in determining what is in a person's interests, or what counts as a *moral* principle, the reasoner must employ the concepts and categories of her particular community; and embedded in the language she speaks and uses to order her world is a particular understanding of the relation of things to her needs and interests, and indeed what her needs and interests are, and hence implicit conceptions of these things as good or valuable to her. This is why there can be no comprehension of moral reasoning or moral terms without a particular broad ethical standpoint from which to rationally criticize or justify aspects of our moral vision and those of others. Moral reasoning itself depends on having substantive moral conceptions, on having a character that is shaped in accordance with a particular moral vision. It is an illusion to suppose that there is some neutral vantage-point from which to assess and justify a particular moral tradition: it is indeed only within traditions that the person is able to acquire the resources by which to understand valuative discourse and justify or criticize particular ethical practices. The person who stands outside all practices is, as Aristotle said,[4] rendered speechless with no grounds for rejecting or defending any particular ethical conception. The person who is completely impartial between particular moralities or between various (necessarily value-laden) conceptions of society or human nature could have no possible basis on which to make a valuative judgement. The only way to remove bias toward any particular position is to efface all (rational) bases for any valuative position. And since the resulting non-cognitivist position is both implausible and unattractive, the only other course open to the moral reasoner is to rationally criticize or justify valuative principles or actions from within the context of a particular tradition.

1. THE SOLUTION: MORAL EDUCATION AND THE MOTIVATION PROBLEM

Many theories which reject the possibility of an Archimedean point outside history emphasize the embeddedness of beliefs, language, and social practices within a particular tradition or culture. This theory is no exception: we have seen that the individualist conception of the person as abstracted from all social relations has severe problems, and that it is necessary to articulate a conception of the person which recognizes the self's historicity and (inter-) dependence on others. I do not, however, think that there is a logical connection between the two: the rejection of foundationalism does not entail that we embrace community and social solidarity; indeed, the recognition that there is no neutral standpoint from which to arbitrate among rival conceptions equally may lead to extreme scepticism or relativism or to a Nietzschean ideal of a *Supermensch*, whose self-created re-descriptions serve as the basis for communal organization. But if there is no necessary or logical connection between anti-foundationalism and communitarianism, there is a close, symbiotic relation between the two: the recognition that our beliefs, our language, indeed our very sense of self are rooted in a particular tradition serves as the basis of the critique of higher-order neutrality; conversely, the recognition that we have no access to uninterpreted facts but are within a concrete historical context serves to underline our dependence on others.

Thus far, I have suggested that it would be fruitful to begin our enquiry from within a particular ethical conception, for that would enable us to avoid the difficulties encountered by the individualist theories of Part I. But the deeper reason or justification for beginning from a starting-point internal to a particular ethical conception is that this is the only place from which reasoning can proceed; ethical criticism and argument is possible only if the moral reasoner is educated in the moral practices and beliefs and modes of justification of her community.

In order to understand how the integrity and motivation problems associated with individualist theories are overcome in a theory that conceives of the person as within a particular culture or tradition, it is necessary to sketch how moral education can overcome the conceptual dichotomy between reason and desire, self-interest and morality.

On the standard historical and internal accounts of moral education, derived from Aristotle, morality is conceived as acquired in a sequence of stages which gradually develop the person's cognitive awareness and affective responses according to a particular ethical conception that she comes to accept. In the first instance, people are conceived of as moved to act by considerations other than morality. In the early stages of development, children tend to identify what is good with what satisfies their pre-reflective desires and what is bad with what hinders them. Judgements are made from the standpoint of whether things frustrate or fulfil their desires. And what the child desires is mainly related to pleasure and pain: the child desires things as pleasurable, with little or no reflective awareness or evaluation of the object of her desires. This does not mean, of course, that the objects of pleasure or desire are solely or narrowly self-related: on the contrary, the comfort and affection of others is essential to the happiness of the young child, and the child naturally develops interests in the interests of others, and these are gradually modified by reflection and generalization. Not only is the individual interested in the interests of others: she also develops commitments to people and ways of life and standards of excellence that stretch far beyond the narrow self-referential conception of the person endorsed in the starting-point of Gauthier's liberal theory. But these moral interests never lose their origins in the desires and interests of the person. What occurs in the process of moral development is that the person's original unformed desires are gradually refined and her affective responses are disciplined in accordance with a conception of the good life: the person comes to see that certain things and certain ways of life are valuable or good and so is moved to act in ways that will achieve these enlarged ethical purposes. Becoming moral does not involve the negation or denial of the person's desires and interests, but, rather, the development of these desires and interests in such a way that they are directed at the right objects. And, indeed, how else could it be? For 'good' and 'bad', like all value terms, are practical concepts: they function to guide the person's choices or goals or objectives for action; and it is necessary for moral action that the person has some commitment to a particular ethical conception or way of life or interest in the interests of others, to enable her to bring about those situations that she perceives as good and prevent those she perceives as bad.

In Aristotle's ethical theory, habituation is identified as the process by which the person comes to be fully ethical. The person must be directed to perform habitual right actions, in part in order that she may learn to take pleasure in good activities, and in part as a method of disciplining herself, so that her affective or emotional responses to a situation are appropriate to her perception of the right thing to do in the situation. The Aristotelian doctrine that virtue is acquired through habituation should not be interpreted to require the person to perform virtuous actions entirely from habit, going through the motions of the right thing to do until she has internalized an entirely mindless disposition to do such a thing in such a situation. What Aristotle's ethical theory affirms is the cognitive dimensions of practice. In order to learn that a certain activity is an instance of a particular virtue, such as generosity, the person must step inside a particular world-view, a particular ethical conception, in which different values and beliefs are ordered and complexly interrelated in a certain vision of the best life to lead. In coming to understand that a particular action is a generous one, say, the person is introduced not merely to one virtue and to one way in which that excellence is exhibited: she sees how generosity is related to the other virtues and to an overall conception of the good life. She comes to see that generosity cannot be reduced merely to certain spontaneous feelings of benevolence, say, or kindness: the virtue of generosity *does* involve cultivating a certain amount of benevolence, but that feeling must be structured by, and so limited by, a conception of the proper scope of the virtue. Generosity is not reducible to other-regarding acts of benevolence, such as giving money to the poor or downtrodden, for sometimes, to be truly generous, one must withhold support.

This conception of moral education has the merit of being able to explain the motivating force of morality. One of the central aims of moral education is to direct the person to find pleasure in good activities: the person is introduced to these activities with a view to learning that they are pleasant, rather as certain foods or drinks only become pleasurable after we cultivate a taste for them. In his excellent article on Aristotle's theory of habituation,[5] M. F. Burnyeat illustrates the relation between virtue and pleasure with the example of learning to enjoy skiing. Burnyeat argues that we learn, in a weak sense of learn, that skiing is enjoyable simply by acquiring that information, but in the strong sense we learn that skiing is enjoyable by trying it ourselves and enjoying it. By analogy, we learn in the strong sense of learn that virtue is good by internalizing that knowledge and coming to take pleasure in performing virtuous actions. Practice is conceived as performing two functions here: first, it leads to knowledge in the sense that it is only through practice and thereby coming to enjoy the activity that we come to fully understand and appreciate a particular virtue. And, secondly, by linking virtue with pleasure, by making the cultivation of excellence part of the person's second nature such that she comes to take pleasure in virtuous actions, this view can overcome the motivation problem that bedevilled liberal theory. There is, on this view, a conceptual connection between having a virtue and taking pleasure in it, with pleasure conceived as derivative on the virtue. This also seems to be a plausible portrayal of the relationship of pleasure to goods, with pleasure conceived of as supervenient on the goods that are pursued. It recognizes that there is not a single homogeneous mental state of pleasure, but that pleasure arises in different activities and is distinctive to the activity. And this conceptualization enables us to explain the motivating power of the ethical life. For it recognizes that part of what it means to have a virtue, or internalized disposition, is for the virtue to be essentially embedded in a certain ordering of the person's emotional or affective responses to the world.

On Aristotle's ethical theory, the virtues represent a mediating device, which is designed to achieve the reconciliation of the subjective and objective standpoints. They are the standards in terms of which the person, in seeking to flourish, develops her natural capacities and potentialities; and this perfectionist quest is developed in the person through her education in the practices of her community, in which she is introduced to the virtues in order that she learn to take pleasure in them and identify her interests with the values in her community. In a liberal society, the person learns tolerance for others and respect for the autonomy of others; she learns the modes of reasoning and justification inherent in liberal critical reflection; and she learns the executive virtues associated with liberal autonomy: self-control and self-mastery, independence, initiative, and resolve.

The conception of ethics implicit in this process of moral education is quite different from that of the two dominant liberal approaches examined in Part I. The liberal conceptions offer a rational justification for the rules of justice—conceiving of justice either as a subset of rational self-interest (Gauthier) or derived from impartial reason (Gewirth, Rawls's original position argument). By contrast, on this conception of ethics, morality is grounded in the first instance in identification with or loyalty to a group. Within the group or moral community, equals are treated equally, and the norms and practices of the group, which are basically directed at the flourishing of the group, are applied to all members.[6] None of this precludes the possibility that members might acknowledge some duties to those outside the group, or that a person may have a variety of nested loyalties or commitments, some to narrower groups and some to wider groups, perhaps encompassing all human beings. Nothing has been said about the *content* of the morality: the chief concern here is to outline the *structure* of morality and the links between the agent's subjective motivational set, the community, and the ideals of the community with which the person identifies. What is noteworthy about this formulation is that it makes the adoption of a moral standpoint dependent on the person's (prior) identification with a moral community: it does *not*—as Rawls's and Gauthier's theories do—make the existence of community and the acceptance of a substantive morality dependent on, or arising out of, the justice of the basic structure of society.

The Problem of Moral Pluralism

The most serious criticism of the proposal that we begin ethical and political enquiry from a starting-point internal to a particular tradition and educate people in the practices of the tradition is that this is impossible. It is alleged that moral education is impossible in contemporary conditions because modern Western societies are deeply plural and divided and there is no common moral standpoint.

This view of contemporary liberal societies has been put forward by both liberals and those critical of liberalism. Liberals such as Rawls and Larmore have sought to defend liberal rules of justice on the grounds that they represent a *modus vivendi* among rival and incompatible moral conceptions. Rawls and Larmore argue that people in Western liberal democratic societies do not share a particular moral conception which could serve as the basis on which to construct the dominant institutions and rules of society. Liberal principles, they conclude, are the best we can hope for, given contemporary conditions, and communitarian politics are quite irrelevant.

Alasdair MacIntyre, in his disturbingly pessimistic account of contemporary liberal democratic societies, also shares this view of modern Western societies. He condemns liberalism on the grounds that it has destroyed the moral vision that bonded people in communities. This has left them without any ethical guideline for their individual lives or their communities, and stripped them of the vocabulary to argue in a way which leads to determinate conclusions.

If this diagnosis of contemporary liberal societies is correct, it would constitute a serious criticism of my proposal. If no common moral standpoint or common ethical conception is attainable, then my claim that a communal standpoint is necessary to overcome the motivation and integrity problems is irrelevant.

The argument of this book challenges this conception of contemporary society, however. On the analysis offered here, the view that liberal principles are neutral among conceptions of the good (either because they are derived from a standpoint independent of all contingency or because they represent a purely political *modus vivendi* among competing conceptions of the good) is a liberal self-delusion. Many contemporary liberals would like to believe that liberal rules of justice permit each person to choose her own particular conception of the good; that, in a liberal polity, each person can choose to be whatever she wants—whether it is to be a Catholic or a feminist or a Christian fundamentalist. But the argument put forward in Part I demonstrates the falsity of this view. Liberalism is itself a conception of the good, on all fours with other conceptions of the good, and deeply antithetical to many moral and religious conceptions. It is committed to the value of autonomy and its principles presuppose the importance of protecting individual autonomy above all else. Because liberal theory values autonomy, it offers people a sphere of privacy or free action in the personal sphere, and so is compatible with those moral theories that accept the liberal public–private dichotomy, and incompatible with many substantive moral conceptions that do not accept the public–private distinction.

In his book *Liberal Virtues*, Stephen Macedo illustrates this with an example favourable to liberalism: he points out that one cannot be a Nazi in a liberal society. A liberal polity requires its citizens to respect the rights of others: Nazis, Macedo correctly points out,

must respect the property, the political rights, and freedoms of Jewish Americans. They may, occasionally, march in Jewish communities, but they must get permits, keep order, and otherwise respect the peace and quiet of these neighbourhoods. They can gather in uniforms, with broadsheets, slogans, music, and other paraphernalia, in legally rented private halls, as long as they do not make too much noise. Nazis must pay taxes to support the liberal institutions they detest, including public schools. The liberal polity requires that the Nazis be law-abiding Nazis and that is not easy. They cannot be 'gung-ho' Nazis, in fact they cannot *be* Nazis at all but only play at it.[7]

And it is not only groups such as the Nazis whose lives are coercively structured by liberal principles. Other groups, such as the Amish in the mid-western United States and the Old Russian Believers in northern Alberta, find the liberal emphasis on individual autonomy and critical reflection threatening to their more communally oriented and simple religious existence. Their cultural survival depends on isolating their children from the many possibilities for choice that surround them: it depends, in other words, on devaluing the exercise of autonomy and emphasizing instead living according to the word of God.

The incompatibility of liberalism with many different ethical theories is testimony to the non-neutrality of liberalism, to the fact that it is a moral ideal in its own right. Liberalism is, of course, not neutral in its *consequences*: the fact that its principles serve a regulative role means that it must deem some actions, some ways of life as acceptable, and some as unacceptable. It does not treat all ways of life equally. But liberalism is also not neutral in its justificatory *origins*: liberal rules of justice are themselves based on a certain broad ethical conception. This became evident in Part I, where we analysed Gewirth's and Rawls's arguments for a thin theory of the good; and we concluded that they were not all-purpose means to a variety of ends, as they purported to be, but were based on the prior acceptance of the importance and value of autonomy. And in Chapter 5, Rawls's and Larmore's arguments for a *modus vivendi* conception revealed, not deep and searing divisions in contemporary liberal societies, as they had argued, but the necessity of a common ethical standpoint from which they derived their liberal principles. On Rawls's own account, the three rival moral theories that could converge on a liberal political settlement were all individualistic theories that placed great value on personal autonomy or choice: Millian liberals, Kantian liberals, and religious believers who believed in the value of religious toleration could, Rawls argued, agree on his principles of justice.

Of course, there are divisions in contemporary Western societies:

there are racial, ethnic, religious, class, and cultural divisions, to name a few; and there are outsiders as well as insiders: there are people in the mainstream and people who live on the margins of Western society. It would be inaccurate to portray contemporary Western societies as some sort of homogeneous Victorian heaven where people share a particular moral vision about the proper ends of human life and the moral virtues appropriate to those ends.

Political conflict emerges not only because each person's self-interested actions conflict with others' self-interested actions in the competition for scarce resources, as many liberals have claimed in their analysis of the 'objective' circumstances of justice, but also because people have different moral understandings of the best way of life for their community. Debates about pornography or abortion or affirmative action are not motivated only by different personal interests but also by different moral understandings. Both liberals and those critical of liberalism who have emphasized moral pluralism (or moral breakdown) have recognized the fact that the traditions and practices in Western liberal political communities are numerous and sometimes conflicting. The rural Christian fundamentalist has a different moral perspective from the materialist urban yuppie or the politically conscious socialist feminist. But these convenient caricatures tend to overemphasize the extent of disagreement in Western liberal societies. People in contemporary liberal societies share a basic commitment to certain moral values: democratic institutions are widely accepted; there is a common commitment to liberal values such as justice and some basic individual rights; and to such basic legal prohibitions as those on murder, theft, and fraud. Without some basic commitments, without a common moral vocabulary, a political community would be impossible and dialogue about the sources of disagreement would be unproductive. When the divisions in society become too intense, conversation at the political level ceases: in that case, the different groups might separate into smaller, politically segmented units; or one group might seek to coerce the other: it might impose its way of life or its favoured political or economic arrangement on the subordinate group. But this book is not about coercion, which is not justified, but always possible and sometimes very effective; nor about foreign relations: this book is concerned with the appropriate justificatory grounds for political actions *within* communities. And it seems, from the argument advanced so far, that the possibility of a political conversation *within* a community presupposes some shared moral ideals.

How do the urban yuppie, the Christian fundamentalist, and the socialist feminist fit into this rather abstract analysis of the necessary conditions for the possibility of a political conversation? The urban yuppie has no difficulty identifying with some of the core values of liberalism; indeed, some would argue that she embodies (the worst) liberal values: extreme individualism, which is expressed in terms of a self-referential 'me-first' attitude; and a commitment to the value of autonomy or individual choice, which is, unfortunately, exercised mainly through consumerism.

By contrast, religious fundamentalism is antithetical to liberal principles: many Islamic fundamentalists, for example, believe that liberal principles of tolerance and mutual respect serve as a mask under which wickedness is allowed to flourish.[8] Liberals, for their part, cannot accept the Islamic fundamentalist view that a society's political and institutional structures should be organized to reflect the laws of God, as laid down in the Koran.[9] Christian fundamentalists, too, find liberal principles compromising to their faith and frequently coercive. This has become evident through demonstrations organized by various fundamentalist Churches to protest against the American interpretation of liberalism's requirement of state neutrality: that religious prayers should not be allowed in public schools. Christian fundamentalists have also protested against liberal abortion laws and against certain movies, books, and music offensive to their moral and religious sensibilities. But it is important to note that Christian fundamentalists in Western societies have become liberalized in important ways: their response to *The Last Temptation of Christ* was positively muted in comparison to the response of Muslims to Salman Rushdie's book *The Satanic Verses*.[10] And this should be no surprise, for liberal societies, if they are to be successful, must inculcate liberal values and beliefs in their citizens. They must ensure that substantive moral and religious conceptions are held in a way that is compatible with liberal values and the liberal public–private dichotomy.

Feminists in liberal societies also experience a tension between their substantive moral commitments and the requirements of liberal justice, but here, too, liberalism has modified feminist practice by shaping the agenda in terms of which public debate is carried on. Although there is a powerful, thoroughgoing *feminist* argument about the sexual division of labour and the devaluing of women's work, this is treated by the liberal state as a *technical* problem of how to compare jobs and so ensure equity in pay between jobs of 'equal value'. Thus the feminist analysis of the patriarchal structure of society is transformed by the liberal state into an issue of 'pay equity'. This formulation succeeds in avoiding the feminist analysis of women's oppression in contemporary capitalist societies by treating instances of oppression in the workplace as specific and isolated examples of inequitable treatment which arise from difficulties attached to evaluating different jobs or anomalous discrimination by individuals (which can be corrected by government action).[11] The fact that feminists have largely supported pay equity initiatives in liberal societies can be seen as evidence of their high awareness of political strategy and their concern to secure for women some concrete benefits; but it is also testimony to the success of liberalism in shaping public discourse and moulding substantive moral conceptions in ways that are acceptable to liberal self-understandings.

It would seem, then, that while contemporary liberal societies are characterized by a diversity of moral conceptions, most of these conceptions are held in ways compatible with liberalism. They are private conceptions, which guide the individual's private life and relations with others, but which are held in ways consistent with respect for liberal rights and liberal rules of justice. The Christian or feminist will of course seek to promulgate her beliefs, but, in Western societies, this is mainly done *in accordance with liberal-democratic procedures for changing people's minds and changing government policy*. This means that the prior commitment must be a liberal one, namely to respect the autonomy of others. While it may be an exaggeration to say that we are all liberals now, the effectiveness of liberal societies in promulgating liberal values and beliefs has transformed many substantive moral and religious conceptions into ones consistent with liberal values. And that means that we, as a society, are *not* characterized by the degree of moral pluralism and disunity that some liberals and critics of liberalism have contended.

It may seem puzzling that I am offering as a solution to the integrity and motivation problems that we begin political and ethical reasoning from within a particular ethical conception, while at the same time claiming, in response to the charge of moral disunity, that liberal societies do in fact adopt the internal starting-point, that they do in fact teach their citizens to value liberal principles and to exhibit those virtues prized in liberal societies. But my proposal is not, in the first instance, a practical proposal: I am not (yet) arguing that we must change our practices; I am attempting to expose incoherences in liberal theory and to raise certain liberal practices to the self-conscious level.

My point is that many contemporary liberals have been wrong about liberal theory: they believe that liberal theory is neutral in the sense that it does not rely on a particular conception of the good, while, in fact, the theory is based on the (prior) acceptance of certain values and prioritizes those values over other ethical values. And many liberals eschew the character-centred approach to ethics, which involves inculcating children into the way of life and values of the community, in favour of an autonomy-centred approach to ethics, according to which conceptions of the good are purely private matters, i.e. objects for the exercise of personal autonomy. But, in fact, liberal societies, if they are to be successful, do and must inculcate liberal values into their citizens and teach them to place moral importance on such liberal values as individual autonomy, tolerance, and equal respect for persons. For liberal principles can work only if citizens value the autonomy of others and give that value priority over competing ideals, attachments, or commitments, that is, if citizens subordinate their other (non-liberal) beliefs and ideals to the requirements of liberal justice. Liberal states survive through time by inculcating these values in their citizens in various ways: through representative institutions designed to express individual choices about politics and governmental authority; through liberal justice which defines the boundaries of individual autonomy according to the principle of the equal freedom of persons; through courts of law which adjudicate disputes among individuals in accordance with procedures designed to embody impartiality; and through various semi-public institutions that embody and help propagate liberal values, such as state schools, universities, and the professions of law and journalism.

2. IMPLICATIONS: FOR THE SELF

The recognition that liberalism is not neutral among, or compatible with, different conceptions of the good, but requires a certain kind of citizen, and must educate the citizenry in liberal ethical values, does have important implications, however. It suggests that the appropriate conception of the person is not Rawls's conception of the person as abstract rational agency, nor Gauthier's conception of the person as essentially non-tuist, with no moral or personal ideals or attachments, nor Kymlicka's conception of a person divided between her beliefs and uncertainty about the validity of her beliefs. These attenuated views of the relationship of the person to her commitments suggest a divided conception of the self which has been at the heart of communitarian criticisms and which has generated the integrity and motivation problems. On the contrary, the person who accepts liberal beliefs *must* do so in a deep way, because liberal principles of equal respect and liberal virtues such as tolerance must regulate and inform all the person's values and private relations. If liberalism is a deep moral theory in its own right, the proponents of liberalism cannot be sceptics or self-interested non-tuists or pure rational agency. They must believe in the value of liberal justice: they accept liberal virtues of individual freedom and responsibility and tolerance, and value personal autonomy and attempt to realize that value in their own lives, through exercising the related (executive) virtues of self-mastery, self-control, and perseverance.

The conception of the person outlined here, as embedded in social practices and traditions, and educated in the beliefs and practices of her community, is associated with communitarian thought, and has been criticized recently by a number of liberals seeking to defend liberalism. One argument employed by liberals is that the communitarian conception of the person as a recipient of communally held beliefs, conceptions, and values denies the possibility of autonomy; and that once communitarians acknowledge that the person can make choices about which communal ends or values she will pursue, their theories become indistinguishable from liberal theories. This argument has been advanced forcefully in Will Kymlicka's discussion of Michael Sandel in his book *Liberalism, Community, and Culture*: 'so long as Sandel admits that the *person* can re-examine her ends—even the ends constitutive of her "self"—then he's failed to justify communitarian politics. He's failed to show why individuals shouldn't be given the conditions appropriate to that re-examining as an indispensable part of leading the best possible life.'[12] Implicit in this passage is the view that appealing to a community's traditions, practices, and values cannot be reconciled with individual autonomy: indeed, this is evident in Kymlicka's definition (or, more accurately, caricature) of communitarianism as involving the claim that self-discovery replaces judgement (although he admits that this view is not actually held by any communitarians).[13] The assumption that autonomy and community stand in fundamental opposition to one another also underlies Kymlicka's conclusion: 'The strong [communitarian] claim (that self-discovery replaces judgment) is implausible and the weak claim (which allows that a self constituted by its ends can none the less be reconstituted), while attractive, fails to distinguish his [Sandel's] position from the liberal view.'[14] What Kymlicka calls 'the strong claim' is a straw man, for it has not been endorsed by any communitarians; and the weak claim—that is, the recognition that the person is both (*a*) constituted by the traditions and practices of her community, and (*b*) can distance herself from these through critical reflection, does *not* lead to a liberal political order in which autonomy is protected and privileged over other values.

The central problem with Kymlicka's liberal argument is that it is based on the false premiss that there is a fundamental opposition between the individual and the community. In fact, however, the development of the individual's autonomy is not defined in opposition to community, in opposition to the acceptance of the rules and ideas and beliefs of the community in which the person develops. Rather, the community is a necessary condition for the possibility of autonomy: the community is necessary to the development of the person's own powers of self-control and self-mastery and competence. Many recent writings, principally by moral psychologists, on the acquisition of autonomy, bear a striking resemblance to Aristotle's description of the process of moral education. Indeed, it is possible to recast the discussion of moral education in the language of autonomy to emphasize this aspect of the person's development.

In his book *Autonomy*, Lawrence Haworth claims that there are distinct stages in the development of the autonomous person, which I have classified as involving: (1) internalization, (2) discipline and self-mastery, and (3) reflective self-awareness.[15] Haworth argues, in his discussion of the initial stages in the development of autonomy, that it is necessary for the person to internalize the community's modes of reasoning, and its standards of behaviour and evaluation. In learning to conform to a particular way of life, the young child's desires and emotions are disciplined and given determinate shape. This discipline is necessary for the person to advance to the second stage, where she acquires a certain amount of competence in the world, to achieve the results that she wants, so that she can interpose herself between domination by others and domination by, say, those of her physically based desires with which she does not identify.[16] It is only by forming intentions, and being competent enough in the world to realize these intentions, that the person can achieve autonomy in the sense of control over her own life.

The third stage outlined by Haworth in the attainment of autonomy involves the acquisition of reflective self-awareness. And this too is acquired in communities, within traditions that develop the person's powers of critical thought and modes of justification. There is, of course, a sense in which the exercise of autonomy affirms the person's independence, and so could be seen as opposed to the community in that sense, but the independence characteristic of autonomy is not a substantive independence, characterized by substantive opposition, but procedural independence, where the salient notion is not that of conformity or non-conformity but the extent to which critical reflection has informed the person's decisions and the person's life is chosen by her.[17]

Reflective self-awareness is an important element of autonomy because it enables the person to understand the grounds of her beliefs or desires and identify with them and so have greater control over her life. Of course, in becoming reflectively aware of the grounds of her beliefs, of her tradition, there emerges the possibility that the person will criticize the practices, beliefs, and conceptions of her community. In adopting the disengaged perspective of critical reflection, the person may become alienated from the practices and beliefs of her society: she may be unable to enjoy the immediate participant relation of individual member to community which characterizes the unreflective person who accepts without question the dominant ideas and beliefs of her community. But it is important to recognize that such reflective criticism is possible only by adopting a standpoint other than the one subject to criticism, and this standpoint must be one that is developed within the tradition in question. It must be a standpoint which can be articulated in terms of the concepts, the language of the particular community, a standpoint which draws, for its persuasive power and plausibility, on the fundamental justificatory conceptions and beliefs of the community. The possibility of such a critique does not imply that the individual stands opposed to the community as a completely independent centre of consciousness: on the contrary, the critique must appeal to the deepest conceptions of the community, to its conception of human nature, for example, or its view of the relation of the person to others, or to God and the world. Thus, although the possibility of critical autonomy depends on the tradition containing a universalist element, on its understanding itself as more than simply a tradition, and the universalist claims of the community may be undermined in the critique, the possibility of the development and exercise of the person's powers of critical reflection depends on that person being within a particular tradition, engaged with at least some of the problems and questions raised by the tradition, and accepting the deepest values or beliefs of the community, for this is the basis on which the critique is made.

What is implied here is that the good of human autonomy is not an individual good, but is essentially communal in nature.[18] It is a communal good, not simply because the promotion of autonomy requires a certain kind of environment or community, such as one in which people's intellectual and reflective powers are nurtured and encouraged, but communal also in the more fundamental sense that the very possibility of autonomy depends on the acceptance of at least some of the tradition's conceptions.

This relation of interdependence between the individual and the community, between the person's capacity for autonomy and the fact that she is (necessarily) situated within a particular tradition, culture, and history, has important implications for how we should treat the value of autonomy. It suggests that the liberal view that substantive ends, purposes, and values are matters of pure subjective choice is unsustainable, for these wider values are absolutely crucial to the acquisition and maintenance of individual autonomy. Liberals should be concerned about values other than those connected directly with individual freedom, since individual autonomy develops in communities and individuals become autonomous through participation in shared practices and through their membership in and affiliation with larger groups. Liberals should be concerned to promote the conditions in which people develop the capacity for autonomy, that is, the shared context (community) which is presupposed in autonomous action and which is an essential precondition of the possibility of morality. Liberals should abandon their traditional preoccupation with external regulatory agencies enforcing spheres of free action and attend to the issue of how social relations—i.e. communities—can flourish.

The insight that individual autonomy and indeed morality is possible only *within* communities of shared practices—that the person both (*a*) embodies communal values and beliefs and (*b*) has the ability to stand back from (communal) values as an independent centre of consciousness—cannot be easily or unproblematically incorporated into liberal theory. This communitarian insight does not serve merely to correct or complete liberal theory: it also has important limiting implications for the scope of liberal principles. We saw in our discussion of liberal theory in Part II that some (revisionist) liberals acknowledge the interdependence of autonomy and community, but they do not permit this insight to affect their (liberal) political principles. Liberals such as Kymlicka and Raz still seek to prioritize liberal principles (which protect the value of autonomy) when they come into conflict with other substantive values, *even though* the value of autonomy is inextricably bound up with, and presupposes, other values. A full appreciation of the interdependence of autonomy and other values would *not* lead to liberal politics in which priority is automatically granted to the value of autonomy when it comes into conflict with other values. Surely, on this conception, it must be a contingent question which value should be given priority: contingent on the importance of the individual freedom that might be impinged; and contingent on the seriousness of the consequences for communal identity or communal practices of permitting the exercise of individual freedom. Sometimes the community will favour the protection of individual autonomy; but one can conceive of occasions in which individual freedom can justifiably be limited to support substantive communal values or the community's way of life.

3. IMPLICATIONS: FOR POLITICS

Any adequate political conception must give expression to the two elements which we have seen are essential to a full and coherent conception of the person: (1) the person's embeddedness in the shared language and practices of her community; and (2) the person's capacity to critically reflect on and choose those practices, values, and traditions with which she wishes to identify. These two elements are given political expression in terms of the concepts of membership and citizenship.[19] The person's communal identity is expressed by the idea that she is a member of this or that community; and the person's autonomy is expressed in terms of her citizenship in a political community, which carries with it certain political rights which entitle her to participate in the collective determination of the conditions of her existence.

The person's membership in a particular community is presupposed by the conception outlined in this chapter of the kind of foundational argument appropriate to political and moral enquiry. The proposal that enquiry should begin from within a particular communal identity assumes from the outset that there is a community of shared values with which the person (initially) identifies. Specifying the boundaries of a particular community is obviously a difficult and contentious issue: the argument from language suggests a bounded linguistic community, although this criterion carries with it the problem of individuating languages. (Is French in Quebec different from French in France? Is English in Scotland different from English in England?) There is an analogous difficulty with the appeal to shared values: if one focuses at the microscopic level, shared values are confined to very small local communities, or neighbourhoods; but if one adopts a more panoramic view of the values that are shared, one could classify the Western world (North America and Europe, at a minimum) as one community.

I do not wish to deny the difficulties that attach to the question of delineating communities, but I think one can address the extreme views.[20]

Some of the communitarians have been very pessimistic about the possibility of situating the person within a particular community. This is because they regard small local communities, where people still have face-to-face contact, and where individuals' attachment to the community is based on their own experience with other members of the community, as the only *genuine* type of community. In some places, where circumstances allow, such local attachments do exist, but in much of the contemporary world, where technological and economic imperatives demand mobility of labour and economies of scale, local communities are threatened. Communitarians such as MacIntyre and Sandel[21] are right to despair about the possibilities of communal identity if they regard as genuine only this kind of community. But this understanding of community is an extremely narrow one, and there seems no reason to dismiss all forms of community but small local ones. Since communal identity is essentially a subjective phenomenon, it makes more sense to identify a community with the set of people who share beliefs about their communal membership, regardless of whether the beliefs are in fact true.

At the other extreme, there are those who hesitate to grant any ethical importance to particularistic commitments and regard the global community as the only relevant moral community. In part, this reticence is based on the experience of extreme nationalism in Nazi Germany, which is anathema to both Marxists and liberals. But the deeper motive for this reticence is the dominant conception of the moral point of view as identified with the perspective of an abstract individual, possessed of reason and a capacity for autonomy, but not fundamentally committed to any particular persons, practices, or values. The moral subject on this universalist theory is disengaged from all particular commitments and symmetrically placed *vis-à-vis* all other moral subjects, who are themselves stripped of all particular commitments and moral ideals. We have seen, however, that this identification of the moral subject with the abstract individual, which underlies the view that the global community is the only relevant moral community, is itself a highly contentious view of moral agency and leads to two serious problems: the integrity problem and the motivation problem. In our ethical life, we *do* pay attention to boundaries: we do regard our duties to our compatriots as more extensive than the duties we owe to strangers; and this fact indicates not some moral shortcoming on our part, but the lack of realism of the universal community view and the abstract conception of the person that supports it.[22]

In the present context, beginning with what people's loyalties actually *are* (rather than what they ought to be), an obvious communal boundary is the national one. People do generally think of themselves in national terms: as Americans or Britons, Japanese or Poles. The particular set of shared beliefs that links people into national groups also binds them into subjective communities: beliefs about their members' distinctiveness; beliefs about their shared history and shared values; and a sense of loyalty to other members of the group, which explains why the individual person is sometimes willing to sacrifice her own personal interests, narrowly defined, for the good of the community as a whole.

Of course, since the concept of community is *subjectively* defined, it is not necessarily restricted to the national level. Many Europeans are starting to think of themselves as Europeans, not merely as French or Italian or German, and are willing to support redistributive policies within the European Community, rather than within the national group only. But national loyalties are the norm in most of the Western world: wider constituencies tend not to attract sufficient loyalty to underwrite a practice of distributive justice; and small local communities are under threat and may not in any case be large enough to support an effective redistributive practice.[23] Whatever the size of the group, it is clear that distributive justice presupposes a bounded community within which distribution takes place. It assumes, that is, a group of people who are committed to dividing social goods, in the first instance, among themselves. And what motivates that commitment, what motivates the adoption of the perspective of the common good, is the person's sense of loyalty to, and identification with, other members of her community, which is acquired through induction in the practices, beliefs, and values of the community.

It may of course be the case that one's beliefs about common membership are false: they may be based on myths about the 'group's' common descent and common history. David Miller has argued that concern about the mythical nature of national communities is one reason why theorists tend to conceive of genuine communities as either global (using rationalist criteria) or small and local (where people share strong personal ties to other members of the community and so have a basis in experience for their feelings of loyalty and beliefs about communal membership).[24] The problem with national communities is that they are constituted by a set of shared beliefs about the members' common identity which has not been acquired by direct experience but has been culturally transmitted, through such means as the printed story or through song or theatre. Nationality is, at least partly, a manufactured item: studies of the nation-building period in Europe indicate the large extent to which national groups have been created to solidify certain power bases.[25] And this fact reminds us of the potential gap between inherited understandings and rational reflection, between membership in a given group and autonomous self-formation.

We have seen, however, that attaching importance to individual autonomy does not mean that we must reject membership in particularistic communities: on the contrary, exercising one's autonomy presupposes a communal context in which choice takes place; and the possibility of any form of morality at all also assumes some communal ties to foster the sense of loyalty which is at the heart of the ethical point of view.

Membership in a particularistic community constitutes the given element in identity: the language, beliefs, and values which the person learns through induction in the practices of the group serve to situate the person in a particular community. If that identity is to be held up to critical scrutiny, the person also requires certain rights to protect rational reflection; education rights, for example, and freedom of speech and freedom of the press. And if the person's communal identity is not to be wholly given to her, and beyond her control, certain political rights are necessary, which entitle each person to participate in reshaping that identity through redefining her community. Membership in a national community must be supplemented by political citizenship, which gives expression to the individual's capacity for autonomy. In the political forum, citizens must be able to (collectively) reflect on their inherited understandings; and shape their lives through choosing the conditions of their existence.

Adopting communitarian premises does not necessarily entail a rejection of liberal freedoms or liberal policies, but it does have implications for our understanding of what politics involves, some of which would be unacceptable to most contemporary liberals. The public–private dichotomy, which involves treating one's moral values as purely subjective, *private* conceptions, and basing political decisions on rules of justice that are neutral among conceptions of the good, is central to most contemporary versions of liberal theory. This liberal idea is challenged by the conception of politics advanced here, and the related view of political judgement, according to which political decisions are reached by balancing the different values involved and, eventually, arriving at a collective decision with respect to the importance of values in a particular case. On this conception, there is no hard-and-fast distinction between public and private decisions: one's moral perspective informs all one's decisions, both with respect to one's own (private) life and decisions which affect the basic structure and policies of one's political community.

The interrelationship between public and private spheres works both ways. It is evident not only in this model of political judgement but also in the earlier description of the behaviour of contemporary liberal states. We have seen that, in contrast to the liberal self-conception, liberalism is in fact a deep moral theory, which is perpetuated through a communal valuing of certain substantive values associated with liberalism. Liberalism is not confined to the public sphere: it is not only a public philosophy which applies to the basic structure of society but a deep moral theory which requires a certain ordering of the individual's own beliefs and values. This (moral education) is achieved through the basic institutions of liberal society, which structure the individual's 'private' life. And the fact that individuals (in their 'private' lives) learn to accept and support liberal principles gives the liberal state the immediate justificatory support that it requires (consent) to continue in its 'public' role.

This suggests that liberals need to re-conceptualize the liberal public–private dichotomy. No longer can conceptions of the good or moral ideals be kept out of the public sphere on the grounds that they are purely subjective, private conceptions, quite distinct from the public conceptions of liberal theory. Liberal ideals are on all fours with other moral ideals and conceptions: liberal principles have no justificatory priority over other moral ideals, which would secure for them primacy in adjudicating among rival moral understandings. Whether or not liberal principles inform the political life of one's community depends on how they fare in the clash and consensus among rival moral (and self-interested) understandings that characterizes political conflict. It depends on the importance of the liberal principle that is at stake, and the importance of the other values that may be threatened by the exercise of individual freedom. On this conception of the relation between politics and society, the state would be justified in acting to protect and promote valuable ways of life. State action in support of certain ways of life may be necessary to ensure a flourishing and valuable culture, in which meaningful choice is possible. Indeed, it follows from the recognition that community and autonomy are important human goods that it is justified to protect a way of life which provides people with a rich and viable culture and with a forum in which the meaningful exercise of autonomy is possible.

Of course, some liberals may argue that they can accept that community is an important good, or that the meaningful exercise of autonomy depends on having a variety of worthwhile options from which to choose, without accepting the republican view regarding the political promotion of valuable ways of life. The characteristic liberal position is to insist that the existence of worthwhile options is best ensured by a neutral liberal state which permits competition among various forms of life in groups and associations below the level of the state. But I have argued that the liberal aspiration to neutrality is impossible to attain: that the liberal dichotomy between the public and private spheres and the conception of politics as neutral among different visions of the good is itself a particular vision of the good; in short, that neutrality cannot be achieved because neutrality itself requires justification. But let us for the moment set aside the difficulties concerning the liberal conception of a 'neutral' state and accept that the question at issue is what mechanisms best secure the goods of reason, autonomy, and community—whether positive government action is sometimes required or whether they are better attained through the operation of a cultural market-place in a 'neutral' liberal state.

The assumption behind this liberal rejection of republicanism is that it is not necessary for governments to actively promote certain values or ways of life: if community or reason or autonomy are indeed fundamental needs or goods, they would not require government promotion but would be secured by the cultural market-place. This reasoning underlies Will Kymlicka's efforts to turn the tables on the communitarian by arguing that it is liberalism which assumes the inherent sociability of persons: 'liberals believe that people naturally form and join social relations and forums in which they come to understand and pursue the good. The state is not needed to provide that communal context.'[26] Kymlicka and other liberals are correct to point out that the forming of social relations is a natural process which normally occurs without state involvement, and to emphasize the important role of groups and associations other than the state in providing a variety of worthwhile options or forms of life.

The problem with the liberal argument is that it is based on a naïvely optimistic view of the operation of the cultural market-place. Rawls, for example, in his 1975 article 'Fairness to Goodness', argues that those forms of life that cannot survive under the neutral state are not worthy of state support and protection and that their demise is no cause for regret.[27] Kymlicka, too, expresses the view that the cultural market-place functions to get rid of trivial or degrading activities or ways of life[28] and indeed that it is 'valued because it helps good ways of life displace bad'.[29] This profoundly benign view of the cultural market-place ignores the possibility that the individualism inherent in such a market-place may make it unfairly biased against the securing of collective goods: it ignores the fact that, sometimes, collective goods can be secured only through collective action. One reason for this is that there is a divergence between individual and collective rationality: a person may have an interest in a certain form of life but not in sustaining that way of life for future generations;[30] or a person may find it individually rational to maximize her share of resources or material goods, but the pursuit of this strategy by everyone will eventually seriously damage the environment, and so jeopardize the quality of life, which is also important to her. In such cases, a public ranking of goods or values, arrived at through political deliberation involving the whole community, and action in accordance with this, might be necessary to secure the flourishing of a certain good or value. What the republican vision insists on, and what is inadequately recognized in individualist liberal theories, is the extent to which a valuable way of life, a way of life supportive of reason and autonomy and community, is a fragile historical achievement, which should not be taken for granted as an assumed backdrop to the neutral liberal state, but may require positive government action in its support.

Another criticism frequently advanced by liberals against the republican conception of a non-neutral state is that it involves an unrealistic aspiration to replace political activity with an organic conception of unity and wholeness, in which the political realm is conceived of as expressing or reflecting in an immediate way the harmonious moral order of society. This is one of Larmore's central criticisms of communitarianism in his book *Patterns of Moral Complexity*. He describes communitarian theory as 'simplistic'[31] in its holistic conception of a society unified by 'a single substantial purpose or conception of the good life'.[32] This crude characterization of communitarianism is also found in Will Kymlicka's essay: he describes communitarians as afflicted with a 'tendency to uncritically endorse existing social practices as the basis for political deliberation about the good',[33] and with another 'tendency'—not obviously compatible with the first one, and so suggesting a more sophisticated understanding of the political than Kymlicka allows—'to assume that anything which is not politically deliberated is thereby left to an individual will incapable of rational judgement'.[34]

But these descriptions of communitarianism, however accurate they may be of some individual thinkers who ally themselves with this tradition, do not represent the relation between politics and society to which a communitarian meta-ethical argument is committed. What communitarianism *is* committed to is a relational conception of morality, such that moral principles and moral beliefs are grounded, at least in the first instance, in their being held or believed or endorsed by a community of people to govern their relations with each other.[35] What makes a group of individuals a *community*, on the conception defended here and in communitarian theory, is their adoption of a common standpoint, which generally consists in shared traditions and practices, which in turn are supported by shared beliefs and ideals. None of this suggests that, on a communitarian view, a monolithic conception of the good or single communal purpose characterizes each society, as Larmore and Kymlicka seem to think. The shared beliefs and traditions and practices of the community may be quite general in scope; there is indeed no reason why a community would not accept or endorse a plurality of different conceptions of the good. The issue dividing liberals from communitarians, and from the conception advanced here, is not concerned with whether values are monist or pluralist, but with the role of conceptions of value in defining the community and the relation of these shared conceptions to the political life. On a communitarian view, there is no point, no reason to deny moral principles a justificatory role in the framing of the political or constitutional structure of society.

Nor does this communitarian conception imply that the moral theory underlying the society is immediately reflected or endorsed in the political realm, with no independent role left for politics or for the exercise of autonomy. On the contrary, what is at stake in political issues is the articulation of this collective identity. Of course, this collective identity can be explored through many intermediate associations, and through ordinary moral discourse, but in political action, where the community must adopt particular policies and pursue some particular course of action, the identity of the community, and the identity of each person as a member of the community, is precisely what is brought into question. Because there are distinct wills, distinct perspectives on the world, it is doubtless true that there will be conflicting interests and disagreements. But if reconciliation is to be possible, if unity is to be created, the political participants must draw on the conceptions, ideas, and practices which they share as members of the same community. Shared practices are presupposed by the idea that the participants can understand the language of the debate, the question at issue; they shape the kinds of arguments and justifications that are thought appropriate in dealing with this question, and are appealed to also in arriving at a solution to the practical problem. In politics, the public interest, the communal identity, is indeed a matter of debate, but the debate takes place within certain parameters, and appeals to the metaphors and practices and tradition and language of the community.[36]

By contrast, the liberal exclusion of rival moral conceptions from political argument suggests a conception of the political as sanitized of all disagreement, as neutral between, because above, the conflict of contested philosophical or religious or moral doctrines. It is a premiss of both Rawls's and Larmore's *modus vivendi* argument, for example, that different people fundamentally disagree over the purposes and aims that they seek to pursue, and so make conflicting claims on the political arena. Since, on Larmore's view, conceptions of the good in contemporary society are bound to diverge, he reasons that it is necessary that the political sphere provide some grounds for adjudicating among them, and the best way to do this is by not basing liberal principles on any particular conception. On this view, political principles are primarily a mechanism for accommodation among competing moral conceptions, and what makes them successful, what makes accommodation and, ultimately, political stability possible, is that these political principles are derived from a basis neutral among all these contending principles. What is presupposed in this procedure is a conception of the person's interests which is antecedent to, or independent of, that person's more determinate conception of her interests. They suppose that it is possible, by abstracting from contested beliefs and ideals and conceptions, to reach a standpoint neutral among all conceptions and yet sufficiently determinate to serve as the ground of liberal principles of justice. This conception suggests that the disagreement in society cannot be so deep as to affect the very language that the person uses to articulate her views, nor so fundamental as to constitute her conception of her interests. The person need only abstract from contested philosophical or religious or moral views to reach a standpoint from which the pursuit of each person's interests can be regulated by rules acceptable to all. The differing interests and the divergent conceptions and beliefs and world-views held by members of society do not impinge at all upon the question of how the basic structure of society should be organized except as a fact to be taken into account in arriving at that standpoint. On this liberal view, the contested or controversial issues are confined to the private realm in order that the public realm can be justified by consensus on principles which serve each person's interests (abstractly defined). Ironically, then, it seems that it is not communitarianism that seeks to banish politics from the political realm, as Larmore's argument had supposed, but certain prominent variants of liberalism.

4. RATIONAL JUSTIFICATION

Central to the conception of ethics and politics advanced here is the view that language is not an instrument with which we *copy* reality, as if we can get outside language to assess the accuracy of the concepts that we use to communicate with each other and think in. On the contrary, all concepts, including ethical ones, receive their force, their intelligibility, from within a particular culture or way of life, and in that sense are grounded in the practices and institutions of a particular society. This implies a conception of rationality as partly constituted by social practices and institutions, beliefs and relations, which have expressive significance for the members of the society. They are rational to those who participate in these social practices because they embody a way of life with which the members of the community identify. But this conception of rationality, this view of language begs the question of the further justification, the further rationale for this way of life or ethical conception. If it lacks this further justification, moral education will appear merely as an agency to maintain the dominance of one cultural tradition over another, without answering the questions: 'Why *this* tradition?' or 'Why this way of life?'

What is presupposed in the further question, 'Why these social practices? Why this way of life?' is the recognition of the possibility of living in a community with different social practices, beliefs, and values. The recognition of the replaceability of one's own form of life destroys the immediate, or *Sittlich*, relation of the individual to the practices of her community, for the person becomes aware that the beliefs, language, and practices that she has been brought up to accept are only one particular set of possible beliefs and practices, and that there are many other

ways of organizing human life. The recognition that these practices and beliefs derive their validity from the fact that the members of a community engage in and are committed to them
involves an awareness that one could be committed to different
practices, a different way of life. It is only by justifying one's
beliefs and practices by answering the further question, 'Why
these practices? Why this way of life?', that the person can reconcile the reflective awareness of her own autonomy in this
regard with her situated position within the practices and way
of life of a particular society or community.

It might be objected that such an exercise of reflective autonomy is impossible on the view defended so far. It might be
claimed that the possibility of a rational rejection of one's way
of life is precluded by the conception of rationality as constituted
by shared practices or traditions of discourse and enquiry.
Endorsing the view that it is only through accepting the values,
beliefs, and language of one's own society that one can reason
at all seems to preclude the possibility of rational dissent from
the beliefs and practices of one's community.[37] But this objection
overlooks the fact that communities encompass a variety of different beliefs, conceptions, and values. There is not one monolithic, and fully coherent, set of beliefs governing a community,
but a plurality of values and conceptions, which are sometimes
in delicate tension with one another. The individual is able to
dissent rationally from the standards and beliefs of her community by subjecting to reasoned criticism some particular subset
of beliefs or practices in terms of other beliefs and practices and
so remaining within the mode of rationality characteristic of her
community.

Richard Rorty, Heidegger, Jacques Derrida, and others who
identify themselves with the post-modernist tradition share with
this account the view that it is impossible to attain a (neutral)
Archimedean point, and they also emphasize the situatedness
of the person within her particular historical community. But
many post-modernists argue that, because there is no standpoint
outside the linguistic practices and modes of life of the community, the individual cannot *evaluate* these practices or this way
of life, as I am suggesting, but can only *redescribe* herself and
her world. Richard Rorty writes in his essay 'The Contingency
of Community': 'To see a common practice as cruel and unjust

. . . is a matter of redescription rather than discovery. It is a matter of changing vocabularies rather than of stripping away the veil of appearances from an objective reality, of experimentation with new ways of speaking rather than overcoming "false consciousness".[38] On Rorty's conception, there is no way of *evaluating* social practices: all one can do is adopt a different vocabulary with respect to them, and (re-)describe them. It is possible, on Rorty's view, for the person to (retrospectively) make her descriptions of society true; but what makes the descriptions true, in Rorty's view, is simply that they have been accepted by the wider community; and even that is not conceived by Rorty as a rational process but as a contingent aesthetic one.

Rorty's claim that our knowledge (in ethics, social science, and natural science) is simply 'redescriptions' contains a great deal of truth: much depends on how the facts are described; and theories are notoriously underdetermined by the facts. But just because there is no theory-independent language in which facts can be expressed does not mean that there is nothing independent of theory, that there are no facts at all, and that re-descriptions are totally unconstrained by any considerations. Even Rorty accepts that redescriptions are subject to *some* constraints: when he writes that the 'redescriptions ... taken together, *buttress*' an alternative understanding, he suggests that there are constraints of consistency on the discourse of redescription.[39] This is also suggested by his endorsement of Sellar's definition of philosophy as the quest 'to see how things in the broadest possible sense of the term, hang together, in the broadest possible sense of the term'.[40] As Charles Taylor has pointed out, this only makes sense if there are some constraints on the redescription: 'otherwise anything could "hang together" with anything, and there would be nothing to "attempt to SEE" here'.[41] And, despite himself, Rorty cannot help relying on some conception of theory as guided or controlled by observation. This emerges when he allows for 'control by less controversial over more controversial beliefs';[42] and, as Roy Bhaskar has pointed out, 'beliefs of the former kind may be less controversial precisely because they were formed in or as a result of (theoretically-informed) observation'.[43]

The conception of ethics as internal to a particular vocabulary or tradition does not, then, preclude the possibility of evaluating

competing conceptions or values or social practices, of disen-
tangling confusions or highlighting questionable assumptions,
or condemning theories for their failure to explain certain facts.
And because it is possible to *critique* particular vocabularies, and
the social practices in which they are implicated, autonomy does
not have to consist in unconstrained self-creation *ex nihilo*, in
redescription without regard for the truth or value of that description, as on the post-modernist conception, but can be conceived,
much more plausibly, as essentially bound up with critical reflection on substantive (communal) values.

We cannot, of course, exclude relativism in principle: to conceive of moral values as social, not existing *an sich*, independent
of human beings, is to recognize that our value-system, our moral
conception, might be only one among a number of equally plausible rival moral conceptions. But this should not worry us in
practice, unless we have reason to think that a better alternative
to our moral theory exists.

As Alasdair MacIntyre has argued in *Whose Justice? Which
Rationality?*, the fact that there are no theory-independent facts
to decide the issue between two rival theories does not mean
that there is no way of demonstrating the rational superiority
of a particular tradition, a particular conception, over other traditions or conceptions. The fact that modes of reasoning are internal to particular conceptions does not preclude the possibility
of rational justification in terms of elements that are common
to different traditions. And unless we make the implausible
assumption that world-views are closed systems, in the sense
of being mutually exclusive and mutually irrefutable, it is likely
that there will be sufficient common ground to permit discourse
and rational argument and justification.

On the view presented here, conceptions are justified in so
far as they make sense of our moral experience, and this involves
offering a coherent and consistent system or ordering of the
external world, and explaining actions and events in the world.
This conception of justification is consistent with this theory in
that it takes rationality to be necessarily constituted in communities.[44] Each tradition of enquiry can be defined in terms of its
own particular problematic, its own programme of unsolved
problems or concerns, by reference to which progress or lack
of progress in the tradition is judged. Progress is neither guaran-

teed nor inevitable: there is always the possibility that the tradition will face an epistemological crisis, either by encountering
new problems, in the form of new facts in the external world
that it cannot explain, or perhaps a rival tradition that introduces
into the community conceptions that it cannot cope with. What
is distinctive about an epistemological crisis is that the old
methods of enquiry and argument fail to solve the incoherences,
or seem only to create new problems, or reveal new inadequacies
in the community's conceptions. It is, of course, possible that
conceptual innovation will occur, which will be able to explain
what could not be explained prior to the innovation, and the
epistemological crisis will be overcome. But what is important
here is that these inadequacies or this progress are recognized
as inadequacies or as progress by the standards of the tradition
itself. And the fact that a tradition may fail to be vindicated
even by the standards of the tradition suggests that it *is* possible
that an adherent of one theory could recognize another theory
as rationally superior to her own, because not subject to inconsis-
tencies or incoherences which plague her own theory, and so
capable of resolving problems that her theory cannot. And this
is precisely what is being claimed here on behalf of this conception. For, throughout this chapter, I have argued for the explan-
atory superiority of this vision over individualist liberal theories,
for the superiority, specifically, of its formulation of the relationship between self-interest and morality, and between the individual and the community, and its conception of the moral point
of view.

NOTES

1. It is true that David Gauthier, in *Morals by Agreement*, does allow
that each person's interests may include love for or dedication to
another person. However, he does not consider these interests as
essential to the person: they are excluded from his construction
of legitimate political principles; and they are not even conceived
as properly moral relations, but merely as preferences that the person has or choices that she has made.
2. David Wiggins, 'Truth, Invention, and the Meaning of Life', *Proceedings of the British Academy* (1976), 341-4.

3. Sabina Lovibond, *Realism and Imagination in Ethics* (Oxford: Basil Blackwell, 1983), 28. I am indebted to Lovibond's discussion of realism and non-cognitivism throughout this section.

4. Aristotle dismisses the person who is outside all moralities as being *apaideutoi*, which means ignorant of communal practices and rational discourse, and so unworthy of our attention. See Martha Craven Nussbaum, *The Fragility of Goodness: Luck and Ethics in Greek Tragedy and Philosophy* (Cambridge: Cambridge University Press, 1986), 252–4; and John M. Cooper, *Reason and Human Good in Aristotle* (Indianapolis: Hackett, 1986), 66.

5. M. F. Burnyeat, 'Aristotle on Learning to be Good', in *Essays on Aristotle's Ethics*, ed. Amelie Oksenberg Rorty (Berkeley, Calif.: University of California Press, 1980), 69–92.

6. This point is from Andrew Oldenquist, 'Loyalties', *Journal of Philosophy*, 79/4 (Apr. 1982), 177.

7. Stephen Macedo, *Liberal Virtues: Citizenship, Virtue, and Community in Liberal Constitutionalism* (Oxford: Clarendon Press, 1990), 260.

8. Alan R. Taylor, *The Islamic Question in Middle East Politics* (Boulder, Colo.: Westview Press, 1988), 99–100, 109–11.

9. Ibid. 105.

10. This example is from Macedo, *Liberal Virtues*, 74.

11. For a more complete discussion of this problem, see Nancy Adamson, Linda Briskin, and Margaret McPhail, *Feminist Organizing for Change: The Contemporary Women's Movement in Canada* (Toronto: Oxford University Press, 1988), 180–4.

12. Kymlicka, *Liberalism, Community, and Culture*, 55.

13. Ibid. 57.

14. Ibid. 56.

15. Lawrence Haworth, *Autonomy: An Essay in Philosophical Psychology and Ethics* (New Haven, Conn.: Yale University Press, 1986), 16–21, 55–7.

16. Parfit denies that the person can be identified with the capacity for autonomy; he denies that the person's identity consists in some 'further fact' beyond the continuity of her aims and projects. Parfit, *Reasons and Persons*, 216. But, significantly, his attempt to jettison the capacity for self-revision from his conception of the person leads him to view each person's awareness of her own identity over time as something which simply *happens* to the person, with no involvement or participation by the person. He is led, that is, into the world of science fiction, conceiving of the construction of apparent experiences, and the awareness of each person as a separately existing entity, a subject of experience, as effected by some evil neuro-surgeon operating on the person.

17. This is a central theme in the philosophy of education. See R. S. Peters, *Ethics and Education* (London: Allen & Unwin, 1966).

18. Haworth, *Autonomy*, 20–1.

19. See David Miller, 'In What Sense Must Socialism Be Communitarian?', *Social Philosophy and Policy*, 6/2, 70.

20. See ibid., esp. pp. 67–9.

21. Michael J. Sandel, 'The Procedural Republic and the Unencumbered Self', *Political Theory*, 12/1 (Feb. 1984), 93–5. See also Miller, 'In What Sense Must Socialism Be Communitarian?', 60–7.

22. Impartial theories (which imply universal commitments) do attempt to bring in boundaries at a later stage of theory-building and thereby conform to our intuitions. This attempt to combine impartial theory with present national commitments (to redistribution, for example) is brilliantly discussed by Brian Barry in his book *Theories of Justice*. He brings out the tension between these elements in an analysis of Rawls and Hume on international and intergenerational justice. However, Barry's solution is to dispense with the self-interested element in these theories (which generate boundaries through the concept of reciprocity) and to retain a purer impartial account. He does not consider how the self-interested element in these theories is designed to overcome the motivation problem; and how his solution does not solve this problem.

23. David Miller, 'In What Sense Must Socialism Be Communitarian?', accepts this point and argues that socialists who wish to support a redistributive programme must therefore take national boundaries seriously.

24. David Miller, 'The Ethical Significance of Nationality', *Ethics*, 98/4 (July 1988), 653–4.

25. A. D. Smith, *The Ethnic Origins of Nations* (Oxford: Basil Blackwell, 1986).

26. Will Kymlicka, 'Liberal Individualism and Liberal Neutrality', *Ethics*, 99/4 (July 1989), 904.

27. Rawls, 'Fairness to Goodness', 549.

28. Kymlicka, 'Liberal Individualism and Liberal Neutrality', 884.

29. Ibid. 895.

30. This is recognized by Kymlicka, 'Liberal Individualism and Liberal Neutrality', 894. Unfortunately, his response to the problem he has raised (ibid. 895) is woefully inadequate. He argues that granting tax concessions to people who act in ways which preserve valuable forms of life would preserve neutrality and support valuable ways of life.

31. Larmore, *Patterns of Moral Complexity*, 119.

32. Ibid. 96.

33. Kymlicka, 'Liberal Individualism and Liberal Neutrality', 898.
34. Ibid.
35. See e.g. Richard Rorty, *Consequences of Pragmatism (Essays 1972–1980)* (Brighton: Harvester, 1982), Introduction, p. xxxvii; Walzer, *Spheres of Justice*, 6–7, 28–30, 31; MacIntyre, *After Virtue*, 218, 219–20; id., *Whose Justice? Which Rationality?*, 392–4.
36. In formulating this conception of the political, I am indebted to Hanna Fenichel Pitkin, *Wittgenstein and Justice: On the Significance of Ludwig Wittgenstein for Social and Political Thought* (Berkeley, Calif.: University of California Press, 1972), 215–16; and Chantal Mouffe, 'Rawls: Political Philosophy without Politics', *Philosophy and Social Criticism*, 13/2 (1987), 112–13.
37. I am indebted here to Lovibond, *Realism and Imagination in Ethics*, 123–32. I do not, of course, accept her view that the community's practices are ultimately irrational, or her conception of moral education as essentially coercive.
38. Richard Rorty, 'The Contingency of Community', *London Review of Books* (24 July 1986), 14.
39. Ibid. 12; my italics.
40. Rorty, *Consequences of Pragmatism*, xiv.
41. Charles Taylor, 'Rorty in the Epistemological Tradition', in *Reading Rorty*, ed. Alan Malachowski (Oxford: Basil Blackwell, 1990), 259.
42. Richard Rorty, *Philosophy and the Mirror of Nature* (Oxford: Basil Blackwell, 1983), 275 n. 6.
43. Roy Bhaskar, 'Rorty, Realism and the Idea of Freedom', in *Reading Rorty*, ed. Alan Malachowski (Oxford: Basil Blackwell, 1990), 208.
44. This does not, of course, mean that all there is is interpretation. The problem is rather that, though the 'facts' do set some constraints on the theories, the constraints are consistent with a wide range of theories.

Bibliography

ACKERMAN, BRUCE, *Social Justice in the Liberal State* (New Haven, Conn.: Yale University Press, 1980).

ACKRILL, J. L., 'Aristotle on Eudaimonia', in *Essays on Aristotle's Ethics*, ed. Amelie Oksenberg Rorty (Berkeley, Calif.: University of California Press, 1980).

ADAMS, R. M., 'Involuntary Sins', *Philosophical Review*, 94/1 (Jan. 1985).

ADAMSON, NANCY, BRISKIN, LINDA, and MCPHAIL, MARGARET, *Feminist Organizing for Change: The contemporary Women's Movement in Canada* (Toronto: Oxford University Press, 1988).

ANDERSON, BENEDICT, *Imagined Communities: Reflections on the Origin and Spread of Nationalism* (London: Verso Editions and New Left Books, 1983).

ANSCOMBE, G. E. M., *Intention* (Oxford: Blackwell, 1958).

—— 'Thought and Action in Aristotle', in *Aristotle's Ethics*, ed. J. J. Walsh and H. L. Shapiro (Belmont, Calif.: Wadsworth, 1967).

ARISTOTLE, *De Anima*, trans. Hugh Lawson-Tancred (Harmondsworth, Middx.: Penguin, 1986).

—— *The Ethics of Aristotle: The Nicomachean Ethics*, trans. J. A. K. Thomson (London: Penguin, 1955).

BAIER, ANNETTE, *Postures of the Mind: Essays on Mind and Morals* (London: Methuen, 1985).

—— 'Pilgrim's Progress', *Canadian Journal of Philosophy*, 18/2 (June 1988).

BAIER, KURT, *The Moral Point of View* (Ithaca, NY: Cornell University Press, 1958).

BARRY, BRIAN M., *The Liberal Theory of Justice* (Oxford: Clarendon Press, 1973).

—— *Theories of Justice* (London: Harvester-Wheatsheaf, 1989).

—— 'How Not to Defend Liberal Institutions', *British Journal of Political Science*, 20/1 (Jan. 1990).

BERGER, PETER, 'On the Obsolescence of the Concept of Honour', in *Liberalism and its Critics*, ed. Michael Sandel (Oxford: Basil Blackwell, 1984).

BERLIN, ISAIAH, 'Two Concepts of Liberty', in *Four Essays on Liberty* (Oxford: Oxford University Press, 1969).

BHASKAR, ROY, 'Rorty, Realism and the Idea of Freedom', in *Reading Rorty*, ed. Alan Malachowski (Oxford: Basil Blackwell, 1990).

BOND, E. J., *Reason and Value* (Cambridge: Cambridge University Press, 1983).

BRANDT, RICHARD B., *A Theory of the Good and the Right* (Oxford: Clarendon Press, 1979).

BRAYBROOKE, DAVID, 'Social Contract Theory's Fanciest Flight', *Ethics*, 97/4 (July 1987).

BUCHANAN, J. M., *The Limits of Liberty: Between Anarchy and Leviathan* (Chicago: University of Chicago Press, 1975).

BURNYEAT, M. F., 'Aristotle on Learning to be Good', in *Essays on Aristotle's Ethics*, ed. Amelie Oksenberg Rorty (Berkeley, Calif.: University of California Press, 1980).

CAMPBELL, RICHMOND, 'Critical Study: Gauthier's Theory of Morals by Agreement', *Philosophical Quarterly*, 38/152 (July 1988).

CARR, DAVID, 'Two Kinds of Virtue', *Proceedings of the Aristotelian Society*, NS lxxxv (1985).

CAVELL, STANLEY, *The Claim of Reason: Wittgenstein, Skepticism, Morality and Tragedy* (New York: Oxford University Press, 1979).

CHARVET, JOHN, *A Critique of Freedom and Equality* (Cambridge: Cambridge University Press, 1981).

COOPER, JOHN, M., *Reason and Human Good in Aristotle* (Indianapolis: Hackett, 1986).

COTTINGHAM, JOHN, 'Partiality, Favouritism and Morality', *Philosophical Quarterly*, 36/144 (July 1986).

DANIELS, NORMAN, 'Equal Liberty and the Unequal Worth of Liberty', in *Reading Rawls* (Oxford: Basil Blackwell, 1975).

DANIELSON, PETER, 'The Visible Hand of Morality', *Canadian Journal of Philosophy*, 18/2 (June 1988).

DAVIDSON, DONALD, 'How is Weakness of the Will Possible?', in *Moral Concepts*, ed. Joel Feinberg (Oxford: Oxford University Press, 1969).

DENT, N. J. H., 'The Tensions in Liberalism', *Philosophical Quarterly*, 38/153 (Oct. 1988).

DOPPELT, GERALD, 'Rawls' Kantian Ideal and the Viability of Modern Liberalism', *Inquiry*, 31/4 (Dec. 1988).

DWORKIN, RONALD M., 'The Original Position', in *Reading Rawls*, ed. Norman Daniels (Oxford: Basil Blackwell, 1975).

—— *Taking Rights Seriously* (Cambridge, Mass.: Harvard University Press, 1977).

—— 'Liberalism', in *Public and Private Morality*, ed. Stuart Hampshire (Cambridge: Cambridge University Press, 1978).

—— 'What is Equality? Part I: Equality of Welfare', *Philosophy and Public Affairs*, 10/3 (Summer 1981).

DWORKIN, RONALD M., 'What is Equality? Part II: Equality of Resources', *Philosophy and Public Affairs*, 10/4 (Fall 1981).

ELSTER, JON, *Ulysses and the Sirens: Studies in Rationality and Irrationality*, rev. edn. (Cambridge: Cambridge University Press, 1984).

FEINBERG, JOEL, *Rights, Justice, and the Bounds of Liberty: Essays in Social Philosophy* (Princeton, NJ: Princeton University Press, 1980).

FINNIS, JOHN, *Natural Law and Natural Rights* (Oxford: Clarendon Press, 1980).

FISHKIN, JAMES S., *Beyond Subjective Morality* (New Haven, Conn.: Yale University Press, 1984).

FISK, MILTON, 'History and Reason in Rawls' Moral Theory', in *Reading Rawls*, ed. Norman Daniels (Oxford: Basil Blackwell, 1975).

FOOT, PHILIPPA, *Virtues and Vices, and Other Essays in Moral Philosophy* (Oxford: Blackwell, 1978).

FRANKENA, WILLIAM, 'Natural and Inalienable Rights', *Philosophical Review*, 64 (1955).

FRANKFURT, H. G., 'Freedom of the Will and the Concept of the Person', *Journal of Philosophy*, 68/1 (Jan. 1971).

FRIEDMAN, MARILYN, 'Feminism and Modern Friendship: Dislocating the Community', *Ethics*, 99/1 (Jan. 1989).

FRIEDMAN, RICHARD B., 'The Basis of Human Rights: A Criticism of Gewirth's Theory', *Nomos XXIII, Human Rights* (1981).

GADAMER, HANS-GEORG, *The Idea of the Good in Platonic–Aristotelian Philosophy*, trans. P. Christopher Smith (New Haven, Conn.: Yale University Press, 1986).

GALLIE, W. B., 'Essentially Contested Concepts', *Proceedings of the Aristotelian Society*, 56 (1955–6).

GALSTON, WILLIAM A., 'Defending Liberalism', *American Political Science Review*, 76/3 (Sept. 1982).

—— 'Moral Personality and Liberal Theory: John Rawls's Dewey Lectures', *Political Theory*, 10/4 (Nov. 1982).

—— 'Pluralism and Social Unity', *Ethics*, 99/4 (July 1989).

GAUTHIER, DAVID, *Practical Reasoning: The Structure and Foundations of Prudential and Moral Arguments and their Exemplification in Discourse* (Oxford: Clarendon Press, 1963).

—— 'Rational Cooperation', *Nous*, 8/1 (Mar. 1974).

—— 'Justice and Natural Endowment: Toward a Critique of Rawls' Ideological Framework', *Social Theory and Practice*, 3/1 (Spring 1974).

—— 'Reason and Maximization', *Canadian Journal of Philosophy*, 4/3 (Mar. 1975).

—— *Morals by Agreement* (Oxford: Clarendon Press, 1986).

—— 'Moral Artifice', *Canadian Journal of Philosophy*, 18/2 (June 1988).

GAUTHIER, RENÉ-ANTOINE, 'The Nature of Aristotle's Ethics', in

Aristotle's Ethics, ed. J. J. Walsh and H. Shapiro (Belmont, Calif.: Wadsworth, 1967).

GEWIRTH, ALAN, *Reason and Morality* (Chicago: University of Chicago Press, 1978).

—— 'The Basis and Content of Human Rights', *Nomos XXIII: Human Rights* (1981).

—— 'Rights and Virtues', *Review of Metaphysics*, 38/4 (June 1985).

GRIFFIN, JAMES, *Well-Being: Its Meaning, Measurement, and Moral Importance* (Oxford: Clarendon Press, 1986).

GUTMANN, AMY, 'Communitarian Critics of Liberalism', *Philosophy and Public Affairs*, 14/3 (Summer 1985).

HALDANE, JOHN J., 'Individuals and the Theory of Justice', *Ratio*, 27/2 (Dec. 1985).

HAMLYN, DAVID, *Perception, Learning and the Self: Essays in the Philosophy of Psychology* (London: Routledge & Kegan Paul, 1983).

HAMPSHIRE, STUART, *Two Theories of Morality* (Oxford: Oxford University Press, 1977).

—— *Thought and Action*, new edn. (London: Chatto & Windus, 1982).

HAMPTON, JEAN, 'Can We Agree on Morals?', *Canadian Journal of Philosophy*, 18/2 (June 1988).

—— 'Should Political Philosophy Be Done Without Metaphysics?', *Ethics*, 99/4 (July 1989).

HARDIE, W. F. R., *Aristotle's Ethical Theory*, 2nd edn. (Oxford: Clarendon Press, 1980).

HARE, R. M., *Freedom and Reason* (Oxford: Clarendon Press, 1963).

—— 'Rawls's Theory of Justice—I', *Philosophical Quarterly*, 23/91 (Apr. 1973).

—— 'Ethical Theory and Utilitarianism', in *Utilitarianism and Beyond*, ed. Amartya Sen and Bernard Williams (Cambridge: Cambridge University Press, 1982).

HARSANYI, JOHN, 'Morality and the Theory of Rational Behaviour', in *Utilitarianism and Beyond*, ed. Amartya Sen and Bernard Williams (Cambridge: Cambridge University Press, 1982).

HART, H. L. A., 'Are there any Natural Rights?', *Philosophical Review*, 64 (1955).

—— *Law, Liberty, and Morality* (Stanford: Stanford University Press, 1963).

—— 'Rawls' on Liberty and its Priority', in *Reading Rawls*, ed. Norman Daniels (Oxford: Basil Blackwell, 1975).

HAUWERWAS, STANLEY, and WADELL, PAUL, 'Review of MacIntyre's After Virtue', *The Thomist*, 46/2 (Apr. 1982).

HAWORTH, LAWRENCE, *Autonomy: An Essay in Philosophical Psychology and Ethics* (New Haven, Conn.: Yale University Press, 1986).

HEGEL, G. W. F., *The Philosophy of Right*, trans. T. M. Knox (Oxford: Clarendon Press, 1942).

HOBBES, THOMAS, *Leviathan*, ed. Michael Oakeshott (London: Penguin, 1968).

HOLLIS, MARTIN, 'Of Masks and Men', in *The Category of the Person: Anthropology, Philosophy, History*, ed. Michael Carrithers, Steven Collins, and Steven Lukes (Cambridge: Cambridge University Press, 1985).

HUDSON, W. D., 'The "Is-Ought" Problem Resolved?', in *Gewirth's Ethical Rationalism*, ed. Edward Regis Jr. (Chicago: University of Chicago Press, 1984).

IRWIN, TERENCE, 'Morality and Personality: Kant and Green', in *Self and Nature in Kant's Philosophy*, ed. Allen W. Wood (Ithaca, NY: Cornell University Press, 1984).

IRWIN, T. H., 'First Principles in Aristotle's Ethics', in *Midwest Studies in Philosophy*, vol. iii (1978), ed. Peter A. French, Theodore E. Uehling, and Howard K. Wettstein (Minneapolis: University of Minnesota Press, 1980).

JAGGAR, ALISON, *Feminist Politics and Human Nature* (Totowa, NJ: Rowman & Allenheld, 1983).

KALIN, JESSE, 'Public Pursuit and Private Escape: The Persistence of Egoism', *Gewirth's Ethical Rationalism*, ed. Edward Regis Jr. (Chicago: University of Chicago Press, 1984).

KANT, IMMANUEL, *Critique of Practical Reason*, trans. Lewis White Beck (Indianapolis: The Bobbs-Merrill Company, 1956).

—— *Groundwork of the Metaphysic of Morals*, trans. H. J. Paton (New York: Harper & Row, 1964).

KEMP, J., 'Kant's Examples of the Categorical Imperative', *Kant: A Collection of Critical Essays*, ed. R. P. Wolff (London: Macmillan, 1968).

KOSMAN, L. A., 'Being Properly Affected: Virtues and Feelings in Aristotle's Ethics', in *Essays on Aristotle's Ethics*, ed. Amelie Oksenberg Rorty (Berkeley, Calif.: University of California Press, 1980).

KOVESI, JULIUS, 'Against the Ritual of "Is" and "Ought"', *Midwest Studies in Philosophy*, vol. iii (1978), ed. Peter A. French, Theodore E. Uehling, and Howard K. Wettstein (Minneapolis: University of Minnesota Press, 1980).

KRAUS, JODY S., and COLEMAN, JULES L., 'Morality and the Theory of Rational Choice', *Ethics*, 97/4 (July 1987).

KUHN, THOMAS, *The Structure of Scientific Revolutions*, 2nd edn. (Chicago: University of Chicago Press, 1970).

KYMLICKA, WILL, 'Liberal Individualism and Liberal Neutrality', *Ethics*, 99/4 (July 1989).

—— *Liberalism, Community, and Culture* (Oxford: Clarendon Press, 1989).

LARMORE, CHARLES, E., *Patterns of Moral Complexity* (Cambridge: Cambridge University Press, 1987).

LEVINE, ANDREW, 'Rawls's Kantianism', *Social Theory and Practice*, 3/1 (Spring 1974).

LOVIBOND, SABINA, *Realism and Imagination in Ethics* (Oxford: Basil Blackwell, 1983).

LUKES, STEVEN, 'Relativism: Cognitive and Moral', *The Aristotelian Society*, Supplementary vol. 48 (1974).

MACCORMICK, D. N., 'Rights in Legislation', in *Law, Morality and Society: Essays in Honour of H. L. A. Hart*, ed. P. M. S. Hacker and Joseph Raz (Oxford: Clarendon Press, 1977).

MACCORMICK, NEIL, *Legal Right and Social Democracy* (Oxford: Clarendon Press, 1982).

MCDOWELL, JOHN, 'Are Moral Requirements Hypothetical Imperatives?', *The Aristotelian Society*, supplementary vol. 52 (1978).

—— 'Virtue and Reason', *The Monist*, 62/3 (July 1979).

MACEDO, STEPHEN, *Liberal Virtues: Citizenship, Virtue, and Community in Liberal Constitutionalism* (Oxford: Clarendon Press, 1990).

MACINTYRE, ALASDAIR, *Against the Self-Images of the Age: Essays on Ideology and Philosophy* (London: Duckworth, 1971).

—— 'Is Patriotism a Virtue?', *The Lindley Lecture* (University of Kansas: Department of Philosophy, 26 Mar. 1984).

—— 'The Relationship of Philosophy to its Past', in *Philosophy in History*, ed. Richard Rorty, J. B. Schneewind, and Quentin Skinner (Cambridge: Cambridge University Press, 1984).

—— *After Virtue: A Study in Moral Theory* (London: Duckworth, 1985).

—— *Whose Justice? Which Rationality?* (London: Duckworth, 1988).

MACK, ERIC, 'Negative Causation and the Duty to Rescue', in *Gewirth's Ethical Rationalism*, ed. Edward Regis Jr. (Chicago: University of Chicago Press, 1984).

MANDEL, MICHAEL, *The Charter of Rights and the Legalization of Politics in Canada* (Toronto: Wall & Thompson, 1989).

MENDOLA, JOSEPH, 'Gauthier's Morals by Agreement and Two Kinds of Rationality', *Ethics*, 97/4 (July 1987).

MILL, JOHN STUART, *Utilitarianism and Other Writings*, ed. Mary Warnock (New York: Meridian, 1974).

MILLER, DAVID, 'In What Sense Must Socialism Be Communitarian?', *Social Philosophy and Policy*, 6/2.

—— 'The Ethical Significance of Nationality', *Ethics*, 98/4 (July 1988).

MONAN, J. D., *Moral Knowledge and its Methodology in Aristotle* (Oxford: Clarendon Press, 1968).

MOUFFE, CHANTAL, 'Rawls: Political Philosophy without Politics', *Philosophy and Social Criticism*, 13/2 (1987).

NAGEL, THOMAS, *The Possibility of Altruism* (Oxford: Clarendon Press, 1970).

—— 'Rawls on Justice', in *Reading Rawls*, ed. Norman Daniels (Oxford: Basil Blackwell, 1975).

—— 'Aristotle on Eudaimonia', *Essays on Aristotle's Ethics*, ed. Amelie Oksenberg Rorty (Berkeley, Calif.: University of California Press, 1980).

—— *The View from Nowhere* (New York: Oxford University Press, 1986).

—— 'Moral Conflict and Political Legitimacy', *Philosophy and Public Affairs*, 16/3 (Summer 1987).

NARVESON, JAN, 'Negative and Positive Rights', in *Gewirth's Ethical Rationalism*, ed. Edward Regis Jr. (Chicago: University of Chicago Press, 1984).

NEILSON, KAI, 'The Choice between Perfectionism and Rawlsian Contractarianism', *Interpretation*, 6/2 (May 1977).

NOZICK, ROBERT, *Anarchy, State and Utopia* (New York: Basic Books, 1974).

NUSSBAUM, MARTHA CRAVEN, *The Fragility of Goodness: Luck and Ethics in Greek Tragedy and Philosophy* (Cambridge: Cambridge University Press, 1986).

OAKESHOTT, MICHAEL, 'Political Education', in *Liberalism and its Critics*, ed. Michael Sandel (Oxford: Basil Blackwell, 1984).

OLDENQUIST, ANDREW, 'Loyalties', *Journal of Philosophy*, 79/4 (Apr. 1982).

PARFIT, DEREK, *Reasons and Persons* (Oxford: Oxford University Press, 1986).

PATON, H. J., *The Categorical Imperative*, 5th edn. (London: Hutchinson, 1965).

PETERS, R. S., *Ethics and Education* (London: Allen & Unwin, 1966).

PETTIT, PHILIP, 'Social Holism and Moral Theory: A Defence of Bradley's Thesis', *Proceedings of the Aristotelian Society*, NS lxxxvi (1986).

PITKIN, HANNA FENICHEL, *Wittgenstein and Justice: On the Significance of Ludwig Wittgenstein for Social and Political Thought* (Berkeley, Calif.: University of California Press, 1972).

PLANT, RAYMOND, *Hegel* (Bloomington, Ind.: Indiana University Press, 1973).

RAPHAEL, D. D., 'Rights and Conflicts', in *Gewirth's Ethical Rationalism*, ed. Edward Regis Jr. (Chicago: University of Chicago Press, 1984).

RAWLS, JOHN, *A Theory of Justice* (Oxford: Oxford University Press, 1972).

—— 'Fairness to Goodness', *Philosophical Review*, 84/4 (Oct. 1975).

—— 'The Basic Structure as Subject', *American Philosophical Quarterly*, 14/2 (Apr. 1977).

—— 'Kantian Constructivism in Moral Theory', *Journal of Philosophy*, 77/9 (Sept. 1980).

—— 'Social Unity and Primary Goods', in *Utilitarianism and Beyond*, ed. Amartya Sen and Bernard Williams (Cambridge: Cambridge University Press, 1982).

—— 'Justice as Fairness: Political not Metaphysical', *Philosophy and Public Affairs*, 14/3 (Summer 1985).

—— 'The Idea of an Overlapping Consensus', *Oxford Journal of Legal Studies*, 7/1 (Spring 1987).

—— 'The Priority of Right and Ideas of the Good', *Philosophy and Public Affairs*, 17/4 (Fall 1988).

RAZ, JOSEPH, *The Morality of Freedom* (Oxford: Clarendon Press, 1986).

—— 'Facing Diversity: The Case of Epistemic Abstinence', *Philosophy and Public Affairs*, 19 (1990).

RORTY, AMELIE OKSENBERG (ed.), *The Identities of Persons* (Berkeley, Calif.: University of California Press, 1976).

—— *Explaining Emotions* (Berkeley, Calif.: University of California Press, 1980).

RORTY, RICHARD, *Consequences of Pragmatism (Essays 1972–1980)* (Brighton: Harvester, 1982).

—— *Philosophy and the Mirror of Nature* (Oxford: Basil Blackwell, 1983).

—— 'The Contingency of Community', *London Review of Books*, 24 July 1986.

SALKEVER, STEPHEN, 'Virtue, Obligation and Politics', *American Political Science Review*, 68/1 (Mar. 1974).

—— 'Aristotle's Social Science', *Political Theory*, 9/4 (Nov. 1981).

SANDEL, MICHAEL J., *Liberalism and the Limits of Justice* (Cambridge: Cambridge University Press, 1982).

—— 'The Procedural Republic and the Unencumbered Self', *Political Theory*, 12/1 (Feb. 1984).

SCANLON, T. M., 'Preference and Urgency', *Journal of Philosophy*, 72/19 (6 Nov. 1975).

—— 'Contractualism and Utilitarianism', *Utilitarianism and Beyond*, ed. Amartya Sen and Bernard Williams (Cambridge: Cambridge University Press, 1982).

SCHAAR, JOHN, 'Reflections on Rawls' Theory of Justice', *Social Theory and Practice*, 3/1 (Spring 1974).

SCHEFFLER, SAMUEL, 'Review of MacIntyre's After Virtue', *Philosophical Review*, 92/3 (July 1983).

SEARLE, JOHN R., *Intentionality: An Essay in the Philosophy of Mind* (Cambridge: Cambridge University Press, 1983).

SHAPIRO, IAN, *The Evolution of Rights in Liberal Theory* (Cambridge: Cambridge University Press, 1986).

SHKLAR, JUDITH, N., *Freedom and Independence: A Study of the Political*

Ideas of Hegel's 'Phenomenology of Mind' (Cambridge: Cambridge University Press, 1976).

SINGER, PETER, 'Sidgwick and Reflective Equilibrium', *The Monist*, 58/3 (July 1974).

SKINNER, QUENTIN, 'The Idea of Negative Liberty: Philosophical and Historical Perspectives', in *Philosophy in History*, ed. Richard Rorty, J. B. Schneewind, and Quentin Skinner (Cambridge: Cambridge University Press, 1984).

SMART, J. J. C., and WILLIAMS, BERNARD, *Utilitarianism: For and Against* (Cambridge: Cambridge University Press, 1976).

SMITH, A. D., 'The Self and the Good', *Proceedings of the Aristotelian Society*, NS lxxxv (1985).

—— *The Ethnic Origins of Nations* (Oxford: Basil Blackwell, 1986).

SORABJI, RICHARD, 'Aristotle on the Role of Intellect in Virtue', *Essays on Aristotle's Ethics*, ed. Amelie Oksenberg Rorty (Berkeley, Calif.: University of California Press, 1980).

STOCKER, MICHAEL, 'The Schizophrenia of Modern Ethical Theories', *Journal of Philosophy*, 73/14 (12 Aug. 1976).

STRAWSON, P. F., *The Bounds of Sense* (London: Methuen, 1966).

SULLIVAN, WILLIAM, *Reconstructing Public Philosophy* (Berkeley, Calif.: University of California Press, 1982).

TAYLOR, ALAN R., *The Islamic Question in Middle East Politics* (Boulder, Colo.: Westview Press, 1988).

TAYLOR, CHARLES, *Hegel* (Cambridge: Cambridge University Press, 1975).

—— *Human Agency and Language: Philosophical Papers, I* (Cambridge: Cambridge University Press, 1985).

—— *Philosophy and the Human Sciences: Philosophical Papers, II* (Cambridge: Cambridge University Press, 1985).

—— 'Rorty in the Epistemological Tradition', in *Reading Rorty*, ed. Alan Malachowski (Oxford: Basil Blackwell, 1990).

TEICHMAN, JENNY, 'Wittgenstein on Persons and Human Beings', in *Understanding Wittgenstein*, ed. Godfrey Vesey (London: Macmillan, 1974).

TEITELMAN, MICHAEL, 'The Limits of Individualism', *Journal of Philosophy*, 69/18 (5 Oct. 1972).

TRIANOSKY, GREGORY, W., 'Rightly Ordered Appetites: How to Live Morally and Live Well', *American Philosophical Quarterly*, 25/1 (Jan. 1988).

UNGER, ROBERTO MANGABEIRA, *Knowledge and Politics* (New York: Free Press, 1975).

—— *Law in Modern Society: Toward a Criticism of Social Theory* (New York: Free Press, 1976).

VEATCH, HENRY, B., 'Book Review of Alan Gewirth's *Reason and Morality*', *Ethics*, 89/4 (July 1979).

—— *Rational Man: A Modern Interpretation of Aristotelian Ethics* (Bloomington, Ind.: Indiana University Press, 1962).

WACHBROIT, ROBERT, 'Review of MacIntyre's After Virtue', *Yale Law Journal*, 92/3 (Jan. 1983).

WALDRON, JEREMY, 'A Right to Do Wrong', *Ethics*, 92/1 (Oct. 1981).

—— 'Theoretical Foundations of Liberalism', *Philosophical Quarterly*, 37/147 (Apr. 1987).

WALLACE, JAMES D., *Virtues and Vices* (Ithaca, NY: Cornell University Press, 1978).

WALLACH, JOHN R., 'Liberals, Communitarians, and the Tasks of Political Theory', *Political Theory*, 15/4 (Nov. 1987).

WALZER, MICHAEL, *Spheres of Justice: A Defense of Pluralism and Equality* (New York: Basic Books, 1983).

WATSON, GARY, 'Free Agency', *Journal of Philosophy*, 72/8 (24 Apr. 1975).

WIGGINS, DAVID, 'Truth, Invention, and the Meaning of Life', *Proceedings of the British Academy*, 1976.

—— 'Deliberation and Practical Reason', in *Essays on Aristotle's Ethics*, ed. Amelie Oksenberg Rorty (Berkeley, Calif.: University of California Press, 1980).

—— 'Weakness of Will, Commensurability, and the Objects of Deliberation and Desire', in *Essays on Aristotle's Ethics*, ed. Amelie Oksenberg Rorty (Berkeley, Calif.: University of California Press, 1980).

WILLIAMS, BERNARD, *Problems of the Self: Philosophical Papers 1956–1972* (Cambridge: Cambridge University Press, 1973).

—— 'Persons, Character and Morality', in *Moral Luck* (Cambridge: Cambridge University Press, 1981).

—— *Ethics and the Limits of Philosophy* (London: Fontana, 1985).

WITTGENSTEIN, LUDWIG, *Philosophical Investigations*, trans. G. E. M. Anscombe (New York: Macmillan, 1953).

YOUNG, ROBERT, 'Dispensing with Moral Rights', *Political Theory*, 6/1 (Feb. 1978).

ZUCKERT, MICHAEL, 'Justice Deserted: A Critique of Rawls', *A Theory of Justice*, *Polity*, 13/3 (Spring 1981).

Index

abortion 179, 180
abstraction, from the individual 21-2, 24, 129-32, 133-5, 145
   Rawls 49, 61, 74, 130
Ackerman, Bruce 10, 34
   Social Justice in the Liberal State 34
affection:
   as constraint on freedom and equality 93, 103, 106, 120, 125
   see also attachments
After Virtue, Alasdair MacIntyre 5
agency:
   Gewirth's human 10, 19-24, 165
   Kant's moral 14
   Rawls's pure 46-7, 50
AIDS 72
altruism 48
anti-foundationalism 171-2
Archimedean point:
   Gauthier's 107-9
   liberal search for 166-8, 199-200
   Rawls's 41, 44, 73-4, 115-16, 140
aristocracy 137
Aristotelian Principle, Rawls's 57-9
Aristotle 1
   conception of the good 45, 47-8
   moral development 171, 172, 173-5, 184
   theory of habituation 173-4
attachments 130-2
   and Gauthier's utility-maximizers 102-5
   and Rawls 64-5, 66, 67-9
autonomy:
   and community 183-8
   and individualism 165, 170
   and liberalism 125-6, 135-8, 140, 145-58, 177-8

   and moral development 184-5
   Rawls's emphasis on 46, 48-50, 53, 59
   reflective 198-202
   and revisability 147, 149-51, 158
   and substantive values 147, 157-9
   and well-being 146-8, 151-2, 156-8
Autonomy, Lawrence Haworth 185

Baier, Annette C. 103-4
Bargaining Problem, Gauthier 81-2, 87, 92-101, 108
bargaining theory, Buchanan 95-6, 97
Barry, Brian 149
   The Liberal Theory of Justice 52-3, 72
   Theories of Justice 34, 37, 69-71
Bhaskar, Roy 200
Bradley, Francis 10
Braybrooke, David 100
Buchanan, J. M. 95-6, 97
Burnyeat, M. F. 174-5

capitalism 170
Categorical Imperative, Kant 11-12, 18-19
choice:
   Gauthier's rational 92-3, 101
   Gewirth's conception of 24, 26-31
   meaningful 152-3, 155, 156-7, 193
   subjective 167, 187
citizenship 188, 191-2
civil peace 134
coercion 179-80
   and Barry 149
   and Gauthier 86, 96-7
   and Gewirth 26
   perfectionist 148-9
   and Rawls 120
collective action 91-2, 194

collective goods 73, 145, 152–3, 186, 194
collective identity 196
communism 138
communitarianism 118–26, 134, 138–40, 195–7
  and anti-foundationalism 171–2
  concept of a community 189, 196
  critical of liberalism 115, 144, 147, 155
  and Gauthier 90–2
  liberal criticism of 183–4, 194, 195
  and Rawls 43, 66, 123–6, 138–40
community:
  and autonomy 183–8
  conception of morality founded in 167–202
  identifying with 175–6
  and the individual 169, 184
  and language 169–70, 188–9, 198–200
  liberal 177–9
  membership of 188–91
  and moral diversity 199
  and Rawls 48–9
  shared conceptions in 167–8, 171–6
  types of 189–91
  value of 147, 149, 151–5, 156
  see also institutions; society
compliance, Gauthier's broad or narrow 85–6, 89–90, 91–2
compliance problem, *see* motivation problem
conflict, political 179
conscience, freedom of 52, 54, 58
consensus, Rawls's 117–23, 128, 139–40
The Contingency of Community, Richard Rorty 199–200
contractarianism:
  Gauthier's 2–3, 81, 100, 105, 107
  Rawls's 52, 61, 80
contractors, Rawls's rational 50–2, 57, 60
co-operation:
  Gauthier's 82–6, 92–4, 97, 101
  Rawls's 35–6
crime 72
Criterion of Relevant Similarities, Gewirth 10, 15–16, 18–19, 23
Critique of Practical Reason, Immanuel Kant 14
culture:
  minority 152, 153–4, 155, 156
  value of 154–5, 156

democracy:
  and freedom 30–1
  and Rawls's principles of justice 117
Derrida, Jacques 199
desert, Rawls's 45–6
dichotomy:
  desire–reason 38
  public–private 40–1, 69, 117, 127–32, 140, 167, 177
  self-interest–morality 38
difference principle, Rawls's 46–7, 52, 56, 69, 81
distribution, Rawls's principles of 52, 72
distributive justice:
  and community 190
  Rawls's 51
Dworkin, Ronald M. 150

education:
  moral, *see* moral development
  right to 25–6
entailment principle, Gewirth 14–16, 20, 22, 24–5, 65
entitlement principle, Gewirth 23–4, 31–2
equality:
  and moral diversity 120
  of opportunity 26
  and Rawls's original position 55–6
ethics:
  and language 198–201
  non-cognitivist 168
  realist 168–9, 175–6
externalities, market 83, 99

Fairness to Goodness, John Rawls 194
families, *see* kin
fascism 138
feminism 120–2, 144, 179, 180–1
  and Gauthier 79–80, 106, 108
  see also women
freedom:
  artistic 146
  of conscience 52, 54, 58
  Gewirth's conception of 15–24, 25–32, 51
  Gewirth's entitlement to 23–4, 31–2
  and moral diversity 120
  Rawls's basic liberties 52–4, 58
  and Rawls's liberty principle 54–7, 72
  of religion 54, 58, 146, 155
  of speech 52, 54, 58, 146

Gauthier, David 79–109, 165–6, 173,
  175–6, 183
  Archimedean point 107–9
  Bargaining Problem 81–2, 87, 92–101,
    108
  contractarianism 2–3, 81, 100, 105, 107
  and Gewirth 79–81, 107, 109
  justice as mutual advantage 9, 34,
    79, 101–7, 132
  Lockian Proviso 94–101
  Minimax Relative Concession 82,
    85–6, 92–7, 99–101
  morality as subset of self-
    interest 65, 80, 91, 107
  Morals by Agreement 2–3, 79–109, 132
  prisoner's dilemma 83–4, 91, 93
  and Rawls 79–81, 100–1, 102, 105–9
  'translucent' utility-maximizers 85,
    87–9, 91–2
Gewirth, Alan 10–32, 145, 175
  Criterion of Relevant Similarities 10,
    15–16, 18–19, 23
  entailment of morality in self-
    interest 14–16, 20–2, 24–5, 65, 70
  entitlement principle 23–4, 31–2
  freedom 15–24, 25–32, 51
  and Gauthier 79–81, 107, 109
  and human agency 10, 19–24, 165–6
  and Kantianism 10, 11–16, 17–18, 22,
    31–2
  Principle of Generic
    Consistency 12–13, 16, 20, 25–41
  prudential goods 13–21, 22–4, 31–2
  and Rawls 49, 51, 61, 63, 73
  Reason and Morality 2, 10, 11–31, 80
  thin theory of the good 17–20, 178
  well-being 27–8, 29, 51
good:
  conceptions of: Aristotle's 45, 47–8;
    diverse 126–9; generic–
    dispositional 17; Kant's 49–50;
    liberal 145
  distinct from right 40–1
  theories of: Gewirth's 17–20, 178;
    Rawls's 47, 49–50, 51–2, 55, 178
good life:
  liberalism founded in 144–5, 151–5
  see also well-being
goods:
  collective 73, 145, 152–3, 186, 194
  Gewirth's prudential 13–21, 22–4,
    31–2
  Kant's 13

  public 99–100
  Rawls's primary 51–9, 72, 127
guilt 65, 67

Habermas, Jürgen 133
habituation, Aristotle's theory of
  173–4
Hampton, Jean, Principle of
  Proportionality 93–4
Hare, R. M. 10
Harsanyi, John 107
Haworth, Lawrence, *Autonomy* 185
Hegelianism 120–1
Heidegger, Martin 199
hierarchies 137
Hobbes, Thomas 36, 84–6, 97, 128
  Leviathan 9
Hume, David 3

ignorance 55–6
impartiality:
  Gauthier's 107
  Gewirth's 38
  justice as 9–10, 34–9, 44, 69
  Kant's 38
  and liberalism 45–6
  and morality 41, 49
  Rawls's 39, 42–4, 48–9, 69
individualism 171–2
  and autonomy 165, 170
  and capitalism 170
  and liberalism 145, 152, 158–9
inequality:
  in families 67, 93, 106, 120, 125
  and Rawls's difference principle 56
institutions:
  and the individual 108–9, 123–5, 169,
    184
  Rawls's just 65–7, 68–9
  see also community; society
integrity problem 165–7, 170, 172
  Gauthier's 109
  Rawls's 38–9
intuitive conceptions 118–19, 122–3,
  124, 127

Jagger, Alison 144
justice:
  as impartiality 9–10, 34–9
  as mutual advantage 9, 34, 36–7, 79,
    101–7, 132
  Rawls's principles of 39–48, 50–62,
    69, 73–4

Rawls's sense of 62–7, 69
Justice as Fairness, John Rawls 16, 118, 122–3, 126, 130

Kant, Immanuel 18, 41, 52, 83, 145
Categorical Imperative 11–12, 18–19
Critique of Practical Reason 14
ethical theory 10–17, 22, 31–2, 49–50, 81
impartiality 38, 41–2, 45, 80, 127–8
kin, as constraint on freedom and equality 67, 93, 106, 120, 125
knowledge:
and 'knowledge requirement' 28–9
redescription as 199–200
Kymlicka, Will 187, 194–6
Liberalism, Community, and Culture 5, 144–59, 183–4

language:
and community 169–70, 188–9, 198–200
and ethics 198–201
Larmore, Charles 140, 167, 195–8
and contextual liberalism 115, 117, 129–38, 140
and *modus vivendi* justification of liberalism 129, 132–3, 138, 176–8, 197
Patterns of Moral Complexity 4, 115, 129, 132–8, 195
'rational conversations' 132–8
Leviathan, Thomas Hobbes 9
The Liberal Theory of Justice, Brian Barry 52–3, 72
liberal values:
basis in liberal communities 177–82
in moral development 182, 183
liberalism:
and autonomy 125–6, 135–8, 140, 145–58, 177–8
and communitarianism 115, 118, 123–6, 134, 140
as a conception of morality 177, 183, 192
contextual 115–40
and feminism 144, 179, 180–1
founded in good life 144–5
incompatibilities 27–9, 131, 152–6, 178–9, 183
and individualism 145, 152, 158–9
neutral to conceptions of the good 45–6, 127–9, 132, 134–8, 144–5, 147

origins 125
and perfectionism 41, 59, 145
public–private dichotomy 40–1, 69, 117, 127–32, 140, 167, 177; revision 192–3
and value of the community 153–4
Liberalism, Community, and Culture, Will Kymlicka 5, 144–59, 183–4
liberty, *see* freedom
Locke, John 82, 97–8, 100
and Gauthier's Lockian Proviso 94–101

Macedo, Stephen 177
MacIntyre, Alasdair 5, 176, 189, 201
After Virtue 5
Whose Justice? Which Rationality? 201
market 83, 93, 97–101, 193–4
externalities 83, 99
maximization of utility, *see* utility-maximizers
membership, community 188–91
Mill, J. S. 53, 58–9
Miller, David 191
Minimax Relative Concession, Gauthier 82, 85–6, 92–7, 99–101
modus vivendi justification of liberalism 126–9, 132–4, 138–40, 176–8, 197
moral development 47–8
Aristotle's 171, 172, 173–5, 184
and autonomy 184–5
and families 67
liberal values in 182, 183
and moral diversity 176
and motivation problem 171–6
Rawls's 64–9
and society 123, 125–6
moral diversity 119–23, 126–9, 139–40, 176–82, 199
moral education, *see* moral development
morality:
Gauthier's subset of self-interest 65, 80, 91, 107
Gewirth's entailment in self-interest 10, 14–16, 20, 22, 24–5, 31–2, 65, 70
Kant's conception of 11, 17, 31, 38, 41
and rationality 12, 27–31
Rawls's conception of 40–1, 43, 45–9, 60
'Morality of Association' 64–5

'Morality of Authority' 64–5, 67
The Morality of Freedom, Joseph Raz 4, 144–59
'Morality of Principles' 65
Morals by Agreement, David Gauthier 2–3, 79–109, 132
motivation problem:
  Gauthier's 81, 82, 84–7, 105–7, 109
  in liberalism 145, 165, 170, 172
  and moral development 171–6
  Rawls's 38, 60–71, 73–4, 81
mutual advantage, justice as 9, 34, 36–7, 79, 101–7, 132

Nagel, Thomas, *The Possibility of Altruism* 80
nationalism 189
Nazism 177
neutrality:
  and Gewirth 17, 19, 20, 21
  of liberal conceptions of the good 45–6, 127–9, 132, 134–8, 144–5, 147
  and Rawls 51–5, 127–9, 147
  unattainability of 170–2, 177–8, 182, 193–4
non-contradiction principle, Gewirth 13, 17
Nozick, Robert 46, 122

opportunity 26, 51, 53
opportunity cost 95
'original position':
  Rawls's 35, 38–44, 48, 50–61, 71–2, 165, 175
  Rawls reconsiders 116, 118

Patterns of Moral Complexity, Charles Larmore 4, 115, 129, 132–8, 195
perfectionism:
  coercive 148–9
  and liberalism 41, 59, 145
person, conception of the 165
  abstracted 21–2, 24, 129–32, 133–5, 145
  Barry's reasonable 70
  communitarian 169–70, 183–4
  Gauthier's 102–5
  Kymlicka's 153
  liberal 133, 135, 145, 158–9
  Rawls's 36, 46–7, 50, 55, 73–4, 80, 145; abstracted 49, 61, 74, 130; changed 116–17, 124–6
  Raz's 146, 153

social 183
Plato 1, 9, 101
pornography 179
The Possibility of Altruism, Thomas Nagel 80
post-modernism 199–200
poverty 55–6
power:
  as primary good 52, 53
  of the state 128
predation 86, 90, 97
primary goods, Rawls's 51–9, 72, 127
Principle of Generic Consistency, Gewirth 12–13, 16, 20, 25–41
Principle of Proportionality, Hampton 93–4
prisoner's dilemma, Gauthier 83–4, 91, 93
prudential goods, Gewirth's 13–21, 22–4, 31–2
public goods 99–100
public–private dichotomy 40–1, 69, 117, 129–32, 140, 167, 177
  revised 192–3

racism 135–7
'rational conversations', Larmore 132–8
rational justification 198–202
rationality, and morality 12, 27–31
Rawls, John 2–5, 34–74, 115–40
  Archimedean point 115–16, 140
  Aristotelian Principle 57–9
  and communitarianism 43, 66, 123–6, 138–40
  conception of morality 40–1, 43, 45–9, 60
  conception of the person 36, 46–7, 50, 55, 73–4, 80, 145; abstracted 49, 61, 74, 130, 165–6, 183
  consensus 117–23, 128, 139–40
  and contextual liberalism 115–32, 136, 138–40
  difference principle 46–7, 52, 56, 69, 81
  Fairness to Goodness 194
  and Gauthier 79–81, 100–1, 102, 105–9
  and Gewirth 49, 51, 61, 63, 73
  impartiality 39, 42–4, 48–9, 69
  integrity problem 38–9
  intuitive conceptions 118–19, 122–3, 124, 127

Justice as Fairness 16, 118, 122–3, 126, 130

liberty principle 54–5, 57, 72

method of reflective equilibrium 38, 41–4, 74, 119, 126–7

and *modus vivendi* justification of liberalism 129, 132, 138–9, 176–8, 197

motivation problem 38, 60–71, 73–4, 81

neutrality 51–5, 127–9, 147

'original position' 35, 38–44, 48, 50–61, 71–2, 165, 175; reconsidered 116, 118

primary goods 51–9, 72, 127

principles of justice 39–48, 50–62, 69, 73–4

pure agency 46–7, 50

self-interest and morality 49–50, 61, 63, 73–4, 117–18

sense of justice 62–7, 69

A Theory of Justice 34–74, 96, 119, 120, 123–8, 140; critique of 115–16, 144

thin theory of the good 47, 49–50, 51–2, 55, 178

universalism 43, 61–2, 72–3, 115–16

'veil of ignorance' 36–9, 44, 60–1, 96

Raz, Joseph 187

The Morality of Freedom 4, 144–59

reason:

   and desire 168, 172

   and morals 13–16, 49–50, 81, 105

   Rawls's conception of 50

Reason and Morality, Alan Gewirth 2, 10, 11–31, 80

reciprocity 66–7, 68–9

redescription as knowledge 199–200

reflective equilibrium, Rawls's method of 38, 41–4, 74, 119, 126–7

religion:

   freedom of 54, 58, 146, 155

   and liberalism 27–9, 131, 178–9

Republic, Plato 9, 101

republicanism 193–5

respect:

   equal, Larmore's principle of 134–7

   self 53

revisability 147, 149–51, 158

right, and good 40–1

rights 15, 25–6, 51, 98, 179

Rorty, Richard 5

   The Contingency of Community 199–200

Rushdie, Salman 180

Sandel, Michael J.:

   communitarian criticism of liberalism 46, 115–16, 144–5, 189

   criticized by Kymlicka 183–4

scarcity of resources 34, 36, 179

self-interest, and morality:

   Barry on 69–71

   dichotomy 38

   and Gauthier 65

   and Gewirth 14–16, 20–5, 31–2, 63, 65, 70

   and Kant 49–50

   and Rawls 49–50, 61, 63, 73–4, 117–18

Social Justice in the Liberal State, Bruce Ackerman 34

society:

   Gauthier on 109

   and the individual 123–5, 145, 159

   and moral development 123, 125–6

   Rawls on 72–3

   see also community; institutions

speech, freedom of 52, 54, 58, 146

state power 128

'strains of commitment', Rawls 61

sympathy theory 11, 63–4, 102, 134

Taylor, Charles 5, 144–5, 200

A Theory of Justice, John Rawls 34–74, 96, 119, 120, 123–8, 140

critique of 115–16, 144

theories of the good:

   Gewirth's thin 17–20

   Rawls's thin 51–2, 55

Theories of Justice, Brian Barry 34, 37, 69–71

'translucent' utility-maximizers 85, 87–9, 91–2

Unger, Roberto M. 144

universalism, Rawls's 43, 61–2, 72–3, 115–16

universalization 16, 18–19, 73

utility-maximizers:

   constrained or staightforward 85, 88–90, 91–2

   Gauthier's 79–81, 83–4, 99, 101–9

   Rawls's 50, 57, 71–2

   'translucent' 85, 87–9, 91–2

value:

   communal 145

value (*cont.*):
    of the community 147, 149, 151–5, 156
    of culture 154–5, 156
    internal 147, 148–9, 158
    Rawls's criteria of 54, 59
    substantive 147, 157–9
'veil of ignorance', Rawls 36–9, 44, 60–1, 96

Walzer, Michael 5
wants, Rawls's 52–3

well-being:
    and autonomy 146–8, 151–2, 156–8
    as Gewirth's prudential goods 15–24, 27–8, 29, 31–2, 51
    see also good life
Whose Justice? Which Rationality?, Alasdair MacIntyre 201
Williams, Bernard 130
women:
    exploitation 125–6
    see also feminism

Zuckert, Michael 46